1450⁄01 EC

SWORDS INTO PLOUGHSHARES

RUFUS M. JONES

SWORDS INTO PLOUGHSHARES

An Account of
The American Friends Service Committee
1917–1937

BY

MARY HOXIE JONES

"They shall beat their swords into plough-
shares and their spears into pruning hooks
Nation shall not lift up a sword against
nation, neither shall they learn war any
more." Micah 4:3

GREENWOOD PRESS, PUBLISHERS
WESTPORT, CONNECTICUT

Originally published in 1937
by The Macmillan Company, New York

First Greenwood Reprinting 1971

Library of Congress Catalogue Card Number 70-109757

SBN 8371-4247-4

Printed in the United States of America

DEDICATION

THIS book is dedicated to Rufus M. Jones, who as Chairman and Honorary Chairman of the American Friends Service Committee from 1917 to 1937, has given twenty years of continuous leadership. His humor, his wisdom and his spiritual counsel have been an inspiration to all the many persons who have gone forth through the gates at Twenty South Twelfth Street and he has guided the Committee through periods of darkness into the light. He has been a never-failing source of delight and help to his daughter, not only in the preparation of this book, but through all the days of her life.

FOREWORD

CROMWELL'S wise saying that "no man ever goes so far as when he doesn't know where he is going," applies in a striking way to the unfolding and enlarging activities of the American Friends Service Committee, whose story is narrated in this book. It was said of Abraham that he went out not knowing whither he was going, but purposing in his mind to find a city with enduring foundations, divinely built. And, as he followed his vision, "God was not ashamed to be called his God," and to go the unknown way with him.

No one dreamed in the sharp crisis of 1917, when the first steps of faith were taken, that we should feed more than a million German children, drive dray loads of cod-liver oil into Russia, plough the fields of the peasants and fight typhus in Poland, rebuild the houses and replant the wastes in Serbia, administer a longtime service of love in Austria, become foster parents to tens of thousands of children in the coal fields in West Virginia, Kentucky, Pennsylvania and Ohio, inaugurate plans for the rehabilitation of the stranded soft coal miners, carry relief to the children on both sides of the warring forces in Spain and create new types of Peace activity which have brought this supreme issue of these times vitally home to the minds and consciences of people in all parts of America.

We verily went out in those days of low visibility not knowing whither we were going, but, like the early Patriarch, we were conscious of a divine leading, and we were aware, even if only dimly, that we were "fellow-laborers with God" in the rugged furrows of the somewhat brambly fields of the world.

The Quakers had always from the time of their rise in the period of the English Commonwealth been sensitive to the ills of humanity and ready as occasions arose to take up the burden of the world's suffering, but in the early and middle periods of Quaker history experiments in the service of love were apt to be spontaneously entered into as the individual concern of a tender heart who followed a leading that seemed to be divinely given to him. John Bellers, John Woolman, William Allen, Elizabeth Fry, Anthony Benezet, and Joseph Sturge are characteristic champions of the Quaker faith. They saw a task that needed to be done. They were recipients of a vision, an inward leading, and they were not disobedient to what seemed to them their heavenly vision. They had a certain amount of corporate backing and support, but in the main they walked a solitary path and went forward on their own uncharted way.

The American Friends Service Committee, as its name implies, was from the beginning, and has all along continued to be, a corporate activity. Many of its undertakings originated in the inward insight of a single individual, and some of its most important concerns had their birth in a sensitive person's soul, but all its decisions have been arrived at through corporate action. Its twenty years of history have given many glowing verifications of the wisdom of arriving at decisions by taking "the sense of the meeting." Nothing in this long period has been settled by a majority vote which overrode the judgment of a strong minority opposed to it. All matters of importance have been luminously presented to the whole group, corporately considered, looked at from many angles, threshed out in clear, open light and decided by unanimous judgment; or referred to a small group to be further studied, matured and brought again to the whole Committee, to be there reconsidered in fuller light and with enlarged wisdom, which usually has resulted in a final unanimous decision.

There were three sisters—the gray Sisters—in Greek mythology, who had one eye in common. They pooled their insights. Whichever one of the sisters had the eye and made a discovery passed the eye on to the others until they all saw what the one had seen. Something like that has been the method of procedure in the Service Committee decisions. When anyone has had an eye that saw he has transmitted his wisdom until all could see what he saw. Thus the work throughout these years of activity has shown a fine blending of individual leadership and harmonious corporate action.

One of the finest features of this book is the successful way in which the writer has fused together in a single narrative the fact-aspect of the enterprises and the epic-aspect hidden underneath the deeds. She has both told the story and at the same time caught the spirit and ideal that underlay the actions. Of course no book could give an itemized account in detail of the various activities and no one could read it if it were told in full. More than forty thousand persons took some part in the German child-feeding operations and the details of that adventure alone would swamp both writer and reader if they were spread out in full length and breadth.

This book reveals a mastery of the sources, an admirable selection of significant facts, events and deeds, with a genuine *feeling* of the pulse of the action, and then, best of all, an effective interpretation of the spirit and way of life that was being expressed in the deeds, the events and the facts. Not less effective is her dramatic and often subtle way of revealing how the various enterprises wrought upon the minds and spirits of those who were the recipients of the services of love. The reader to a marked extent will feel what was *moving* the actors and what was taking place in the hearts of those who were the sharers. The narrative passes beyond a record of relief to a human story of fellowship in suffering and a communion of life. It has been written, not to glorify any person, nor to trumpet the fame of the Society of Friends. It has been written to tell a moving human story, and to show the splendor of unselfish love in the midst of the dark epoch of violence, confusion and hate. It was worth telling. It is well told and it will be read and pondered.

RUFUS M. JONES

CONTENTS

xi

ILLUSTRATIONS

INTRODUCTION

I am writing an introduction because I feel that I must
explain some of the chapters which constitute this account
of the American Friends Service Committee during its
twenty years of existence.

I was asked to write a book which would be a history of
this Committee, giving, as one expects a history to do,
accurate information concerning achievements now accomplished. I have made every attempt to make this
information accurate. But I was asked to do more than
write a history. I was asked to make this book an interpretive volume which would lay stress on motives for
action, which would gather together more than facts and
which would, in the process of telling the story of twenty
years of service, show the subtle, intangible forces behind
the facts revealed.

This book will come to the attention of a variety of
individuals who may be divided into three specific classes.
First, those who have been closely associated with the
Service Committee either on the field, in the office, or on
committees; second, those who know of the Service Committee without being well acquainted with it; and, third, those
who have never heard of it.

Those who have been closely associated with the American Friends Service Committee will find immediately that
I have skimmed hurriedly over the surface. They have
been looking forward, no doubt, to reading a full account
of their particular interest or field of work and they will

feel that justice has not been done to it. But let those readers consider the size of a book which could do justice to every phase of the American Friends Service Committee. Those who have never heard of this organization will find in this volume sufficient material to give them a conception of a unique service rendered for twenty years.

In the early part of October 1936 I was asked to write this book which was to be finished in time to appear in print at the World Conference of Friends in September 1937. There were put at my disposal all the files of the last twenty years—nearly one hundred drawers crammed with correspondence, documents and miscellaneous material. There are, by a rough estimate, three thousand individuals who have served in one capacity or another and from whom I could obtain first-hand information. It became obvious the instant I accepted the task of writing this book that I could not go through every drawer nor interview every person who might be able to give me vivid accounts of his particular type of service.

As I mapped out the kind of volume which I hoped to produce I became convinced that if I were to cover the entire period of twenty years and if I were to write a book which would be both interpretive and readable, I could not begin to include every single episode which had occurred from the first committee meeting in 1917 to the last in 1937. If I were to finish the book in time for the World Conference I would be forced to omit a great deal.

Let any one who may be disappointed to find how little space has been given to Russia, for instance, start to write it up himself, beginning in 1916, including the two years in Russia after that and the six months in Siberia, later work in 1920, the period of the famine, the medical work which continued after that and finally the less spectacular period until the center in Moscow was closed in 1931. It would make a complete book in itself and this is true of every phase of the Service Committee. One volume has been written on the reconstruction in France. *A Service of Love in War Time*, by Rufus M. Jones, published just as this work was being concluded, gives a complete story of that first great venture. A. Ruth Fry in *A Quaker Adventure* tells the English side of the European relief work from 1914 to 1926 and Lester M. Jones in *Quakers In Action* gives a brief, though detailed, history of the Service Committee from 1917 until 1928.

This book which I have written is not like any one of these three. The first chapters which I wrote were dull and swamped in masses of detail. How was I to interpret and give facts too? I remembered, one day, what L. Violet Hodgkin had done for the history of Quakerism in her volume, *Quaker Saints*, where she took stories of the early Friends and re-created them, making these people vivid and alive because of her imaginative genius. It occurred to me that perhaps I might attempt the same method. I scrapped my first chapters and began again.

I have created purely imaginary stories based on material which I have read. I used fictitious names and jumbled members of Units together to make one person, as in Russia, for example, where I have taken the experiences of several people and made them happen to one person. I took, also, the liberty of portraying actual individuals, as in the opening chapter, "Committee Meeting," and in a later chapter, "Keeping Typhus Out of Europe," making them utter sentences which they can say in great truth that they never did utter. As they are all persons whom I know I have tried to have them say what I imagined they might have said under those circumstances.

This method which I have pursued has made the book

become a living one for me and these imaginary individuals have become real people. There were, of course, two or three thousand individuals whom I could have used instead of creating new ones, but I believe that I have achieved my end with less difficulty and with sufficient vividness to allow me the liberties I have taken. I have prefaced every story with a "footnote" chapter in my endeavor to give accurate information concerning every phase of the work. In one or two cases, because of the increasing length of the book, I have abandoned the story and left merely the introductory chapter.

Abby Worthington, who appears for the first time in the chapter, "The Spirit of the Mission," is not based on any one person and is purely a fictitious character. I had not intended, at first, to have her appear in more than one chapter, but later I decided that through her I could give continuity to and a feeling of growth and development in the Service Committee itself. It was impossible to have her serve in Russia because the work was contemporary with that in France and Germany. She is not, therefore, the author of the "Diary." When she first appears she is a young woman of about twenty-five so that when the book closes she is forty-five and she represents the enthusiastic and devoted service of the young person, the growing comprehension of the purpose of the Service Committee and the wisdom of mature years coupled with a long period of service. All three of these phases have been typical of many workers during twenty years. She has become, in my mind, the interpretation of the Service Committee, and the symbol for all the workers whom it is impossible to describe in a volume of this size.

I started to write this book because I was asked to do it. I am completing it, not only because I was asked to but because I have come to feel, during these intervening months, that it is of vital importance for people to understand the variety of tasks which the Service Committee has undertaken since it arose, over night in April 1917 to fill one definite need in the crisis of war, and for people to feel the spiritual life underlying every one of these tasks. It is not perfect by any means but it holds a challenge for every man and woman who believes that the Kingdom of God can come on earth and in the hearts of people of all races and nationalities.

I am grateful for the use of the lines quoted from Rupert Brooke from "Collected Poems of Rupert Brooke," copyright, 1915, by Dodd, Mead & Company, used by permission of the publishers, and for the verses from Alice Meynell, used by permission of Charles Scribner's Sons.

The list of persons who have aided me in the preparation of this volume is too long to mention by name but I wish to thank all the members of the staff in the office at Twenty South Twelfth Street, especially Clarence E. Pickett, whose counsel and advice have helped me immensely. I owe a debt of gratitude to both my parents and to Frances C. Ferris for reading this book in manuscript and giving me criticism and encouragement.

SUMMER IN ENGLAND
1914

. . . "Most happy year! And out of town
  The hay was prosperous, and the wheat;
The silken harvest climbed the down;
  Moon after moon was heavenly sweet,
Stroking the bread within the sheaves,
Looking 'twixt apples and their leaves.

And while this rose made round her cup,
  The armies died convulsed. And when
This chaste young silver sun went up
  Softly, a thousand shattered men,
One wet corruption, heaped the plain,
After a league-long throb of pain.

Flower following tender flower; and birds,
  And berries; and benignant skies
Made thrive the serried flocks and herds.—
  Yonder are men shot through the eyes.
    Love, hide thy face
From man's unpardonable race . . ."

ALICE MEYNELL

CHAPTER I

COMMITTEE MEETING

June 1917

Alfred G. Scattergood: "Well, Friends, I think we are all present. Perhaps it would be in order for us to settle down for a few moments of silence before we begin the business of the afternoon." The room becomes quiet immediately and the silence is not broken for several minutes until Rufus M. Jones rises from his seat to offer prayer.

Rufus M. Jones: "Eternal Father, at the beginning of this overwhelming task we turn to Thee and ask that Thy everlasting arms will uphold and strengthen us. Guide us during these dark days and give us wisdom for our momentous deliberations. Help us in a time when there is no peace to know Thy peace which passes all understanding. For Christ's sake, Amen."

Alfred G. Scattergood: "The first item of business is a report from our secretary, Vincent D. Nicholson."

Vincent D. Nicholson: "Friends will remember that a committee of two was appointed to visit Rufus Jones and ask him to become chairman of the American Friends Service Committee. I want to say that we paid the visit, and Rufus Jones is willing to accept this position, although he says that he is very busy and does not believe that he will be able to spend a great deal of time attending meetings. We told him that we would not need to call on him unless there was an emergency. It has seemed to

3

us that Rufus Jones is peculiarly fitted for this office because he is a member of the Five Years Meeting who lives in the Philadelphia area and who is well known among Friends everywhere. Our temporary chairman, Alfred G. Scattergood, has consented to serve as vice-chairman."

Alfred G. Scattergood: "Thank thee, Vincent. Rufus Jones' acceptance is a source of great satisfaction to me. Will thee come forward, Rufus, and take the chair?"

The group: "This appointment is most gratifying."

Rufus M. Jones, taking the chair: "It has not been easy for me to decide whether I ought to accept this appointment or not. I am already carrying a heavy load of responsibility and it has been only after a period of careful consideration that I have felt willing to accept the chairmanship of this new committee. However, it has been laid upon me that I ought to accept. We have no way now of knowing how wide the area of our service will be in the years to come but I feel that this is a momentous occasion, perhaps one of the most important steps of my life. We have met together a few times and already we are deep in plans for a piece of relief work which will demand sacrificial lives and consecrated hearts. We are, all of us, dedicated to this task to which we have set our hands and we are also dedicated to our beloved Society of Friends. There are only a few of us but I hope we shall be able to keep ourselves free from prejudice while men are torn with bitterness and hate. We must be great in spirit if we are in any way to rectify the results of war.

"Vincent, will thee read the Minutes of the last meeting?"

Vincent D. Nicholson: "Minutes of the American Friends Service Committee, held Fifth Month 28, 1917 . . . Minutes of previous meetings were read and approved. The change of name from Friends' National Service Committee to the American Friends Service Committee was approved . . . The

Ploughshare

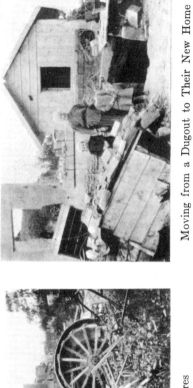

Reaping in France

Moving from a Dugout to Their New Home

The Équipe at Evres

Committee on Executive Secretary reported that after conferring with the Friends in Richmond, Indiana, they found the Five Years Meeting would support the work. Vincent D. Nicholson has agreed to accept the offer to be Executive Secretary of the Committee and he will take up that position on June first . . .

"Grayson M.-P. Murphy, Chief of the American Red Cross in France, has requested a commission of two Friends to sail with him on the *Touraine*, June the second, for France. After careful consideration of the personnel of this commission it was agreed to ask J. Henry Scattergood and Morris E. Leeds to go . . . It was felt that the commission should also get in touch with Friends in England . . .

"The Committee on Foreign Work reported that it had enough applicants from which to choose four women for Russia . . . We are still waiting for details to come from England regarding the seven Friends who are to work with their relief committee in France. It is estimated that it will cost $2000 for each of the persons going to Russia. The committee is to finance both the Russian and the French Unit, meeting all expenses but paying no salary . . .

"It was decided to begin the training of one hundred men to comprise Reconstruction Unit number one at Haverford College as soon as possible after Commencement. The following were appointed as a committee with full power to determine the qualifications of the men and pass on applicants for this Unit and to organize the training: Rufus M. Jones and others . . .

"Sympathy was expressed with the idea of sending women also . . .

"Then adjourned, J. Barnard Walton, temporary secretary." [1]

[1] Minutes for Meeting held May 28, 1917, with a few slight changes in wording.

Rufus M. Jones: "Unless there are any corrections, the Minutes are approved. Thank thee, Vincent. Lucy Biddle Lewis, will thee report on the plans for sending workers to Russia?"

Lucy Biddle Lewis: "We are very happy to be able to say that six women have offered their services for Russia, four of whom have been chosen by the sub-committee, subject, however, to satisfactory medical certificates. We were not able to have these reports in before this meeting today. The women in question are, my daughter, Lydia Lewis, Anna Haines, Nancy Babb and Amelia Farbiszewski. The last named is not a Friend, but holds the views of Friends with regard to war, and is eminently fitted for the work as she speaks Russian and is experienced in social work. The first three named are Friends with wide experience in social work. The sub-committee recommends sending the other two applicants, Esther White and Emilie Bradbury if English Friends so desire."

Rufus M. Jones: "Thank thee for this interesting information. What is your wish concerning our Russian Unit?"

Hannah Clothier Hull: "I should like to express my gratitude for the great amount of time and labor which this sub-committee has spent on this matter. It seems to me that the fact that Miss Farbiszewski is not a Friend will not make very much difference and her knowledge of the Russian language and country will make her a valuable asset to the group. I hope very much we shall see our way clear to send these four women with the prospect of sending the other two when we hear from Friends in London."

Willard Swift: "In view of the great expense entailed in sending workers to Russia would it not be expedient to limit ourselves to four only, at least for the present?"

Rufus M. Jones: "I hope it will be possible to send all six but I believe we must wait until we hear from London. I should like to add that these six women named by Lucy Biddle Lewis are splendid persons, qualified to undertake the extremely difficult tasks which will await them. I hope nothing will prevent them from going."

Lucy Biddle Lewis: "They are planning to sail in July."

Rufus M. Jones: "Henry, will thee report on the workers for France?"

Henry J. Cadbury: "You all know the poem where the little girl, when asked how many brothers and sisters she had, replied, 'Oh, master, we are seven!' I can report that we still have seven volunteers although one person has withdrawn, but there will be no difficulty in filling this vacancy. We have cabled to London that we had seven workers to send over at once and they cabled back that they would be glad to use all seven though they had asked for only five. English Friends will welcome any number whom we can send and I foresee that as our work becomes organized we are going to be swamped with applications for service. George V. Downing, Eleanor Cary, Douglas Waples, Ernest Brown and Howard and Kitty Elkinton are expecting to sail on June 23rd and we may consider them as heralds to the larger number whom we hope to send later. We have interviewed these Friends and feel that they are well qualified."

Stanley R. Yarnall: "It seems to me, Friends, that the way is opening in a remarkable manner for this new venture of ours. I hope we may be truly thankful for these young men and women who are volunteering to go to Russia and France."

Rufus M. Jones: "Perhaps we might leave this subject and pass on to the matter of the Reconstruction Unit, about which I am to report. I have had a long conference

with Isaac Sharpless who is willing for us to use Haverford
College during the Unit's period of training. Barclay Hall
will house one hundred men and President Sharpless will
turn over the college's equipment for our project. We have
had inquiries from several Quaker men but the application
blanks are still at the printers' and until they can be distributed to every community where there are Friends we
cannot handle the applicants satisfactorily."

Barnard Walton: "I hope our secretary will inform President Sharpless of the gratitude of this committee for his
generous offer. There is a question in my mind on which
I should like the thinking of this group. Will the Unit
of a hundred men be made up of Friends only, or do we
expect to welcome conscientious objectors from all denominations?"

Rufus M. Jones: "Barnard has raised a very important
question. There will be many, especially among the Mennonites and the Brethren, who will share our testimony
concerning war. I hope that we can co-operate with other
sects in every way that is possible but I feel that we ought
to make this first Unit primarily a Quaker group. It will
be easier to settle this question as the applications come in.

"We are going to be faced, of course, with the fact that
many Friends will not share in our testimony and will feel
that they must join the army. This has happened already
in England and is sure to happen here. We want to make
it clear from the start that this Unit is not being formed
to give Friends a way of escaping hardship. It is to offer
an honorable service to those whose consciences will not
allow them to defend their country by carrying arms. As
was said at our first meeting of this committee on April
30th, 'We are united in expressing our love for our country and our desire to serve her loyally. We offer ourselves
to the Government of the United States in any constructive

work in which we can conscientiously serve humanity.'[2] There will, doubtless, be Friends who will want to use this Unit as a way of escape and who are trying to evade the draft. We must guard against receiving any men who are 'on the fence.' We cannot make up their minds for them. This crisis calls for the most profound searching of heart and conscience that has ever faced the Society of Friends, and I hope it will be possible for the Society to stand out, firm and unwavering, for our testimony against war, but in the hysteria and propaganda which is sweeping America after her entrance into the war, the youth will be swept off their feet. We must be lenient with their perplexities and bewilderments, but the issue is for them to decide and we must not urge them to think what we believe they ought to think.

"Our major problem will lie in getting conscientious objectors, whether they are Quakers or not, exempted from the draft. While I believe that the Secretaries of War and of State in Washington will be able to make some arrangement for releasing these boys from the draft to do reconstruction in France, I think it is important to appoint a small group to visit these Secretaries and lay our concern before them. I should like to see Vincent Nicholson one of such a group."

Vincent Nicholson: "Well, Rufus, I am glad thee is optimistic about so much interest for the peace cause in Washington just now. Personally, I think we are going to find it difficult to convince these Secretaries that we are being just as patriotic in our way as the army is in its way. Theoretically the world knows that the Quakers are pacifists, but we are in the minority and at a time like this we may be ignored. It is going to be extremely diffcult to secure passports for the Unit."

[2] From the Minutes of the Meeting on April 30, 1917.

Rufus M. Jones: "Thee is too pessimistic, Vincent. We must present this concern so that it will take hold of the Washington officials. I feel sure they will make some arrangement for us."

Arabella Carter: "I hope that Rufus Jones will go with Vincent Nicholson on this visit to Washington."

The Committee: "I hope he will also."

Alfred G. Scattergood: "I hope Hollingsworth Wood can go also, and that these three Friends can report back to us as soon as possible. The whole program of sending men to France depends on being allowed to secure passports for them. I should like to say, while we are on the subject of sending workers to France that I have been asked several times whether we are going to send women as well as men. What are we to decide on this matter?"

Anne Walton: "It seems to me that it is impossible for us to decide anything about the needs in Europe until we can hear directly from the two commissioners whom we have sent over for the express purpose of investigating just such matters as this. Two women are going in this first group which sails this month. We shall be able to learn from them also whether it will be advisable to send any more."

Harold Evans: "I approve of Anne Walton's suggestion. It is likely that a few women workers will be needed but I feel that we should begin with the Haverford Unit and then proceed as way opens."

Harold Watson: "I have been wondering how we are to reach all the outlying Meetings. This committee is so new that many Friends will not have heard of it."

Rufus M. Jones: "The American Friends Service Committee represents the two Philadelphia Yearly Meetings and the Five Years Meeting. It seems to me that we can work through existing organizations in all these Yearly Meetings and be a central office and clearing house. We may need a Field Secretary besides our Executive Secretary, but Vincent has written already to every Yearly Meeting in the United States and each Yearly Meeting is writing to all its local meetings. This should greatly simplify our task and will make it possible for us to be in touch with every Quaker community. As soon as the plans are organized for the Unit I do not think we shall have much trouble in announcing ourselves.

"We can have no way of telling how long the war is going to last, but it is my hope that the Service Committee will be a connecting link for all of these scattered meetings throughout the United States and one of the great pieces of service which we can perform is the amalgamation of the Society of Friends. We have no way of knowing what the future holds for this newly created child.

"The Finance Committee has a report to make before we adjourn."

Harold Evans: "Friends will remember that it was decided to ask Charles F. Jenkins to serve as Treasurer. He has signified his willingness to serve in that capacity."

The Committee: "This is very satisfactory."

Rufus M. Jones: "I know of no further business for this afternoon. Shall we close our meeting with a few minutes of silent hush?

> "Thou, O Christ, convince us by Thy Spirit,
> thrill us with Thy Divine passion, drown our
> selfishness in Thy invading love, lay on us
> the burden of the world's suffering . . ." [3]

---

[3] Prayer by John Wilhelm Rowntree.

This chapter is a composite account taken from the Minutes of three committee meetings. Those whose names are given as being present were in attendance at one or all of these meetings, and their conversation is imaginary although the topics were discussed at these meetings.

CHAPTER II

PREPARATIONS FOR FRANCE AND
THE FRENCH MISSION

THE casual observer in Philadelphia who walks along Twelfth Street between Market and Chestnut Streets will see on his right a high, iron fence with two heavy iron gates. Behind this fence, set back from the pavement, is a two story brick building, rather dingy, not very impressive in size because it is overshadowed by higher ones around it. The "yard" is covered with brick paving except for a small plot of ground in which, during spring and early summer, there flourishes a fairly respectable growth of grass. Children run in here to find their ball which has come over the fence from Clover Street, the alley which runs off from Twelfth Street at a right angle. At Christmas time the fence is hung with holly wreaths and mistletoe which are sold to passers-by. In the autumn the chestnut man stands on the corner with his little stove and his roasted chestnuts and in the spring a man sells catnip to cat lovers.

The observer will see that a building juts out nearly to the fence and that it has a roof over a small porch, supported by yellow columns. If he looks through the gate, however, he will see that there is another door, farther back, and that there is a bay window to the left of the door, filled with plants and flowers. On the second floor he may see someone moving about.

If he sees any of these things as he hurries past he is

conscious only that here is a building unlike any of the others along the street and he wonders why it has not been torn down to make room for something modern and useful. Why should a valuable piece of land in the centre of Philadelphia be wasted for a dingy, two story brick building?

In 1917 there were young men and women who had come to Philadelphia for the first time and who were hunting for the address which had been given to them, Twenty South Twelfth Street. They were more than casual observers. They came to the iron fence and paused, wondering whether this was the place for which they were looking. At the gate they paused again to be sure that this was the Quaker Meeting House and the Friends Institute. Here, they had been told, was housed the American Friends Service Committee and they had come to offer themselves for service in France. For twenty years messenger boys, mail carriers, girls and boys, men and women have been going in the gate to carry on the business of the American Friends Service Committee, coming out again to a larger life in other countries and other cities.

Twenty-four days after the United States entered the World War a group of fourteen Friends met together in Philadelphia at Fifteenth and Race Streets on April 30, 1917, to discuss what should be done in a crisis which would affect every Quaker man of draft age. These Friends who met together represented both Race and Arch Street Yearly Meetings, Hicksite and Orthodox, and the Five Years Meeting to which body neither of the Philadelphia Meetings belonged. But theological differences of past generations were forgotten in the more important problem which faced them all,—the desire of all Friends to bear a testimony against war and to do a constructive piece of work in an area which had been used as a battlefield.

When the American Friends Service Committee was organized its first requirement was an office for its new secretary, Vincent D. Nicholson. The Friends Institute was a wing which had been added to the meeting house in 1892 to provide club and reading rooms for members of the Society of Friends who had no suitable place in the city where they could spend their free time. It contained six rooms altogether for the use of its members and it was willing to allow a room on the first floor to be turned over for the Service Committee. Vincent Nicholson moved in on the first of June and began to interview the candidates for the Haverford Unit. Here also he wrestled with the almost insuperable difficulties of the draft, for the task of obtaining exemption for conscientious objectors did not prove to be as simple as had been expected. English Friends had been carrying on relief and reconstruction in France since 1914 and it had seemed to American Friends that it would be a comparatively simple matter for Quakers of draft age to be released to assist English Friends in the work which they had started.

It had been understood that members of religious bodies who did not believe in war were automatically liberated from military service, but it was soon learned that the exemption was from active service only and that Friends would be expected to give some form of non-combatant service, which for the conscientious objector, was more distasteful in some ways than going to the front and carrying a bayonet. Non-combatant service gave him a safe, comparatively easy job, while the man without religious objections to war was sent off to the front where he was more than likely to be killed or severely wounded. A Quaker who was not willing to fight but would join the army and be a cook for the mess would seem to be a hypocrite. It meant that a sincere conscientious objector could not join the army in any way and if he could not get exemption from military service he was treated as a prisoner in the military camps.

In the early days of the war, English Friends had met this same problem. They had been brought before a Tribunal where they applied for complete exemption and when they refused to take any form of alternative service, as many of them did, they were sent to prison. The last question put before them was, "If you are not willing to undertake any kind of work of national importance as a condition of being exempted from military service, state precisely your reasons; and also how you reconcile your enjoying the privileges of British citizenship with this refusal?" The following is a typical answer to this question.

"I am not prepared to take on or continue what is called work of national importance merely 'as a *condition of being exempted.*' When a man holds such beliefs as mine, he must be prepared to suffer for them until he can get the law of the land and the majority of his fellows to accept the validity of his beliefs. I hold that the law has allowed my convictions are worthy of complete respect, even in war time, and I claim the *complete exemption* the Military Service Acts permit. The only alternative which my conscience tells me it is my duty to accept is the alternative of the prison, and, if need be, of the atrocities which have been committed upon the conscientious objectors. I am not willing to wriggle out of that alternative by accepting the bargain of 'work of national importance.' None of the privileges of British citizenship have been won by war. It was the strong hearts of the past who resisted, even unto death, the growth of the belief in, and practice of, militarism, who have given us such privileges as we possess. It is my duty to continue in my present course in order to hand down at least some of those privileges to the generations to come. When this war is over . . . British citizens will find their privileges have been gradually filched away from them. The memory that I stood, as I conceive it to be my duty to stand, for the privileges which war taketh away, will be, I think, the best contribution that I can make to the rebuilding again of that Faith in Liberty, whose destruction has been the most terrible consequence of this war." [1]

The path of a conscientious objector during the years from 1914 to 1918 was not an easy one.

A committee of three Friends visited the newly appointed Chief of the American Red Cross in France, Major Grayson Murphy, a former student at Haverford College, and Henry P. Davison, the Director of all Foreign War-Relief Work. The former "heartily welcomed the suggestion of the formation of a Quaker Unit to work in co-operation with the civilian service of the American Red Cross in France and he suggested that a small commission of Friends be sent to France to work out plans on the field." The latter "fell in heartily with the proposal and gave it his official approval and endorsement." [2] J. Henry Scattergood and Morris E. Leeds sailed for France June second to investigate the field at first hand.

In the meantime plans were made in the office at Twenty South Twelfth Street to organize a Unit of one hundred men to be trained during the summer at Haverford College under the direction of Dr. James A. Babbitt and to reach Paris early in September, but the question of obtaining passports for the members of the Unit proved to be more difficult than any one had anticipated and while the Unit went through a summer of strenuous preparation,—road building, ploughing, lessons in French and first aid and various other necessary

[1] Question and Answer taken from *Why I am a Conscientious Objector,* published by The No-Conscription Fellowship, London, 1916.
[2] Jones, Rufus M., *A Service of Love in Wartime,* p. 10.

information, Rufus Jones and others with him made frequent trips to Washington in an endeavor to get permission for members of the Unit to sail. But in the end "every man of the Haverford hundred got passports, except the one man whose local board in Indiana refused to the last either to transfer him or to grant him a permit." [3]

There was not room in any of the ships crossing the Atlantic to transport the entire Unit at one time. The first men to arrive in France reached Paris on September 7, 1917. These were followed by fifty-one men and three women a week later. It had been decided to include a small number of women although they did not have any such period of preparation at Haverford as the men had received. Work began from the start as a "triangular merger"—the War Victims Committee of the English Friends, the American Red Cross and the American Friends Service Committee—and this arrangement continued until the work in France was finished in 1920.

Charles Evans was chief of the American Unit from September 1917 until November 1918 when Charles J. Rhoads took his place. During the last period of the French work Wilmer J. Young was in charge of the headquarters in France, from which all the work of the "Mission" as it was called, radiated. This work was divided into five specific headings, medical, agricultural, transport, building and relief. There were hospitals at Châlons-sur-Marne, Samoëns, Sermaize, Bethincourt and Brizeaux. Portable houses were made at Dôle and Ornans. Although members of the Mission were awarded definite jobs under these special classifications, in times of crisis, of which there were many, as in Caesar's day, everything had to be done at the same time. Everyone tried to give as much assistance as he was physically able to render.

[3] *Ibid.,* p. 58.

During the last big push of the German army in the spring of 1918 whole villages had to be evacuated which meant getting transportation, food and lodging for these refugees until they could return to the places which had been their homes. After the Armistice, the Mission undertook the rebuilding of the destroyed Verdun region and it was at this time that they tried two daring schemes. First of all they bought, for a comparatively small sum, five American army dumps which were now useless to the army, and which contained tools of all kinds, machines, barbed wire, everything which the Mission could use for its task of rebuilding. Whatever it could not use was sold at a minimum cost to the French peasants and this unexpected sum of money and that which came in from sales in the co-operative stores was used later to erect a new building for the Maternity Hospital at Châlons and to provide the equivalent of wages for the German prisoners who assisted the Mission workers in rebuilding the Verdun area. Use of German prisoners was the second daring scheme. These men were idle and the French Government allowed the Friends Mission to employ the prisoners on the two conditions that no man should be permitted to escape and that no wages should be paid. This agreement was carried out but a record was kept of the amount of time which the prisoners gave to the work and their "wages" were given to their families in Germany.

"Though many things from the dumps were given to needy families or sold at low prices, most of the materials not shipped were sold at market prices to people of the community who could afford to pay for what they wanted. Not only was it interesting to see these war materials turned over to civilians for the arts of peace, but it was also a satisfaction to have a hand in persuading French men of means to aid French people made needy by the war,—that is, persuading the well-to-do to help the poor indirectly through the Mission. Thus, during the last spring and summer when the Mission might have been short of funds it was able to continue with its full program by means of additional resources from one of its own departments, and these funds will be a large factor in the success of our Maternity Hospital project at Châlons-sur-Marne.

"The financial success of the Dumps Department directly expanded the work of the Mission in its various departments and the operation of this one expanded the influence of the Mission by putting us in vital contact with French commercial life and with the American army, through each of which I am convinced the work of the Mission, and hence its ideals, are getting favorable advertisement. This is also true of the German prisoners whom we employed. Looking back to compare my early anticipations concerning the Dumps with my experience in this department, I find that what had appealed to me as a venture into 'no man's land' with many unfavorable possibilities has really been a venture in 'practical idealism' with many gratifying phases emphasizing to me the desirability of a Missionary proposition being self-supporting." [4]

"According to the latest reports, December 1919, relief in some form or degree has been given by Friends to 1666 French villages and over 46,000 families have been assisted. The Mission has planted 25,000 trees, mostly fruit trees, in the Verdun area, five trees per family and many communal trees. Of the group still on the field, more than half are eager to go, when their work in France is done . . . to one of the new fields of labor and relief which have already opened in Serbia, Poland, Vienna and Germany." [5]

While the members of the Unit in France, clad in their

[4] Liechty, O. R. in *Reconstruction*, January 15, 1920.
[5] Jones, Rufus M., *A Service of Love in War Time*, p. 240.

gray uniforms and wearing the red and black star on their arms, labored to restore French villages, the office space at Twenty South Twelfth Street became too small. The Friends Institute granted the request that the office should be moved upstairs into "the two east rooms." The Service Committee was still a temporary, emergency Mission, but it was increasing its outreach and its field of service all the time. As the war continued more men were drafted and suddenly the Committee found itself without an Executive Secretary. Vincent Nicholson had been drafted and sent to camp. This occurred in August 1918 and while efforts were being made to obtain a furlough for him, Wilbur K. Thomas was appointed Acting Secretary in his place. He became Executive Secretary in September when Vincent Nicholson resigned. Two months later the Armistice was signed and the fighting stopped. The war was over, everyone believed, so that life could return to its normal routine. Service abroad would be needed no longer.

The signing of the Armistice did not miraculously restore French villages, nor feed German children, nor give coal to Austria, nor prevent famine in Russia, nor remove typhus fever from Poland, nor do away with the need for constructive peace, international and interracial programs, nor give work to unemployed miners.

The Mission remained in France until 1920 but their return to America was the beginning of another great period of service.

"Now, God be thanked who has matched us with His hour,
And caught our youth and wakened us from sleeping . . ."

"We have built a house that is not for Time's throwing . . ."

RUPERT BROOKE

Chapter III

"THE SPIRIT OF THE MISSION"

The following is an imaginary account of a Sunday afternoon in June 1918. The two women, Abby Worthington, an American, and Myra Reynolds, English, are living outside of a French village where they are giving relief. Dick Allen, American, from the Agricultural Department, Stephen Barrett, English, from the Transport, and engaged to Myra, Tyler Wilson, American, from the Medical, and Jack Harris, American, from the Building Departments, have come to spend the afternoon with the girls.

The late afternoon sun threw long shadows in the courtyard and fell warmly on the white-washed statue of the Virgin who, with her gentle outstretched hands, guarded the entrance to the old house. Every foot of land, except the path and a grassy plot beneath the clump of trees, had been made into a garden. The dark green leaves of the potatoes, so coarsely marked, and the pinkish white blossoms nodded in the slight breeze. There was a long row of lettuce and another of carrots. Close against the house there was a small garden edged with stones where nasturtiums were growing, the orange and yellow flowers half hidden under the round flat leaves. There was a rosebush winding itself in and out over the old arbor and the delicate perfume of the roses was blown by the breeze over the courtyard.

Because it was Sunday the church bells in the distant

village were ringing for the evening service. Two old ladies in clean white caps walked down the path toward the gate, their thick, clumsy boots grating on the path as they scuffed their heavy feet. Abby heard them coming in spite of the conversation around her.

"Grandmère, Madame," she called, "You must not go to church. It is too far, the walk is too long for you and the road too steep. I beg of you to stay here." Abby left the table under the trees and caught up with the two old women. "Grandmère, you cannot walk so far and by the time you reach the village the service will be finished."

"It is no matter, ma fille. If the service is over we shall return. Last Sunday it rained, and the one before that the wind blew, and the one before that the air was too cold. To-day the sun is warm and the good God will know that we have attempted it, at least. Let us go."

"You are both foolish," Abby replied.

"No more than you, ma fille," Madame answered. "Do you not wear yourself out all day and every day? Now you are having rest. Go back to your friends. We shall be too late if you keep us standing here." Grandmère and Madame scuffed along and Abby went into the kitchen. She came out bringing a jug of boiling water.

"Those old women will drop dead on the way," she announced to the group under the trees. "They have no business to walk so far but I can't stop them."

"Oh, don't worry about them, Abby. They'll walk a kilometer, sit down for a rest and walk back. They'll never get to church and they don't mean to. Spring's just got into their blood, that's all. Turn your attention to us, please. How about a little more butter for a starving refugee?" Dick handed an empty plate to Abby.

"You just put that plate down, Dick. Do you think we run a dairy here? I'll have you know that you boys have eaten up a half pound of butter this afternoon. We don't get more than a pound a week, anyway."

"Hard luck, old girl. A swarm of locusts descends on the belle mademoiselle and eats her out of house, home and butter. Is there any more honey?"

"I'm saving that for next Sunday. After that when you come you can eat your bread without anything."

"Never mind next Sunday, Abby. We may be bombed before then. Give us the honey today. Where is it? I'll get it."

"No you won't either. And you needn't hunt for it for you'll never find it. You've all had enough."

"Had enough!" Dick exclaimed, "but, Abby, we've hardly had a thing. Look at this table! It's perfectly bare. I know just how Mother Hubbard's poor starving dog felt."

"Do you? Then let me give each of you a teaspoonful of cod liver oil. Children around here are practically crying for it."

"Maybe, but their sense of smell is the type which would relish that foul stuff. How about letting us have the honey now and giving us a rabbit pie next week, if we come. We may all be dead and think how badly you'd feel to realize you hadn't fed us up properly. These rabbits of yours look remarkably fat and juicy."

"Look here, my dear boy, was I sent out to France to care for these old ladies or to feed the Mish? Am I raising these rabbits for Sunday afternoon teas and spending my time making special dishes for this hungry horde? If you're still hungry you can eat some of those carrots. They're awfully good for you, raw, right out of the ground, with the dirt still clinging to them. Makes them more filling."

"Oh, come on, Abby, don't get sore. We know you've raised these rabbits yourself, that is, the rabbits have done a large part of it themselves, and hoed the potatoes and done everything up here to make it a swell place. But English cooking at the équipe does get monotonous, begging your pardon, Myra. This is the only place where we can get butter and honey and sit down for a good time. Where else can we come and play with rabbits? You'd better put them in a pen, Abby, they'll eat up everything in the garden if you don't and then you'll blame us, I suppose."

"Well, then, Dick, you entertain yourself catching them all."

"Gosh, everything lives on everything else, doesn't it. What a world, but do you know, one of the few things I have really learned is that I am always hungry."

Abby pushed her cup and saucer away and tossed her large, floppy hat on the ground. She ran her fingers through her hair and the breeze loosened the tendrils around her face.

"Isn't it funny," she sighed, "here I sit, so thankful to be cool when last winter I thought I could never be warm enough again. Do you remember, Myra, the hot bricks we took to bed, and the sleeping bags and the layers of clothes? Did you ever picture yourself sitting out here in a thin dress, trying to keep cool? Thank heaven winter is over. I don't see how I can go through another."

"I don't believe you'll have to. All this last push of the Germans is a final effort. No one believes they can keep it up much longer."

"Steve! Is that really true?" Myra leaned forward, tense with eagerness. Steve's sock, which she was darning, fell from her hand. "These last raids have been pretty awful and they've got on our nerves. That's why Abby seems cross. She isn't really."

"Oh, I know," Dick said.

"It's pretty well got us, too," Steve went on, "but I think it's the end. The Americans are pouring in and they're dying like flies, but the Allies are going to push the Germans back. If we have to go through another winter everybody'll go mad. You can't carry on a massacre like this forever. After a certain length of time it makes everybody sick, like too many sweets. But I've been out here so long that I can't imagine life without the war. What would it be like to be back in England, with a regular job, wearing proper clothes?

"I keep thinking about my brother. What's he going to do when the war is over? He's been in prison since 1915 and all he's been allowed to do is read and write letters to mother about what he has read. What kind of a life is that for a brilliant boy just down from a University? He always has liked to study and at first he didn't mind the chance to go on. But after rotting away, year after year, reading Thucydides and *Paradise Lost*, where's it getting him? He'll lose his mind if he stays there much longer."

"Steve, couldn't he have been released for service in the Mish?" Abby questioned.

"Yes, if he would have. But he didn't approve of alternative service. We British C.O.s were taken before a Tribunal. First of all we had to state why we were applying for exemption from military service and then we were asked ten questions. It's not so hard to refuse the military. After all, that's fairly obvious, but it's a nice point for your conscience to decide whether you will go to prison and do nothing, or whether you will take an active part in any reconstruction service. My brother refused everything and there was no question in his mind that alternative service was wrong. I did not come along until 1916. I'd had a year of reading his letters to mother. What was I to do? I couldn't fight, but prison didn't seem the right thing, either. That's where every man's conscience has a different interpretation of what's right and what's wrong. I believed it was better to be doing something positive. I'd have gone stark crazy in a month cooped up in a cell. If anybody had handed me a gun by the end of that month I'd have grabbed it just to have something solid in my hands. It was better for me to grab tools and be working with the transport. A man's conscience isn't all there is to him. It would be a lot easier if it were but there are flesh and blood and muscle which undermine the soul if the body is shut up. My brother is a stronger man than I am and I respect his stand. It's right for him. I believe I am right, too. I know I would have joined the army and been in the front line of the trenches if I couldn't have had alternative service."

"Steve, I can't imagine you in the trenches, no matter what. You're much too kind hearted."

"That's what you think, Myra, but you haven't seen me yelling at the peasants or swearing over the petrol or cursing the American boys who don't understand English cars!"

"Listen to Stevie!" Tyler slapped his leg and roared with laughter. "Myra, he's so mild that the cars roll over him and he doesn't know it! As for the peasants, they think he's priceless. He could no more fight anybody than he could fly. Fly away, birdie!" Tyler waved his arms at Steve and threw some bread crumbs toward him. "He's so soft hearted, Myra, that I know he's in agony watching you darn his socks. The needle hurts their feet!" Every one laughed.

"Jack, tell us what you've been doing this week," Abby asked, when the laughter had died down. "We're marooned up here and never know anything." Jack was silent a minute before he answered.

"I've just been counting up. In the seven days since last Sunday I've had nineteen meals. That is not enough."

"Kill him, somebody," Tyler expostulated from the grass where he had thrown himself down. "There is a limit. Dick, you tell the ladies your experiences. I'm going to sleep."

"That's right. Spend the afternoon with two ladies. All you boys can think of is food and sleep. Myra and I are flattered."

"Really, Abby," Tyler said, "you can say the nicest things. I suppose you wouldn't be a bit sleepy if you'd been up half the nights in the week, operating on the lame, halt and blind, with the lights so feeble that the nurses have to hold bug lights, excuse me, Myra. I forgot the English sensitiveness to that word, 'bug.' I mean, of course, insect lights, so that I can see. You would be fresh as a daisy, I know, after such peaceful evenings."

"Oh, Tyler, I am sorry to be so nasty, but here we are, simply starved for talk and all you boys can think about is food and sleep. I know you are tired to death, but so are we."

"Well, we've been running a three ring circus in our hospital. I guess I haven't seen you since you sent me that boy with meningitis. I was sorry to send his body back in the middle of the night, but if the officials had found him there, with no papers, we would have been in a hole, since he lived in another district. How'd the mother take his death? Hope she didn't blame you."

"Steve brought him back, you know. He banged on the gate, frightening poor old Madame out of her wits. She came puffing up into my bed room as fast as her lame knees could bring her, shouting that it was the Germans at the gate."

"I told you so," Tyler interrupted, "Steve is awfully fierce when he is aroused!"

"I was so dead asleep," Abby continued, "that I couldn't make out what was the matter and when I got down there was Steve, expecting Myra instead of me. That was a disappointment. He told me the child died on the operating table and that you had sent the body back into his own district before morning."

"Why didn't you send the kid down sooner, Abby? There wasn't a ghost of a chance for him by the time he arrived."

"Did you ever try to make one of these French peasant women do something when her mind is set against it, Tyler? I'd been trying to get her to send the boy for three days but she wouldn't hear of such a thing. Finally, she came wailing to me and begged me to do something, and of course by that time he was desperately ill. I wish you could have seen me hunting for a horse to pull the old cart that's over here in the shed. All the horses having been sent off, supposedly, to the army, there wasn't one to be had for love or money. I went to every house in the village and was just getting on my bicycle to come home and give it up, when a man whom I had never seen appeared and told me there would be a horse and cart standing near the sick boy's house. I thanked him and said nothing more. It was, obviously, one of those occasions when you ask no questions. We got the boy in the cart as fast as we could and refused to take the mother. I should say it was one of the outstanding dramas of the Mish, because French peasants are not easily balked. You should have seen the road and my driving. The horse turned up as an answer to prayer, so to speak, and I took it as an omen that the boy might get well."

"Not a chance. But you're a plucky one, Abby. I've got to hand it to you. Not many women could have scared up a horse. Well, tell us the rest."

"When we got around to the mother's house she was even

deader asleep than I was. I banged on the door until she came, dirty and disgustingly drunk. Steve handed her the body wrapped up in an old coat and he told her the doctor was very sorry but the boy got there too late and was dead. I told Steve to go and I'd stay with the woman. The place was full of bottles, the mess and the stench were beyond anything. After I got out I couldn't get enough clean air into my lungs."

"You'd have enjoyed living with the peasants as I did. Not a window open, not a door. The goats and the chickens, grandpa, grandma, mama and the children all crowded in together. Papa was off to the war, thank goodness, but the air couldn't have been much richer if he had been there. I almost joined the army so I could get hold of a gas mask. It's going to be fun when we live with them during the threshing season. Chaff and dust will make it even sweeter."

"Poor old Dick! Well, if the atmosphere was so rich it must have helped to ease the pangs of hunger. Have another crumb, do!" Tyler flipped an invisible morsel in Dick's direction.

"Abby, you know this is a swell place here. Will you kindly tell me how you got this? What do you do besides hoe potatoes, encourage the propagation of rabbits and hide honey under your pillow?"

"You've been quiet for a long time, Jack. I was getting worried about you. I came here because nobody else wanted to. This particular spot was the great problem in the Mish. No one wanted to be shut up here in this remote place with ten old women, but it looked like heaven to me. I applied and they sent me, although they were worried that I was too young to be up here alone."

"Yes, but after all, you had the ten old women. They're good chaperons. How many have their eyes glued to the windows to see whether you are behaving like a lady?"

"You might go and see, Tyler. The first six weeks we spent in an old château several miles on the other side of the village. I thought I should pass out. It took me all day to saw cnough wood to burn for one evening. It rained practically every day that we were there and I sawed wet wood which wouldn't burn every single one of those days. There was never time to do anything else. What I have to do here is a mere nothing in comparison and anyway I have Myra to help me. What about yourself, Jack?"

"We're putting up some more houses and leveling the land again. You know it was bad enough when we got here last September and found villages flat and the land full of shell holes and the peasants living in cellars, but when we got new houses up and the land ready for crops it just never occurred to me that this would be destroyed. It's nothing but the work of the devil to wreck a place twice, especially when it's been built up again after the first raid."

"I know, Jack." Abby pushed back her hair with a fierce gesture of her hand. "The whole business is the work of the devil. Here I am, taking care of old women who will all be dead in a year or two, anyway, war or no war, and everybody else putting up houses that are made of nothing but wood and can be knocked down, the whole lot of them, by one shell. Everything we're doing seems so futile. Children die before we can get them to the hospital. What's it all for?"

"There's more use to what we're doing than what *they're* doing." Tyler indicated with the sweep of his hand the sound of guns which could be heard toward the horizon. "I suppose I notice them more here because it's so quiet and peaceful sitting in this garden. What if they are killing Germans? Killing off men isn't going to settle anything. A kid was brought into the hospital the other day with his hand blown off. He'd found a hand grenade, thought it was a stick, picked it up, and, whoops! off it went. It was meant for an adult enemy, but instead it struck a ten year old French boy who'll go through life without his right hand. Well, suppose it had been a French man or a German man who'd picked it up? It's like burning the martyrs at the stake. It may or may not prove a doctrine, but in any case it burns a man. Maybe there was some glory and hallelujah to this war in the first month, though I doubt it, but believe me, the excitement has worn off and it's plain Hell."

"Tyler, were you in camp before you came over here?"

"No, Abby, I came straight from Haverford. But I'll tell you about somebody who was. You know Bentley, don't you, who has to be so careful of his eyes and wears dark glasses a lot of the time? I thought it was funny they let anybody over here with such poor eyesight but Barton was telling me the other day what happened to him. Bentley never says a word, of course. He was in camp and was so badly treated it's a wonder they didn't kill him. They gouged thumbs in his eyes, that's why he has to be so careful, put a rope around his neck, beat him and I don't know what all. Barton said he had never taken much stock in the stories about martyrs in the old days and thought that a lot of hysterical people had manufactured most of them, but he said if ever there was a martyr for a cause it was Bentley. It would have been a kindness to him if they had killed him, he suffered so. They weren't gentle with Barton but they had some special spite against Bentley. He wouldn't do a thing he was asked to do, they thought he was crazy and tried the tactics on him that were used on the insane before people knew any better. Not one complaint was ever heard from Bentley, though Barton said he was so bruised that he could not lie down and that his eyes hurt him so that the pain was unbearable. His conscience was clear and he knew what he was doing, and if a man can go through that sort of treatment without a whimper, he's got a religion worth talking about.

"I didn't want to fight but I don't know whether I could have stuck to my principles if I'd been sent to a camp like that. I had a hard time to get a passport, but Rufus Jones did all the work getting that fixed up. We came straight here from Haverford, and by the time the draft hit me it was all fixed up. It's been a path of roses for me. Speaking of Rufus Jones, did you hear how he accepted the chairmanship of the American Friends Service Committee? He said he'd take the position and be chairman, but he didn't feel he could spend a great deal of time on the Committee. The joke's on him all right. He spent most of the summer of 1917 down in Washington getting our passports fixed up. From all I hear he spends more time on this job than he does at his teaching!"

"Well, I guess we're all surprised at the amount of time we're spending on this job! What would you do, Tyler, if there was something wrong with your papers and they told you you'd have to come home?"

"Don't breathe such an idea, Myra. For all my light talk, I'm heart and soul in this Mish Hospital. My conscience may have been vague last summer at Haverford but I'm not vague any more. I didn't know what it was all about. I didn't believe in war but then I didn't know what war was like. I had a cheerful picture of men in red coats, black boots, carrying nice, shining swords and riding on coal black chargers. You can't get awfully wrought up about an affair that looks like that. Because I was brought up to believe that war was wrong I did my best to persuade myself that I didn't want to join the army and wear a red coat, but nine months of living in the midst of modern warfare has made me so damn sure that I never want to have anything to do with it that I guess the camp could do what they liked, but they couldn't make me fight. This method of settling a row is just plain silly, besides being anti-Christian. Sometimes I wonder how God can let this sort of thing go on."

It grew so dark that Myra could no longer see to darn Steve's socks and she folded them up neatly in her large mending basket. The six of them sat in silence for a while when Tyler finished speaking. He was not a man who spoke very often about himself. Abby uncrossed her knee.

"I can't help being impressed," she said, "at what Tyler says. I suppose it makes all the difference if you're a man. Myra and I could have stayed at home and it wouldn't have made any difference. Then of course Myra came partly because of Steve. When he came, it was natural for her to come. But I wasn't in love with anybody and I didn't have to choose between this or camp. I just didn't want to miss anything."

"If you weren't in love then, are you now?"

"You know there are times, Steve, when I wish you were in prison with your brother, reading Xenophon, or some other Greek. I most certainly am not. How anybody has the time or the energy to fall in love, I can't imagine. If you had to take care of ten old ladies and hoe a garden and—"

"And feed starving members of the Mish! But joking aside, Abby, why did you come to France? For a good time or to help save the world?"

"Oh, there were lots of reasons, Dick, I suppose. I wanted to get away from home. I wanted something different. I should have been driven entirely by altruistic motives, and having been born and brought up a Quaker probably I did have a small element of a concern to be of some use where there was need. How does one ever know, exactly? I wanted excitement. How much was that and how much concern it's hard to say."

"Not having been 'born and brought up a Quaker' like the rest of you, may I ask, as an interested observer whether excitement or concern is uppermost in your mind after these months here?"

"Dick, I didn't know you weren't a Friend. You mean that without benefit of clergy, as it were, without having been brought up in the principles of the Society of Friends, you thought it all out by yourself?"

"Well, hardly that, Abby. I'm a Mennonite and we hold the same views about war that the Quakers do. I have had a thorough training in the idea that war is wrong. I am hardly to be considered original in thinking it out for myself."

"What bothers me now," Abby continued, "is that while my conscience hadn't begun to work before I left home, it's working over time now. I don't feel as though I were getting anywhere. Yes, I know I was sent here to take care of these old ladies. That's simple enough. Here is a job, go and do it. I can speak French and I seem to be able to use my head, and what's more I can get along with the English, but twenty years from now what will my having done relief work in the war mean to me or any one else? We're all doing useful, practical jobs, like building houses, threshing grain, planting gardens, taking care of the sick, helping people who need us now. We're busy, we're fairly happy and we're appreciated. I suppose that ought to be enough. But it isn't enough. The war will end sometime and we'll all go home. Myra and Steve will get married and the rest of us will find other jobs, if we're lucky.

"We ought to be doing something that's more *vital*, more creative. We ought to be getting something of our own convictions over to these people. Quakerism never meant an awful lot to me until I arrived in France and began to try to put some of it into practice. If we're supposed to make

Quakers out of these Catholic peasants we have failed completely because they can't conceive of anything except the Catholic Church. They think Quakers are fine,—'Les Amis sont devoués'—but they were doubtful when I said you couldn't be a Catholic and a Quaker too. I suppose they look on us as some kind of a fraternity, or a club, like the Rotary or the Elks, which specializes in doing kind deeds. We've been here all this time and haven't done more than convince them that we're kindly people, yet we're members of a religion which has a dynamic, spiritual, contagious power. What's the matter with us?"

"Nothing's the matter with us," Steve replied. "We weren't sent out here to make converts. We've come out for a definite purpose, to build up in a spirit of love what has been destroyed in a spirit of hatred. We have professed that we could not fight because we did not believe, first of all, in killing our fellow men, and second, in using this method in settling disputes. We're merely a demonstration in a practical way of the spirit which does away with the occasion for war. We're not missionaries."

"But, Steve, what good is it if five hundred or more Quakers spend all these years in France giving a practical demonstration and not one single person is interested enough in the beliefs behind our demonstration to be converted to Quakerism?"

"You can't tell, Abby. Things like that don't happen in a hurry. When our work is finished it doesn't mean that our influence dies with it. These people are Catholics, as you have said, to whom Quakerism with its lack of form and ritual is not likely to appeal. We haven't come out here to show the world how wonderful we are, nor to impress these people with the fact that Quakerism is better than Catholicism. It may be for us but it would leave most of these peasants utterly cold. No, the thing that seems most im-

portant to me is the fact that while the world is waging a
war in the name of Christ, we can bind up the wounds of war
in the name of Christ. Religion means very little until it
is translated into positive action. Of course the men in the
trenches believe that's what they're doing, and you can't con-
demn them. We talk so much about the conscience of the
C.O. but the soldier has one too which makes him believe
it is right to defend his country with arms. 'For God, King
and Country' is no light, meaningless phrase. He considers
himself a Christian just as much as we think we are. How
can one be consistent? The Germans are praying to the same
God that we and the Allies are on this side of the Front.
Don't you think, Abby, that every one of us has gained a
real religious experience as the result of the Mish? Isn't
that worth something?"

"I know I have." Jack lit a cigarette and the six faces
gleamed suddenly in the light of the flickering match. "I
haven't said much before. I hadn't ever thought much
about religion except to dislike it and when the war came
along I was a student at Haverford so I was swept into the
Unit pretty easily. But I thought I'd see how things were
and maybe I'd join the army after I got over here. Building houses sounded like a sissy job when there were so
many more important things to be doing. That's what I
thought. You see I got turned against religion when I was
a kid. My folks were too strict and there was too much
talk about not being able to do this and it being wrong
to do that, and God would punish you if you disobeyed Him.
My folks are good and sincere, but their kind of religion
won't do for me and when I got to college I tried to forget it.

"My little plan to join the army passed out of the picture when I'd been here a month. Of all the stupid, inane
pieces of folly, trying to settle a dispute by killing a lot

of men is it. What right has one side of the line to fire bullets at the other? If you shoot a man on the streets of Philadelphia, you can be killed for it. But if you shoot a German over here you get a medal for it. The man's dead just the same. No, sir. Any religion that says it's all right for men to kill one another is obsolete, I don't care what Steve says.

"I guess the main thing the Unit will get out of this work in France will be a real, honest to goodness belief in Quakerism. I never thought I'd ever feel such a thing as the inner voice my folks talked about, but I know what it means. I know what Luther meant when he said, 'Here I stand, I cannot do otherwise.' You know that phrase about the ocean of light and love flowing over the ocean of darkness and death? It never meant a thing to me except so many words. Why, it's what we're trying to do! The trouble with my folks' religion is that it's always telling you what you can't do and shouldn't do, but religion if it's going to be any good tells you what you should do and you go ahead and do it. Instead of crushing you down into a little insignificant nothing at all it makes you grow into something big."

"I guess Jack has hit the nail on the head." Tyler sat up and rubbed his leg. "Got a cramp from sitting still so long. I'm not used to it. There's a problem on my mind, though. Suppose we'd been sent to Germany to do what we're doing here. We might have, you know. After all, they must be suffering a lot and for all we know need help more than anybody. Would we have rushed to get into the Mish or would we have found our Quaker principles balked at that prospect?"

"It wouldn't have been practical," Myra said. "They'd have thought we were spies and locked us up."

"That's evading Tyler's point which is a good one," Abby

replied. "It seems to me that if we find they do need relief then we ought to go to them just as much as to the French."

"Would you go, Abby?" Tyler asked.

"I might. I'd consider it more seriously if they'd fix the language so that there were no irregular verbs. My goodness! Grandmère and Madame haven't come back yet. I forgot all about them. Do you suppose they're lost?"

"Don't get excited, my dear. They came back long ago, tip-toeing gently so that you wouldn't hear them and ask about the service. They never got near the church. I knew they wouldn't." Dick's smile of satisfaction was lost in the dark. "We've got to clear out of here. It's getting late. The lights in that car are none too good."

"Oh, dear!" Myra exclaimed. "Must you go? It's such fun having you."

"Never mind, they'll come again next Sunday. You will, won't you?"

"Listen to Abby, the bounteous hostess. She's actually inviting us to come and feast on her groaning board!" Dick struck his empty cup with a spoon. "Listen to that hollow ring! Not one single drop and yet I am invited to come and drink. She'll hide the honey and tell us there is no butter and she'll go vegetarian and not kill her rabbits. Is that cricket? as the English say." Myra took hold of Steve's arm.

"You're mean, Dick. Abby let you boys take all her share of the butter. She won't have any at all this week. And she'll have something extra special for you. Maybe you do get hungry but after all we haven't got such bounteous supplies."

"I'm sorry, girls. You're regular trumps and we've had no end of a good time. Look how the statue stands out in the dark. I should think the poor soul would hate all this bloodshed. It's a kind of incessant crucifixion, isn't it? She watched her own Son hang on the cross and then they stick her up so that she can keep on watching the world at the same business. Well, good night, everybody."

"Good night."

"Myra, what a sweet day it has been!" Myra and Abby stood by the statue watching the lights of the car as it climbed up the hill and then vanished on the other side. "And what nice boys they are. They all have so much that's real about them. You know the slogan of the army or the navy, I forget which it is, that says, 'We build men!' The Mish builds men without any doubt."

CHAPTER IV

RUSSIA

IN April 1916 a small group of English Friends visited Russia in order to investigate conditions there. They went to the district of Samara and made their headquarters in Buzuluk, fourteen hundred miles from the German frontier and a thirty-six hour train ride from Moscow when the trains were running on schedule. In Buzuluk and its surrounding towns and villages they found the hospitals closed because the Russian doctors had been sent off to the Front. Hundreds of refugees had crowded into the already over-crowded peasants' homes. There was a great lack of employment, food and clothing.

After obtaining permission from the Zemstvo, or local governing body, the English Friends took a large country house at Motogova, several hours' drive north of Buzuluk, in which to care for orphan children. In November 1916 a hospital was opened and continued under the care of Friends, who sent doctors and nurses into Russia, until April 1918. To the south of Buzuluk, at Lubimovka, there was an empty hospital, containing fourteen beds. This was opened in July 1916 and remained under Friends until April 1918, when, as at Motogova, the return of many Russian doctors made outside help unnecessary.[1] At Bogdanovka and Andrievka, forty miles to the south, were medical centers. At the former were stationed a relief worker

[1] Because of the signing of the Russian Peace Treaty at Brest-Litovsk.

42

and a nurse and at the latter a doctor, a nurse, a dispenser for medical care and a relief worker. There was a hospital at Andrievka, but although attempts were made to use the in-patient department, only two wards for male patients were opened, and most of the work at this center was in the out-patient department, opened in October 1916. One of the buildings of the hospital was used for a refugee work room.

District nursing centers were established in Effimovka in December 1916 and Bogdanovka in March 1917. Nurses were in charge at each of these centers and a dispensary was open during the mornings. In the afternoons the nurses visited among the homes. The efficiency of this work was increased by weekly visits from a doctor. The latter center was closed at the end of August 1917 and the former at the end of April 1918.[2]

In Moscow, undernourished orphan children were placed out in orphanages situated in country districts, a total of five hundred children in three colonies. In Buzuluk there were workshops, feeding stations, a trade school, library, labor bureau and book-binding departments.[3]

Six American women, Esther White, Emilie C. Bradbury, Nancy Babb, Anna J. Haines, Lydia Lewis and Amelia Farbiszewski, all trained social workers, reached Russia in September 1917, one year after English Friends started their work. Due to the difficulties described later, all members of the Unit left Russia by October 1918. Lydia Lewis married Dr. John Rickman, one of the English doctors, and they left in the summer of 1918. Amelia Farbiszewski

---

[2] Material taken from the Annual Report of Russian Work of the Friends War Victims Relief Fund, 1916–1917. Reports of medical work in Southern Centers and of Motogova Hospital, August 1917–April 1918.

[3] *Relief and Reconstruction Work of the Society of Friends in Russia* and *Relief Work in Russia 1916*. J. Burtt.

left at that time also. Esther White went to Moscow with Theodore Rigg to see what could be done about bringing the orphans out of that area, which was threatened by famine, into the Samara district where food was more plentiful, but she finally left for England without having been able to accomplish anything. Nancy Babb, Anna Haines and Emilie Bradbury crossed into Siberia where they continued to give in Omsk a type of relief similar to that which they had given in Buzuluk.

This Unit, from the time it arrived in Russia until it left Siberia in July 1919, going by way of Vladivostok to Japan and across the Pacific Ocean to America, was isolated from the rest of the world to a degree which few people have realized, and it worked under conditions which were probably more difficult than those which confronted the Mission in the war zone. As an example of the Unit's isolation, Emilie Bradbury received no communication of any kind from her home for sixteen months after she arrived in Buzuluk. Letters sent into Russia from the offices in London and Philadelphia often never arrived and the same was true of letters sent from Russia. When the three women cabled to Philadelphia from Siberia asking for permission to remain and work with the Red Cross, the cable, sent on the 22nd of November, did not arrive in the office at Twenty South Twelfth Street until December 16th. They did not know that Vincent Nicholson had left the office in August and that Wilbur K. Thomas had taken his place.

In the summer of 1920 the Service Committee asked Anna Haines to return to Russia. With Arthur Watts, an English Friend, she distributed milk, soap, fats and medicines to people in Moscow and in the summer of 1921 she was the only foreign member of a group of Russian physicians and teachers who investigated the Volga region because of reports of famine in that area. She sent word to the Philadelphia office that a Unit of workers would be needed for the coming winter and Nancy Babb came out ahead of the Unit in order to take Anna Haines' place while she went back to the United States and carried on a publicity campaign to secure funds.

This Unit, headed by Murray S. Kenworthy, arrived in Russia on October 28, 1921. Several of these workers caught typhus, among them Murray Kenworthy himself who was very ill from December until the following March. There was some criticism that the Quakers were careless in their methods of precaution and that they took unnecessary risks, but this criticism was unwarranted because utmost measures were taken to prevent illness. The domestic end of living was complicated because all water had to be boiled for drinking and all food had to be cooked. Water for bathing was not easy to obtain in large quantities and the Unit, to be of any use at all, had to visit among the homes and be in close contact with both peasants and refugees. Members of the Unit wore a special kind of silk undergarment, supposed to be lice-proof since lice cannot crawl on silk, but even with this protection and caps over the hair, lice were so plentiful that it was impossible to escape them.

Besides these difficulties, the Unit was under a continual mental strain. The suffering around them was so terrible that, although their food was sufficient, they had little desire to eat when every one around them was starving. One can only marvel that this little band of workers came through this experience without losing their sanity.

The famine, caused by a continued drought and also by the blockade set up against Russia, was bad enough in itself, but in the summer of 1922 refugees swarmed into Russia from Turkestan, bringing with them the most virulent kind of malarial mosquito, so that a terrible epidemic of malaria was added to the many troubles of that year. Cholera was always prevalent during the summer. Actual famine relief continued until the summer of 1923 after which the work carried on was mainly medical care in centers for mothers and children. Anti-malaria clinics were open as late as the spring of 1925 and a great effort was made to check tuberculosis. This phase of the work was not an independent Quaker program but was done in connection with the Health Department of the Soviet.

The Quakers were by no means the only persons giving relief during the Russian famine. "The American Red Cross aided Russia through the Quakers. They made contributions of medicine and clothing" to the extent of a hundred thousand dollars.[4] The American Relief Administration, of which Herbert Hoover was chairman, and with which the American Friends Service Committee had been working in Germany during 1920 and 1921, asked the Friends to co-operate with them in Russia. This meant that the American and English Friends had to work as separate Units, since the A.R.A. was entirely an American organization. In almost every instance the Soviet Government was extremely co-operative with the Service Committee and gave them help whenever it was possible.

"The Russian work done by the Friends Service Committee in 1917 and 1918 seems to me to have quite a different basis from that done in 1922. The motive behind the work of the Friends for the refugees during the war bore a distinct relation to our traditional pacifist attitudes and, therefore, had a closer connection with our basic religious beliefs than had the service during the famine. In the latter period, when famine relief for the population at large was the dominant service, many other groups were also active.

[4] Statement made by Anna J. Haines.

"I believe that the Russian Government, whether it was Czarist, Kerensky or Soviet, recognized in our war time relief a protest against war, since it was known that many of the men working in our Unit would normally have been in the army had it not been for their pacifist beliefs. The recognition by England and America of the validity of such beliefs could scarcely fail to make some impression upon a country whose successive governments have not respected such conscientious scruples in their own subjects.

"The relationship between the work in Poland and Russia is also somewhat complicated. Most of the refugees for whom we cared in 1917 and 1918 were residents of Poland who, as Russian subjects, had been driven out of their homes by the advancing German armies. When Poland became an independent country it did so on the basis of sharp antagonism with Soviet Russia. When peace was declared the Polish refugees were evacuated from central Russia as soon as possible. There were groups of Friends working at that time in both countries, but there was no opportunity for much co-operation between the two groups, since each one must obtain permission to work from governments who were mutually suspicious and antagonistic. The type of work was also quite different, the Polish groups going in for rehabilitation and resettlement of returning refugees while the small group remaining in Russia continued to carry on refugee relief work for the civil war sufferers in Siberia. I believe the Polish Unit was of considerable assistance to the later groups of famine relief workers since many of them had to travel through Warsaw to enter Russia."[5]

[5] Letter from Anna J. Haines, March 3, 1937.
Material for this chapter has been taken from reports on Russian work; *Quakers in Action,* Lester M. Jones; *A Quaker Adventure,* A. Ruth Fry and material given by Anna J. Haines, Nancy Babb and Emilie C. Bradbury.

". . . The world's great altitudes of pain . . ."
MICHAEL FIELD

Chapter V

THE DIARY OF AN UNKNOWN RUSSIAN WORKER

1

July 1917. We're off and I can't believe it. Everything has happened so fast and I've been in such a scramble to get ready that I feel as though I were in a dream. We're sailing from Vancouver and have to go all the way around by the Pacific Ocean, Japan and the Trans-Siberian Railway because women aren't allowed to enter Russia by way of Europe, so here we are, six of us, starting off by sailing down Puget Sound which was simply beautiful in the sunset light.

We've started our study of Russian already and it's not exactly an easy language to attack. I have moments when I wish I were going to France instead and I keep trying to analyze the reason why I decided as I have because I could have brushed up my French in no time and while I'd have been near the Front, perhaps, and in danger, I wouldn't have had this peculiar sensation in the pit of my stomach. Still, if I had the chance to choose over again, I don't believe I'd have done differently as I seem to have some kind of a concern for the Russians. Everybody else will go to France because it's the obvious and logical thing to do. Any place is better than America right now and I'm thankful to get out of that fearful hysteria where people are just going mad with their "Buy Liberty Bonds," "Sacrifice for our Boys," "For God and Country." It doesn't prove a thing to blow anybody's brains out except make a filthy mess to clean up.

It's sickening. I don't know how long it will take the Service Committee to bring any kind of order out of this chaos.

It would be interesting, just as a record, to know how many of us who go off to France and Russia, go for "God and Country" as we are told the soldiers are doing, and how many go for a change and excitement!

August 1917. After all our rush to get off and be in Russia as soon as possible, we're stuck in Tsuruga, Japan, of all places. We were actually on the gang plank of the boat which was to take us to Vladivostok where we get on the Trans-Siberian Railway, when we were stopped, our passports examined, and, although we had visas for Russia which we obtained in Washington from the representatives of the Kerensky Government, we were turned back from the boat and not allowed to get on. It took us a while to find out what the trouble was and in the meantime there was nothing for us to do but settle down in Tsuruga and await developments. They thought we were a bunch of radicals swarming back into Russia! It seems that the Czar exiled hundreds of citizens who were considered radical and the minute the Kerensky Government came in these exiles came over from America and tried to get back into Russia. A lot of them did, and by the time we came along, the Government was alarmed and put a stop to every person coming from America. They had never heard of the Service Committee or the War Victims' Relief from England and were adamant about our entering Russia. We are now waiting until our visas are approved by the authorities in Petrograd. Things don't move quite so swiftly in the Orient as they do in the United States! [1]

We've taken a house with a Japanese maid who can't speak anything except Japanese. We are getting along all right and of course the delay gives us more time to study

[1] Information from Anna J. Haines.

Russian. I know how to say: "I should like to have my soiled clothes washed," but I have a feeling that this phrase won't be of much use as I shall probably wash my own clothes. The people here can't make out what six young women expect to do in Russia in the midst of the war. I suppose it is a little startling to the conventional minded. I feel less and less adequate for the job, about which I know almost nothing, and have had a chance to let down from the excitement of getting off. The social work that I have done in Philadelphia won't be much help, I imagine, in a country where conditions will be so different. How different, I am beginning to realize.

On the other hand, I am glad I came. Russia has always had a fascination for me ever since I went to school and heard about the "Czar of all the Russias." The phrase brings pictures of a rich, fertile country, where fields of a vast size are waving with yellow grain, or in winter, miles and miles of white, dazzling snow over which sledges are drawn by horses galloping to escape the pack of wolves following them. The men are magnificent in their high boots and fur caps and the women are blond and gay, dressed in brilliant embroidered dresses. There are always samovars full of tea and tables covered with peculiar foods. Swift and dangerous, the Volga rushes down from the mountains through forests of dark pine trees. How much of this will I find to be the truth or just my own imagination?

September 1917. After waiting a month in Japan they let us go. It was proved in Petrograd that we weren't returning exiles. We've only just arrived in Buzuluk where the English Quakers welcomed us most enthusiastically until they found that not one of the six of us was a trained nurse. It seems they had been counting on us all to be used in hospitals as they are short on nurses as it is, and one or two of them are returning to England. I don't know what happened between the English and the American Committees, whether they got their signals mixed, or whether the English thought they had said nurses, when they hadn't.

As briefly as I can I'll give the history of conditions in Russia and tell what the English Friends have done.

In 1915 the German and Austrian armies made their big advance right through Poland into Western Russia. In that advance they drove before them some fifteen million refugees who suffered terribly on the road. They finally got in trains where they fared as badly. They got infectious diseases, especially dysentery, and died by thousands, and on the trains the dead bodies had to be taken out first at every station before the passengers who were still alive could get off.

About eighty thousand refugees were taken into Russian Turkestan by the Russian, then Czarist, Government where they were housed in Russian military barracks. They were overcrowded, had no proper food supply or sanitation, which latter at its best is none too good, so that in less than six months fifty thousand of them died. The remaining thirty thousand were brought back into European Russia to the district of Buzuluk, a department of the Government of Samara about the size of Belgium, and this is where we are.

Our work is right on the Buzuluk steppe which is an almost flat country, quite bare with no trees, no fences, no hedges, nothing to break the monotony of the landscape, except big steppe villages, which consist for the most part of one straight street with two rows of houses, generally containing only one room. When the refugees arrived they had to share these one roomed huts with the local steppe peasants who are the most primitive in Russia and the refugees from Poland found them very distasteful.

This was the condition of things when the English Friends came out in 1916. They secured a big house which had been standing empty for a few years and filled it with about one hundred children who were orphans with no one to look after them. The Friends fed and clothed these children, found a Russian schoolmistress to teach them, and have taught the boys carpentering and elements of other trades. The children have responded quickly and there is a decided change among both boys and girls. In addition to this, canteens have been opened for the distribution of clothing. Six thousand pairs of boots were bought and given to the refugees. It gets so fearfully cold here in winter that it is impossible for anyone to go out of doors without the felt boots which the Russians wear.

One of the most important aspects of the work has been industrial relief. In several of the centers, two or three rooms have been taken, the refugee women have been assembled and given work similar to what they would do in their own homes, in general the production of cloth from raw wool, flax and hemp. They have done the cleaning, combing, etc., on the old fashioned hand wheels and looms which the refugee men have made and several thousand yards of cloth have been woven and made into clothes. The women are paid only ten cents a day for their labor but it has had a wonderful psychological effect on them to have something which keeps them occupied.

The Russian Government called up a majority of the doctors from the country for the Front. Many districts were left without any doctors at all and with the addition of the unwelcome refugees who brought cholera, typhus and malaria with them, the situation was desperate. The Friends have workers in three hospitals, but one doctor and his wife who is a nurse, are working among a population of eighty thousand. English Friends say that the attitude toward them is far more friendly than it was when they first came. The peasants were suspicious and thought that the foreigners were just trying to get something out of them, but they have learned, to some extent, that the red and black star shows that the wearer is trying to help those in need.[2]

Where is my picture of the kingdom of the Czar of all the Russias?! We seem to be a thousand miles from anything, as indeed we are. We are buried in this flat land of steppes and we seem so far away from the war that I can hardly believe it is going on in the same continent, although everywhere around us are the effects of war—these refugees who have been driven back and forth and bring desolation wherever they stop. The crops are pitifully meagre, due to the lack of rain. If famine is added to the sufferings of these people it will be terrible and yet it looks now as though there will not be enough food to carry them through the winter. *October 1917.* I am to be sent to the hospital in the south in spite of the fact that I am not a nurse. The other five are going to different centers and it remains to be seen how we get on. I can't imagine how we thought we could do anything out here without being nurses. I have been working hard on the language and am making more progress now that I hear it all the time but it is a discouraging language. There is so much to do that there's no time to sit around and mope. I've been helping in the work room and have done some visiting around in order to see for myself how the Russians live. A good many of them are living in cellars, but the climate and soil are dry so that it's not so unhealthy as it would be at home. Sometimes as many as eighteen people are living together in one room, and even though there may be windows in the houses, they are never opened because the Russian peasant has an antipathy to fresh air, especially in winter when heat is so difficult to obtain. I suppose I shall get used, sometime, to the smells and the dirt and the lack

---

[2] This description of the work of the English Friends has been taken almost verbatim from an address by Dr. J. Tylor Fox, given at Central Hall, Westminster, London, March 6, 1918.

of interest the peasants have in being clean. Russia is a strange country. It isn't Europe and it isn't Asia but a mixture of both.

November 1917. Dr. Preston[3] has been treating me as though I were a graduate nurse and knew everything. As soon as I arrived here he said, "I shall expect you to do what I ask you." I replied, "Suppose I don't know how?" He laughed and said, "I need some one who does know how so you'll have to do the best you can."

I began helping in the out-patient hall which is always filled with patients waiting their turn or besieging the dispenser's window. Now in cold weather with stoves burning and windows sealed, the air is almost unbearable. Patients who are sicker than the rest lie on the floor, the children always cry and everybody talks. Few can read, labels are unknown and much explanation is necessary. We take the name, age and address of each patient, also the diagnosis and treatment, and enter them all in a book, after which a slip of paper also giving these details is handed to each patient to keep so that he can get the right medicine. But these get lost, or torn up and a second or third examination has to be made.

One day we had in the same room a Russian from an adjoining village, a refugee, an Austrian prisoner, two Tartars, a Cossack and a Kirghese. There is no race monotony for we treat about one hundred and fifty patients regularly. Yesterday we had an accident case which interrupted all our work for a while and there were several who were too ill for the dispensary. As the hospital was full we had to send them back to the carts which brought them. How can we do anything when the parents won't make their children take their medicine? "Has he had the medicine?" Dr. Preston will ask. And the answer invariably is, "No, he didn't wish it." I

[3] The name is fictitious.

mentally throw up my hands in the utter futility of trying to help people who are so ignorant.[4]

Everybody is so dirty that I want to give each one of them a bath, using strong disinfectant and soap. It seems to me most of their ailments would disappear if the peasants and refugees would only be a little cleaner. I am amazed at Dr. Preston's patience and long suffering and his cleverness. In the first place he has me, totally inexperienced, to train in. Then, instead of being able to get through the line of patients quickly, each one wants to talk a long time about his or her trouble. Often he thinks one thing is the matter with him when it's obvious even to a novice like me that it's something entirely different. Then he has very set ideas about the kind of treatment he ought to have. I have learned that there are two great remedies, "drops" and "ointment." If you have skin trouble or a sore eye, all that is needed is an ointment to rub on the afflicted part, or if you have a cough, it can be cured by rubbing a good ointment on the chest. If the ointment doesn't have any effect, drinking some drops will certainly cure the trouble. Of course, if the illness does not depart it also stands to reason that the doctor has prescribed the wrong drops or the wrong ointment. However, in this hospital the peasants have witnessed some remarkable cures and they are inclined to believe that Dr. Preston knows what he is doing, though they are very partial to pink pills and will try to bribe him to give them these instead of what he has prescribed. They bring ducks and eggs and all sorts of things with the idea that after receiving these gifts, Dr. Preston will instantly swing over to their point of view. But the opening of closed dispensaries, or starting new ones, has created a good feeling among the local peasantry.[5]

---

[4] Account of the dispensary taken almost verbatim from the Report for Russia of the War Victims' Relief Committee, 1916–1917.

[5] *Among the War Victims in Russia,* J. Tylor Fox.

December 1917. I've been promoted to the operating room and have given ether under Dr. Preston's supervision several times. The first time I did it I was so scared that my knees shook under me. Suppose I gave too much and the man died, or too little and he woke up in the middle of the operation? I wasn't able to breathe naturally until he had come to, but having done it once I have more confidence. Pretty soon I shall be blasé about it, no doubt. I never told Dr. Preston that I was deathly sick after I saw my first operation. I managed to stick it out, though I know I went white as a sheet, until it was over and I could escape.

I told him I didn't see why we couldn't train in one or two of the refugees around here who haven't a thing to do and could at least do laundry and scrub floors. Not that I object to hard work but there simply aren't enough hours in the day to get things done. We're so busy that I've hardly had time to worry over the fact that I've never had a single letter from home since I left. I haven't the vaguest idea what's happening in France or anywhere else. My life consists of fourteen beds of patients, some hundred and fifty out-patients, attempts to train in these refugee girls and make them do what I tell them while I try to do what the doctor tells me, and, incidentally, keep on with my Russian. Of course I pick up new words every day, but I'm still pretty poor.

The interpreter who is helping me now with the out-patients worked in a Ford factory in Detroit for a short time, but his vocabulary is limited to car parts which are different from the Russian peasant's internal workings.

I've moved into a small room in the hospital where I sleep in order to be near enough for Eulicina, one of my refugee girls, to call me if I am needed. My quarters are not exactly palatial, as I am sleeping on a board supported by a tin bath tub! I'm so dead tired by the time I relax on my board that I go off to sleep as though I were lying on springs and a feather bed. The adaptability of the human frame is wonderful. I'm even getting fond of these Russian peasants, once I begin to understand them a little better.

June 1918. Just as I was beginning to get really useful in the hospital all the Russian doctors came home from the Front so Dr. Preston and I left. He'll be going back to England soon, but I don't have any expectation of leaving. Ethel Hall,[6] an English nurse, and I plan to make up a travelling clinic and visit among the villages where trachoma is so prevalent. There's so much eye trouble of every sort that something must be done and I am hoping that I can get a few people in each village to help me. This will make a beginning in my plan to get the people started doing things for themselves.

In the meantime Buzuluk is a milling mass of humanity. The warm weather has come and all the refugees are pouring in from the outlying villages to take the train at Buzuluk station. Here they sit because the railways have been cut by the little invasion of the Czechoslovakians. So far there has been no epidemic of anything but one never knows when it will break out and of course all these people have to be fed. We've opened soup kitchens and we're trying to get more work for all these additional people.

There's one thing to be said for being in Russia. There's never a moment to spend wishing there was something to do. If one plan miscarries, another can always be tried. If the hospitals close you can always feed refugees!

July 1918. As I was saying, if there aren't any refugees to feed there's always the possibility of a war. The Czechoslovaks and the Soviet have staged a battle over Buzuluk and shelled the town. This would be nothing to the French Unit, I suppose, since they must have air raids frequently,

[6] Name fictitious.

but it was a little too much for me, though I have grown accustomed to every other form of discomfort.

We all got up about three A.M., ate some breakfast, and then with mattresses, candles, samovar, money and food, went down to the cellar with about fifty or sixty people from the neighborhood. I had often looked at refugees lying about on their belongings, but had never supposed that I'd be reduced to doing the same. It was a funny sight, with several of us in a row in the darkest, blackest corner of the cellar trying to make ourselves comfortable by the light of a feeble candle.[7]

No damage was done to any of our buildings, however, and when it was all over we emerged into daylight again. Theodore Rigg arrived from Moscow to find us still gasping; he was a joyful sight as he brought us enough money to last for some length of time and this is a relief as we hadn't much left. We are completely cut off from the world without any communications from anywhere. The journey from Moscow took him ten days and he never knew from hour to hour whether he would arrive or not and he couldn't get any word to us that he was coming.

When he and Esther White go back to Moscow as they plan to do very soon, to try and establish more colonies for the Moscow children with the help of the Russian Committee for Relief of starving children,[8] they will drop out of our ken entirely, for we shan't know whether they arrive or not.

One becomes immune to this kind of existence. I've been in Russia nearly a year and don't know anything about my family. For all I can tell, they know nothing about me.

[7] Account of the air raid taken, almost verbatim from a letter written by Esther White after she reached Moscow and dated October 2, 1918.

[8] Account taken from a letter written by T. Rigg, Buzuluk, July 7, 1918.

Shall I ever go back and see people whom I knew before I came here? Russia has become the only place that has reality. It must have been in another incarnation that I went to school and college. All I can think of now are refugees, peasants, dirt, medicine and food.

November 1918. It seems there are other places besides Russia and here I am in Irkutsk, Siberia.

I settled myself down in Buzuluk and was taking charge of the workroom after we finished our "trachoma travellings" and expected to stay until next spring, but on the fifteenth of September Jack Catchpool appeared out of the blue, having come from Moscow and told us that the Bolshevik attitude toward English and Americans was becoming more hostile than it had been. Esther's and Theodore's work was so hampered by suspicious Bolshevik authorities in Moscow that they had come to the conclusion it would be better to leave. It was good to know that they had even arrived.

In addition to the feeling in Moscow there was a probability that our work would be curtailed and perhaps entirely disrupted by the impending Bolshevik capture of the Samara district. We were getting very short of money, so that our work could have been carried on for three months more only.

On the second of October we received a telegram from the American Consulate in Samara stating that they were leaving immediately for Siberia, as the Trans-Siberian Railway might be cut at any moment, and, after quick consultation, five of us, Emilie Bradbury, Nancy Babb, Mr. Catchpool, Mr. Baker and I, decided to do the same, being guided by the above reasons and also by the fact that for some time we had felt that Buzuluk was no longer a district where the refugee situation was critical. There was work for able bodied men, bread was cheaper than it had been for two years and our workroom gave livelihood to the women.

After a hurried packing we five left in a freight car early

on the morning of October fourth and made a quick, that is, quick considering the distance and the circumstances, and safe trip to Omsk which is over a thousand miles from Buzuluk. The next day the train stopped running. We heard afterwards that the position became so threatening and the Bolsheviks so hostile to English people that the three workers who had stayed on in Buzuluk to look after the industrial classes, the orphanage and the refugee work room, left by cart three days after we did.

The refugees in Omsk are in the worst plight that we have seen anywhere. In Irkutsk, about eighteen hundred miles from Omsk, where we are now, the refugees are fewer in number and the people in the local government seem to be more awake to their responsibilities. We want to open work rooms for spinning, weaving, etc., like the ones we had in Buzuluk, for widows with children and single women who have no man to support them. We have wired the Philadelphia office asking for $50,000 to support relief work in Omsk for six months and saying that if this money isn't forthcoming, we shall join the Red Cross and work as one of their sections. In any case we shall leave here for Omsk on November 23 and start our work, hoping to hear favorably from Philadelphia. We still have some money which we brought from Buzuluk to tide us over. I for one am eager to be back at work again after two months of roaming around.[9]

News of peace came as a surprise to us and though peace seems far from us here just now, it may come and the refugees be able to go home. And when they do start going home, what a tremendous amount of work it will mean to do it systematically.[10]

[9] Account of leaving Moscow and arrival in Omsk and Irkutsk taken almost verbatim from a letter written by Anna J. Haines from Irkutsk, November 22, 1918, to Vincent Nicholson, Philadelphia.
[10] From a letter written by Emilie C. Bradbury under the same date to Vincent Nicholson.

January 1919. We received a cable from the Philadelphia office dated December 16, and we sent ours November 22. I suppose it took all that time to reach the office but the delay certainly made it difficult for us to know what to do. They say that we can go ahead and work with the Red Cross and that they'll pay our personal expenses. Not a word about the money we asked for, but they're waiting for more information which they'll get when the four English Friends, Keddie, Tatlock, Catchpool and Hoffman, who've left by now, arrive in Philadelphia. I don't believe anybody who hasn't been through it, will have the vaguest idea about our Russian work. Everybody's attention has been focussed on France whereas Russia is so remote that no one can picture what we've been doing. Probably everybody thinks of Russia as I did, fields of grain and peasants singing Russian Easter music.

I'll be glad enough to go home when this particular job is over but I'll never be satisfied if I can't come back. After I tell people what the work's been like they won't believe it when I say I want to come back again. If everything had been beautiful I don't believe I should have had a chance to get so close to Russia but we've been through so much together that I can't leave it, permanently. I'd like to have a chance to get some medical training, nurse's probably, rather than a doctor's which takes so long, so that when I do come back I could do more than I could this time.

I nearly went under at the beginning with the confusion of so many things to be done at once when I didn't know the language. The dirt and the poverty and the suffering seemed beyond any help or remedy but I'm thankful I stuck it out. Suppose I hadn't come to Russia and had missed such an experience!

2

November 1921. Back again to Buzuluk, after three years' absence. I'm not an R.N. yet, but I shall be someday. When word came that the Service Committee was sending a Unit for famine relief I took a leave of absence, so to speak, from my training.

Never has any place seemed more like home than this. We crossed the Russian frontier about noon on October 28, coming from Riga to Moscow, no more Vladivostok and the Trans-Siberian! and, after some days in Moscow conferring with Arthur Watts of the English Mission, we set off for Buzuluk, arriving here November 8. Along with my joy at returning to Russia I feel the most horrible sadness. Conditions that seemed desperate when I was here three and four years ago are so much worse that I do not see how anyone will get through the winter. There was no harvest to speak of. There has been no rain for months and the steppes are burned dry. They tell us that seed which was sown in the autumn of 1920 and this last spring has never sprouted but is lying in the parched ground.

There is more than the drought to blame for the failure of crops. Under the new regime, when the landed estates were broken up, the peasants tilled only enough land for themselves, not realizing that Russia depended on the surplus supplies which came from the estates. The male population has been greatly reduced, of course, and comprises a pitiably small number, the armies, first for the war and then for the revolution having taken thousands. Refugees have not taken the place of these men at all, but have sat down heavily, demanding food, when there wasn't enough for the Russians themselves. Last of all, there is the blockade, so that nothing is being imported.

The situation is desperate in the Samara region. Although winter is only just beginning, thousands have died and thousands are on the road, seeking food wherever there is a rumor that food is available. They are dropping dead along the way, in the trains, wherever they happen to be, leaving their children to struggle along by themselves. Russia will have thousands of orphans to care for, and there will be terrible epidemics of cholera, typhus and the rest.

In the short time I have been back I have seen dead people lying in heaps by the roadside, their clothes stripped from them, so great is the need for warm clothing. Babies are brought to us every day because the parents are dead or because the family cannot care for another individual. But we can't take care of them, either. Everywhere we go, people fall on their knees in front of us, begging, in the name of God, that we will give them something to eat.

December 1921. We waited a few days longer in Buzuluk for the lost cars of food from the A.R.A. to come up and then, when they came, it was discovered that some seals were broken. The railroad people are responsible for the safe transport of the food, so they insisted that the food must be examined to see whether there had been any loss. This meant unloading the cars and more loss of time and after a day of this we decided to have the food stored in the Buzuluk warehouse and go on to Sorochenskoe without it. We were all ready to start when it was reported that something was wrong with the wheel on one car and that it could not be mended until the next day. This was too much for our patience and we left one man with that car and went on, using the engine from the post train, which had just come in. We made the trip in three hours after living at the station for eight days waiting for a chance to start. The train whose engine we took did not get here for several days. It was snow bound!

When we arrived at the Ispolcom, the executive committee of the Soviet, in Sorochenskoe we found that two men had been appointed to look after our interests, one was the chairman of the Board of Education and the other was his assistant.

Then we looked at the house selected for us. It had been cleaned up but there is old and much bedraggled wall paper on the walls, the windows are, most of them, pasted shut for the winter, and, Russian fashion, we sleep with our windows closed at night, although the temperature has been only slightly below freezing. Our furniture is scarce and very old, what there is of it. We have four rooms upstairs and we use three for sleeping and one for a dining room and living room although we live mostly in the office. Below is the kitchen in which there was only a big Russian stove when we arrived and the cooking had to be done by setting kettles into the fire. Back of this our two servants sleep, really on the stove, and off from the kitchen are two rooms which we are using for office and bed room. Russian stoves are built into the walls and we can heat two or three rooms with one stove.

All day Wednesday, Murray Kenworthy had been sick and Thursday morning his temperature was sufficiently high to warrant getting a doctor. He was an Austrian and asked me various questions by which I knew that he suspected the case might be typhus. In the meantime we were still at the station, waiting until the boys finished unpacking at the warehouse before we moved into the house. We were all ready to start but through some misunderstanding no sleighs had been ordered and the night was stormy and windy. Everybody advised us to wait till morning but we said it was impossible with Mr. Kenworthy sick.

The chairman of the Board of Education himself went out to get the sleighs and while we waited the men entertained us with tales of cannibalism in the surrounding neighborhood. Some parents eat their children to keep them from suffering more, others are eating dead bodies and the cases are increasing. Some are eating plants that only camels can eat, and hemp which poisons them so that they go mad. When the sleighs came Beulah went with the first load to get a bed ready and I came with Mr. Kenworthy who was comfortable, wrapped up and stretched out in the sleigh. After we got home, we had supper to get.

Two days after that a Russian nurse appeared on the scene and I was called in only when she could not understand what Kenworthy wanted and to interpret for the Austrian doctor who could not talk to Kenworthy! Amidst the confusion of new nurse, new cook, many callers, we calculated and made out orders for food for the children's homes. Just as we were getting into bed someone came to tell us there was a thief in the warehouse.

This morning, Christmas, we rose late. When I went in to see Kenworthy he wished me a rather weak Merry Christmas and we celebrated by moving him from the iron bedstead with no springs to the bed with springs which the doctor has sent from the hospital. He has typhus all right. His heart and lungs are both affected and the doctor thinks there will be days when he will be worse.[11]

Now we've just had our Christmas dinner,—sardines, bread, cocoa, and dried apricots. I've spent the evening trying to decide how to distribute this first shipment of A.R.A. food which consists of forty thousand rations, just enough to feed forty thousand children for one month. It seems hopeless. Not knowing when the next shipment will come in, we don't dare use this food up so fast and it seems dreadful not to feed as many children as we can but we shall have

[11] Account of moving to Sorochenskoe taken, with some alterations, from a letter written by Miriam West, dated, Sorochenskoe, December 29, 1921.

to cut it down to twenty thousand children for two months and hope by the end of that time we shall have more supplies. But what are twenty thousand when there are hundreds of thousands who are starving.

We've heard that Nancy Babb has typhus at Buzuluk but she's not so ill as Murray Kenworthy. After all the precautions every one takes I can't imagine how they caught it though after visiting in the filthy houses it's a wonder we all haven't caught something. I keep hunting for lice on me all the time. It's terrible to have Kenworthy so ill when he came out to direct the rest of us and organize the whole work. We're trying to do the best we can, but we're not organizers.

Thank goodness there has been more snow to cover up the dead bodies. Perhaps for a little while the land will look clean. I keep thinking of the Christmas dinners the people around me have been eating. Soup made from boiling harness leather, bread made from powdered bones and grass, stuck together with glue from a horse's hoof. There aren't any animals left to eat. I'm glad the baby that was left here last night died. I shouldn't have taken him in but on Christmas Eve I couldn't refuse him. He'd been without milk for so long that I suppose the little bit I gave him was too much of a shock. Poor thing, but I don't want to get fond of anything or anybody. I've got to keep all my energies for work and staying sane.

January 1922. Money and food aren't coming in as fast as we thought they would and I suppose the reason is that people in America are anti-Bolshevik and don't care what happens to all these Russians. They're afraid that their precious capitalistic system will be destroyed if Red ideas permeate the whole world, and if the Russians die because of the famine, so much the better. Why can't people understand what's been happening here? You can't damn the present government without knowing something of Russian history, because while the Bolshevik Government may be terrible, it's less so than the Czarist régime and you can't expect people of a nation of this size who have lived for centuries under violence and oppression to change in a night.[12] After all, this revolution wasn't so different from the French Revolution except that that happened over a hundred years ago.

Anybody who studies that period is appalled at the conditions and is sympathetic with the peasants who had no rights and no education. There's no difference between those French peasants and the Russian peasants of 1917 who were no better than slaves. America with all its talk about being the land of the free and the home of the brave has no conception of what freedom would mean to a peasant.

I'm glad the eyes of the world are focussed on Russia because this country is going to point the way, I believe, not to the communism that the rich capitalists are so afraid of, but to the freedom that our pseudo-democracy prattles about but doesn't practice. It was these same capitalists who invented the slogan, "make the world safe for democracy," I'll be bound and hauled in fortunes while the world went to the devil. Now they won't let a penny of that money leak in here because it will restore the Bolsheviks to health and strength and they will destroy the world's economic system.

Oh, why can't the rich understand the oppression, the poverty, the ignorance under which the Russians have lived, the sort of system which no civilized land ought to have in this day and age? Why don't they come and see for themselves? They can afford it. It would do them good to see

---

[12] A statement, with some alterations, made by Vincent D. Nicholson in *Reconstruction*, October 15, 1919.

homes where people are eating powdered bones and bark off the trees, and even one another, so I am told, though I haven't seen it. Then they might forget their capitalism for a day or so and turn a finger to do something about this suffering which goes on, day after day. Those of us who are here can hardly bear to touch food of which we have enough when everybody around us is starving.

Bolshevism! It's nothing but a name to which people in their ignorance have attached a poisonous label. The time will come when workers in factories and mills in the United States who are oppressed by these rich men are going to rise up and smite them. The capitalists would do well to stop sneering at Russia or being afraid of it and study the situation pretty carefully. They're going to have trouble in their own country some day.

February 1922. Murray Kenworthy is better. That is, he isn't going to die, but it will be a long time yet before he can be on the job. We hear that more workers are on the way to help us. Food and money are coming in a bit better, but the winter gets colder and longer, and when we aren't numb with the cold, we're numb with all the suffering we see. I don't know how we thought we could distribute the food from a center when the children haven't proper clothes or boots to wear in this bitter weather. We've been sending supplies to the homes and letting families cook their own meals. This means that adults are getting fed as well which makes me feel better. Otherwise there would be nothing but orphans left. I try not to think of all the homeless people, wandering around hunting for food, and dropping dead to be buried in the snow.

March 1922. I may never believe that I really saw with my own eyes the sight I witnessed today. I had seen everything ghastly and horrible except this. I heard there was a family living in an old shed near here. They had managed to get to

Sorochenskoe somehow, having heard that food was being given out but they were half crazed by all that had happened. I arrived to find the woman dead and the man eating her.

On the way back I remembered how I felt when I saw the first operation which had made me sick. I think it's a mistake to send new people to help us, much as we need them, because no novice can stand this sort of thing. If one only could be sick and forget the memory of this experience.

Something happened the other day, though, that made me even more upset. One of these rich Americans came through our town in his private car given him by the Russian Government for his tour of investigation. We heard that he was down at the station, sitting in his car, for several hours until another train could take him on, so I marched down to see him. He said he understood that people weren't dying from hunger any more and that things were a great deal better. I assured him that nothing was farther from the truth, that people are dying by hundreds all the time and that if he would come out of his car for ten minutes I could show him a heap of bodies near the station. He refused to leave his car and I know it was because he was afraid I was telling the truth and that he might see something disagreeable which would change his rosy point of view. Then, of course, if he left his hygienic car, he might run the risk of getting typhus.

I wish now that I had told him what I really thought of him and if I had seen him today I should have gone off the deep end. He would have believed I was just an hysterical woman, trying to get money. I did try to convince him that I knew what I was talking about but he smiled and said he knew because after all that was why he had come, and he had been investigating all over the country. "This is one of the very worst districts in all Russia and until you see with your own eyes that what I am telling you does exist you have no right to go on saying that conditions are better."

It had no effect so he has gone on to broadcast that the Quakers are liars, as we must be if he is telling the truth, and that the Russians are growing fat and healthy. I wonder how he'd like living on herrings and beans and tinned milk, day after day, with no roast on Sundays. Oh, I wish all the lice in Russia would crawl over his soft, flabby skin and bite him! How can there be such people? He's somewhere safe by now, eating good food and having the best champagne, while in a shed behind our house a man is driven to eat the flesh of his dead wife.

May 1922. Spring has never seemed so beautiful. The warmth of the sun penetrates into my bones at last and I am beginning to relax. I'd been holding myself tense so long just trying to keep warm.

With the thaw came heavy rains and the snow melted, uncovering all the dead bodies which had been buried, mercifully, for the winter. We were frightfully busy getting squads of men to dig graves and bury these bodies so that they would not lie around and spread disease. But the squads were so weak that they couldn't do any work unless we gave them extra food and even so it was pitiful to watch their feeble attempts at digging. In every shed, in every remote corner were piles of bodies, horrible enough to have around but a real menace to health with the coming of warm weather.

There has been a fearful jam at the Baltic ports. All the food which should have been sent earlier for use during the winter was caught in ships which were stuck in the ice. Even the Kiel Canal was frozen and nothing could be done. Now when the thaw has broken up the ice everything is being sent at once, and transport is in a chaos. When the first cartload of cod liver oil was brought up from our station, one of the barrels leaked so that the oil dripped out and ran down through a crack in the cart. A few children, who were strong enough, walked under the cart and caught the drippings in cups, drinking the stuff down as though it were nectar.

We have some tractors which were bought in Warsaw. Some of the boys here have been taught to run them but if anything happens to these machines the nearest repair shop is two hundred miles away. The land is beautiful where it has been ploughed. Everyone is rejoicing to start sowing the corn and we are praying that this seed will yield a fine harvest.

July 1922. There has been no rain at all. The ground is cracked and burned so that nothing is growing. Potatoes have not even sprouted. All day long the sun beats down on the fields and the peasants look up at the brilliant sky, hoping to see a change in the weather. But there are no clouds, there is nothing except the heat and the burned fields. All our hopes for a good harvest are gone, for there will be no harvest at all and unless Russia is fed for another winter every one will die.

They are sending me away for a rest although I do not want to leave. I can't bear to see people who have plenty to eat and whose crops are growing well. But they say I have to go. They're anxious because one man, not working with us, has committed suicide and a woman has gone mad. I should not do either one and I should be happier to stay on with these people and share their misery.

I am too tired to argue and I realize I am too tired to be of very much use so I am willing to do as they say and return before the winter comes. I shall go to England and try to forget for a little while that there is suffering. But how can I forget, because my life is bound up with Russia?

Material for this chapter has been taken from two reports written by Murray S. Kenworthy; from general reports and letters.

CHAPTER VI

GERMANY

As early as October 13, 1918, twenty-nine days before the Armistice, Carolena M. Wood wrote to Wilbur K. Thomas at Twenty South Twelfth Street: "For the past two or three years I have felt a concern for service among the people in Germany. As the opportunity for such service seems to be approaching, I write to volunteer under your leadership. I believe that Friends have, awaiting them in that country, an important service in spiritual healing and reconstruction."

Carolena Wood sailed for Germany April 18, 1919, and wrote from France early in May: "I have had five days of great joy in seeing with my eyes the wonderful service of love which has been given to Friends to do in France. The delay in the Peace Treaty makes it very doubtful about getting into Germany at once and brings a question as to whether this is, or is not, the psychological moment to proceed. Ruth Fry, J. Thompson Eliott and Hilda Clark, English Friends, are here planning for service in Poland and Vienna and they will go on to look over the ground there at once. They are also moving all stones to find a way for my service, both through the English authorities and Mr. Hoover who seems to have entered wonderfully into the spirit of my concern and to feel that it is possible thus to meet one of the needs of the hour. Lucy Biddle Lewis goes to present a tentative offer of service from Jane Addams to go with us under the red and black star. She will go *only*

with us and to represent our spirit and point of view . . .
In Germany the suffering is very great and they need to
feel that some one cares. Hoover will let us use his passports and sell us all the food we can buy. He thinks our
service is primarily to the morale of the country, but thinks
we can go better with something in our hands . . . "

"On Sunday June 6th our party crossed the German frontier, Miss Addams, Dr. Alice Hamilton and I, with a Dutch
woman physician, Dr. Aletta Jacobs, who has been asked
to make a report on conditions in Germany from a neutral
standpoint . . . It is evident that the suffering both in mind
and body is intense . . . The German authorities are very
appreciative and will admit our supplies free of duty . . . "

"August 1 . . . Germany has built so well of stone and
tile that their buildings do not show the neglect which one
notices in France . . . There are practically no animals
visible from the trains . . . There are few horses, a few
goats and almost no dogs left . . . The thirty-five tons of
milk is, I hope, on its way from Hamburg. I am now hoping
to get three thousand pounds of sugar from the Czechoslo-
vakian Government and hope to find some cocoa in Holland before long . . . I spent a few days in Silesia and have
been in Berlin since, pushing the purchase of the food and
the organization on a broader basis of the plans for distribution . . . I am very happy in this service and count it a
great privilege to represent the Society of Friends as an ambassador of Christ when my Government has as yet no representative here."

In a report to Wilbur Thomas, written some time during
her stay in Berlin, she said: "By this time you have all the
appalling figures about the diseases. The tuberculosis charts
make one sick at heart . . . Since the 'turnip year' three
years ago when they had no potatoes, but only turnip mar-
malade for breakfast, boiled turnip for dinner and turnip

soup for supper, they have had greatly reduced powers of resistance to disease. Dr. Sigmund Schultze, who was formerly the Minister at Potsdam said to us, 'we carried on the war to the point of collapse.' . . . When I was in the destruction left in the battle fields of France I wished that all the world might go there to see what war is, but this is no less a battle field with its deep, awful lesson . . .

"The old over-fat Germany is gone. Everyone has lost from twenty-five to fifty pounds and the red cheeks have nearly all disappeared. Many have a strange gray-white look . . . The bread is very dark and heavy because there is not enough wheat flour to make the yeast work successfully. It still has eight or ten percent of sawdust besides a good deal of ground peas and beans . . . At this time of year the vegetables are coming in and relieve the desperate monotony of the sour bread and substitutes of all sorts. Milk is given more as a medicine than food. It can be had only on a doctor's prescription . . . A well child over six cannot have any. For those under six, the pint of milk allowed each child per day is inadequate . . . The mothers *will* give the milk which has been prescribed for them to the children . . .

"When I saw Mr. Hoover in Paris he said, 'We may count food values in calories, but we have no way to measure human misery.' We may go about the streets here looking at the shop windows and at the well people we see and not know the sorrow of Germany. It is only as we enter humbly and tenderly into the room of suffering that our hearts can in some sense measure the pain . . . "

On August 25, she wrote: "The German people have used their curtains and sheets for clothes . . . and they use linen table cloths on the beds and paper table cloths on the tables . . . The small boys do not look badly in plush trousers made from curtains or furniture covering. Even this has come to an end, however . . . If America sent munitions to their enemies in the last war shall we not send them munitions of food and clothes? . . . Tuberculosis seems to follow every cold. How can children do without woolen stockings if they have no leather shoes? Of course there is no rubber at all in Germany to use for rubber shoes. Mothers here are very clever at knitting so I have cabled for wool yarn to knit stockings. If we put our love in the yarn they can put their love in the knitting and the stockings will surely be doubly warm! . . ."

It was decided at a committee meeting of the American Friends Service Committee held on September 25th after Carolena Wood and Jane Addams reported in full their visit to Germany that a group of workers should be sent into Germany and Austria to distribute food and clothing. While plans were being formulated and an effort was made to raise money for this purpose, Herbert Hoover, Chairman of the American Relief Administration and the European Children's Fund wrote to the American Friends Service Committee on November 1, 1919: "(Our Administration has) not organized such a service for Germany . . . I have some funds remaining from the operations of last winter under the Supreme Economic Council, which funds are applicable to this purpose. I have been approached by various societies in the United States comprising citizens of German descent, who are anxious to be of some service in this matter. I, therefore, would be very glad to know if your Society would be willing to undertake the expansion of your activities to the extent of becoming the repository of any funds which may be subscribed in the United States for this purpose, and to the extent of increasing your personnel in Germany to organize and safeguard the distribution of food to this specific purpose . . .

"I suggest that your Society undertake this work for Germany for obvious reasons. The first is the experience you have gained in initiating this work. The second is the fact that this effort in sheer humanity should not be allowed to develop into political propaganda in either the United States or Germany and it seems to me, therefore, that some society such as the American Quakers, which is beyond all question of political interest, should become the filter through which such an effort should pass . . .

"In order that there should be every encouragement to undertake such an effort, I am prepared to guarantee from the funds at my disposal the purchasing department expenses, and to pay the entire cost of overseas transport from Atlantic ports into German ports of any food stuffs thus delivered for child relief and for which your society is to furnish the purchase money . . .

Signed, Herbert Hoover."

"With some realization of the great responsibility and wonderful opportunity involved, the committee voted to accept Mr. Hoover's invitation and to undertake the relief work for the children of Germany."[1]

Carolena Wood wrote to Charles J. Rhoads from Berlin, August 1, 1919, " . . . As thee may know the Peace Treaty simply said that the prisoners of war should be returned (to Germany) . . ." Two hundred of these prisoners had been working for the Friends Mission in France without wages, since that had been the agreement made by the Mission with the French Government. It has been stated previously that a record was kept of the exact number of hours which these men spent in labor for the Friends. In the late autumn of 1919 pictures were taken of the prisoners and

[1] Minutes of the American Friends Service Committee, November 5, 1919.

four Friends, Constance Gostick, Mary Kelsey, Ronald Hotson and Solomon Yoder entered Germany in December and remained until March 1920 for the purpose of visiting the families of these men, showing the photograph to indicate that the father, son or brother was in good health and paying to the family the sum of money which the prisoner had earned and which could not rightfully, because of the promise to the Government, be paid to him, himself. In nearly every case families had been cut off from news of the prisoners and did not know where they were or whether they were alive. The visits of the four Friends made a profound impression and brought help and encouragement. The prisoners did not return for some months.

Soon after this group had come into Germany, a Unit of nineteen American Friends, under the leadership of Alfred G. Scattergood, first chairman of the American Friends Service Committee, sailed for Germany, arriving in Berlin on January 2, 1920. There was a delay in the arrival of the food, however, and it was difficult at best for the German people to understand why the Americans had come. They were bewildered by the blockade which the Allies had imposed on their country. "Having been deceived by their political and military leaders they were now at an utter loss to understand why the world hated them so much . . . They could not understand why the Allies had imposed a food blockade upon them, why their little children were permitted to starve to death, and why they had failed as a nation." [2]

Relief work in Germany can be discussed in three specific categories.

The first period was from February 26, 1920, when the first meal was served to children in Berlin, until August

[2] Minutes of the American Friends Service Committee, September 25, 1919.

Six Years Old

MEDICAL EXAMINATION IN VIENNA

Boys Hoping They Are Sufficiently Undernourished to Get a Meal
Ticket

Quäkerspeisung

1921. During this time the American Friends Service Committee distributed food purchased with funds from the A.R.A., Mr. Hoover's American Relief Administration, and with money contributed from individuals for this purpose. "Mr. Hoover and those directly connected with the work, see the need for feeding one million a day from January 1921 to July 1921 and plans are underway to secure sufficient funds for that purpose. Mr. Hoover has contributed two million dollars' worth of food toward the feeding for the coming winter and the German Government has voted to give us all the flour and sugar which we use . . . Cash on hand, including the contributions from the German Government and food supplies on hand, totals four and a half millions toward the feeding this coming winter." [3]

The feeding was limited to children who were decidedly underweight with serious signs of malnutrition, or who had diseases as a result of malnutrition. At first the age limit was made for children from six to fourteen years old but later it included children from two to six years. Nursing mothers were given supplementary meals, also. Food was cooked in central kitchens and transferred from these in carts to the feeding centers which were generally schools. The small American Unit was assisted by forty thousand Germans who helped in the preparation and distribution of the food and "during the third week in June 1921, the feeding reached the high peak of 1,010,658 persons in 1640 communities receiving a supplementary meal each day from 8,364 feeding stations supplied by 2,271 kitchens." [4]

The second period was from August 1921 until the end of July 1922. It had been hoped that Friends could withdraw in the summer of 1921 but conditions remained so

[3] Minutes of the American Friends Service Committee, September 30, 1920.
[4] Jones, Lester M., *Quakers in Action*, p. 55.

serious that it became evident that food would be needed for another year. The Service Committee did not have sufficient funds, either of its own or from the A.R.A. to continue the work, but at a meeting of prominent German-Americans from the eastern part of the United States "the future of mass child-feeding in Germany had been discussed and the necessity for Americans of German descent to unite in raising the money to support this work for another year." [5]

This group of German-Americans co-operated with the Service Committee and worked with them on the most friendly terms. They carried on a campaign for $3,000,000 with which to buy food to be sent to Germany and distributed under the auspices of the Service Committee. Enough money was secured to feed five hundred thousand children a day until July 31, 1922, at which time the relief work was handed over by the Service Committee to the German Central Committee for Foreign Relief which had been working in close co-operation during the entire time of child feeding.

As will be shown in a later chapter dealing with the Quaker Centers in Europe, cessation of relief did not bring all members of the Unit back to America. The work in Germany was not entirely closed and when need arose again it was a comparatively easy matter for the Service Committee to organize another Unit.

The third period was from February 15, 1924, until October 7, 1924. "In August 1923 the German Government made an appeal to Friends in America through their representative in Washington, Ambassador Wiedfeldt, asking that they return to Germany and become responsible for the child feeding there. Later the fall of the mark (which was 4.2 trillion to the dollar) and other signs of economic disorder brought to the world a realization that the worst was

[5] From the Minutes of a Joint Meeting of the Executive Board and the German Committee, April 5, 1921.

not yet over in Germany. At this time, General Henry T. Allen, who commanded the American forces at Coblenz after the war, being much disturbed by the prospect of a food shortage in Germany, agreed to become chairman of a committee composed of prominent Americans, organized for the purpose of collecting money for the feeding of German children, provided that the American Friends Service Committee would agree to act as trustees for the fund." [6]

There were three reasons why the German situation was serious in 1923:

"1. The inability of merchants or the Government to finance the usual margin of imports.

"2. The breakdown of currency and consequently of distribution of domestic supplies from the farms to the cities.

"3. Widespread unemployment both in occupied and unoccupied Germany and consequent inability of large masses of people to buy, even if supplies existed." [7]

On December 11, 1923, the German President, Herr Ebert, cabled asking that Friends take quick action in coming and five days later Henry Tatnall Brown and his wife sailed with Dr. Haven Emerson, the former to supervise the child-feeding program in Germany and the latter, Professor of Public Health Administration in Columbia University, to make a thorough investigation of the entire situation. Henry Brown remained until the end of March and in June, D. Robert Yarnall sailed with his wife to become head of the child-feeding program.

The first carload of Allen food arrived in Berlin on January 28, 1924, and on the 15th of February a cable from Philadelphia authorized Henry Brown to begin feeding a

[6] From a speech made by Henry T. Brown at a conference of the Mittelstellen of the Deutsche Zentral Ausschuss, February 29, 1924.
[7] Report on German Food Situation by C. E. Herring, United States Commercial Attaché for Berlin, and on the staff of the Department of Commerce.

million children a day. Robert Yarnall remained in charge until October 7 of that year when the Service Committee withdrew and transferred the child-feeding once more to the Deutsche Zentral Ausschuss für die Auslands Hilfe, the German Central Committee for Foreign Relief.

"Brother Juniper marvelled . . . for it seemed to him that these temporal things were naught, save in so far as men of their charity shared them with their neighbors . . .
And they ate of the pottage of flour by reason of his importunate charity. And they were refreshed much more by devotion than by food."

The Little Flowers of St. Francis of Assisi

Chapter VII

INTO THE ROOM OF SUFFERING

December 1919

FRIEDA climbed the bare, carpetless stairs and closed the door behind her as she entered the cold room.

"Hans, I've come back," she said and the small bundle of clothes moved on the bed as the thin face of a child turned towards the voice.

"How is Mama?"

"Hansi, Mama is dead. They told me at the hospital that she died this morning." The boy made no sound but stared at Frieda with large, round eyes. "It is better so. There is no food for her to eat and at least she is happy now." Frieda sat down on the bed and took her brother's thin hand in hers. Tears rolled down her white, drawn cheeks and fell on her ragged coat, but Hans did not cry. He lay very still and watched his sister. Finally he spoke.

"I am going to die, Frieda. I have been waiting so long for you to come back and the pain has been bad and I was so cold. No, no, you must keep your coat on. It will not make me any warmer, because the cold is inside me, too."

"Don't talk like that, Hansi. Now that Mama is gone perhaps I can get you into the hospital. I keep thinking I shall find some food which will make you stronger. I was gone a long time this afternoon because I was looking for some coal. Perhaps in a day or so we can have a little fire. That will make you warm all over."

"Don't you see, Sister, that if I were dead, you could manage better. You can't take care of me and hunt for food, too. I don't believe there is any food in the hospital, either. Now that Mama is dead I don't mind dying so much. I could be with her again and perhaps with Papa, if he is dead, too. Tell me about Papa, once more, Frieda."

"But I've told you about him so many times, Hans."

"Never mind, tell me again."

"Will you go to sleep if I talk about him? See, I will lie down beside you and that will make you warm." The boy moved slowly under the torn, dirty cover and Frieda, still wearing her coat, lay down by him. There was no other furniture in the room except the small iron bedstead. There was a stove in the corner but it was empty and the only heat came from the bodies of the little boy and his sister. There were a few dishes piled on the floor but they were empty.

Frieda was not crying any more. Grief for her mother was to be endured better than the lack of food and warmth for Hans and she had no strength with which to cry. Now that Mama was dead Hans was the only person left in the world because surely Papa had died long ago in France where the French soldiers had captured him and been cruel to him. If Hans died then she would kill herself and be buried with him.

"Close your eyes and try to go to sleep. Tomorrow I think I can get some potatoes. What shall I tell you about Papa?"

"Was there always enough to eat when he was at home?"

"Always. Papa was a baker and people said he was the best one in all Berlin. Mama used to scold him when he gave me little cakes because they were so rich. But he used to laugh and say, 'They are good for her and will make her grow fat and rosy.' He used to tease Mama and we

would both laugh. He gave you little cakes too, don't you
remember?"

"I can't remember ever having any cakes."

"You were five when Papa went away to the war, and
you were a big boy. I remember when he lifted you up in
his arms to say goodbye. I was thirteen and felt very old
because Mama let me sell things in the shop that day but I
was frightened too because I couldn't understand very well
why Papa was going. Mama tried to explain to me that
there was a war in France and that the French and English
were fighting against Germany. I couldn't see why Papa
had to go and fight with Helène who was a French girl in
my school the year before. She was the only French person I knew. Mama cried and cried after Papa left and held
you in her arms for a long time, I remember, praying that
the dear God would send him back soon. She tried to keep
the bakery going but it was hard work because none of the
other men could bake as well as Papa and then Gretel was
born in October. Mama was sick for quite a long time and
Gretel was always delicate so that Mama couldn't leave
her. I stopped going to school so that I could help Mama
take care of you and Gretel but she died the next March
before Papa ever saw her.

"Pretty soon after that there came a letter from him saying that he had been wounded but not very badly and that
he was in the hospital. We were happier for a little while
because he was safe and we knew where he was. He came
home before he went back to the war and Mama used to
hear from him once in a while. That was in 1915. Mama
was having a hard time with the bakery because there
weren't any men left to work in it. Then letters stopped coming from Papa but we didn't get any notice about his being
killed, so we didn't know where he was.

"We had to move and Mama told the post office because

she hoped every day to hear from him and at last one day there came a post card from France which said, 'I am their prisoner but I am safe. I hope you and the children are well. Josef.' "

Hans had fallen asleep, soothed by the sound of Frieda's voice, but she lay rigid and wide awake as she tried to think what she must do next. She was too hungry to think clearly and yet now that Mama was dead there was no one else to look after Hans except herself. But she couldn't buy any food or coal for him because she had no money. It was hard to believe that Mama was dead but it was better so because she had been suffering a long time and now that was over. Hans was ill and wanted to die but he mustn't die. If only she could get some food for him. She began to think about the bakery and Papa and the little cakes which had been so plentiful and so good and which Papa had given to her. If only some one could give her little cakes now.

Frieda heard steps in the hall outside but she paid no attention because no one ever came to their poor little room. Someone was knocking on a door but it must be the one across from theirs, Frieda thought. Suddenly, to her amazement the door opened and a lady came in. Frieda sat up and tried to smooth back her hair as she patted the heavy yellow braid which was wound around her head.

"I beg pardon," the lady said, "I was told that Frau Heinrich lives here. Is that so?"

"Yes, only my mother is dead. Did you wish to see her? I am Frieda Heinrich, her daughter, and this is my brother, Hans, but he is ill."

"Is your father a prisoner in France?"

"We heard from him a long time ago and he said he was a prisoner, but we know nothing about him at all. We are afraid he is dead too. Who are you, please? You are a foreigner?"

"I am Fräulein Abby Worthington, Frieda, from America, but I have been living in France. Your father was one of many German prisoners who worked for us. Do you remember him?" Abby opened her handbag and took out a photograph. "He sent this picture to you." Frieda took it in her hands and gave a cry.

"But it is Papa! Hans, Hans, wake up! The lady brings us a picture of Papa! He looks thinner and older, but it is he and Josef Heinrich is written on the back. Tell me, Fräulein, where is he? Will he be coming back to us soon?"

"I can't tell you when he can come back, Frieda. Not for a while, but perhaps in a few months."

"But Fräulein, you have come a long way, all the way from France and you must be tired and hungry." Frieda looked anxiously around the room, as though she hoped to see a chair which she could offer to her guest. "I must apologize for not giving you a chair to sit on, or something to eat."

"Never mind that. I am not tired, but you are if you have been taking care of the little boy. I cannot stay very long but I will tell you about your father. I have been living in France since 1917. Did you ever hear of the Quakers, Frieda, or the Friends? Die Freunden?" Frieda shook her head.

"The Quakers do not believe that anyone should fight. When the war started they did not want to kill Germans any more than they wanted to kill men in their own country. After a long delay the American Government gave the Quaker men permission to come to France and build houses in the villages which had been destroyed. They planted gardens and worked in hospitals."

"But I do not understand what you mean, Fräulein," Frieda said. "We have been told that all the Allies have been cruel and have done terrible things. How then could they build houses and plant gardens? They have put this blockade against us to keep food from coming in to our country. Why have they done that?"

"I cannot answer that question because I cannot understand. It is wrong and wicked. The war is over but people do not always think about what they are doing. But about your father."

"Yes, yes, tell me more about Papa."

"There was a great deal of work to do in France, more than we could manage by ourselves. We knew there were German prisoners nearby who had nothing to do and who would be glad to work so some one asked permission of the French Government and they allowed us to use two hundred German men. Your father was one of these. We asked the men what they used to do at home in the Fatherland and your father said he was a baker. He was made cook for the two hundred men."

"Why didn't he write to us? Surely if the Quakers are kind, they would let him write."

"He did write but the letters must have been lost. I had a very hard time to find you. I have been looking for several days. A letter, perhaps, could not ask so many times. He was afraid that you were all dead because he heard nothing. He is well and strong and happy because he is back in the kitchen."

"Won't you let him come back soon, Fräulein? Now that Mama is dead there is no one but me to look after Hans and I have nothing."

"I can't promise when he will come back, Frieda. That depends on the French Government. I think perhaps in a few months, they will let him come. I have brought something for you."

"Oh, then we may keep his picture! How wonderful to have Papa's picture and to know that he is well and strong and will be coming home. If only Mama could have known. She died this morning, Fräulein."

"That is very sad. Of course, the picture is yours, but I have brought you the money your father has earned while he has been working for us." Abby opened the bag and took out a packet of bills. "This is for you and Hans."

"Money?" Frieda stared at Abby while her hands twisted her ragged coat. Money would buy coal and food and clothes and it would keep Hans from dying. "Why do you bring money to me? Prisoners have to work for nothing. I cannot understand."

"It is for you. We were not allowed to pay the prisoners but nothing was said about paying their families. We kept a record of the time each man worked and so we know what your father would have earned if he had received wages. We do not expect to have work done for nothing. Some day you will understand. Your father has been much liked by every one. Give me your hand, child, and take the money. I must go now, but I will come back again, before I leave Berlin." Abby turned to go, but Frieda stopped her.

"Fräulein, you have come a long way to Berlin. You must have spent many marks to come so far. Let me give you some of this money."

"This money is all for you and Hans, Frieda, every pfennig. I do not want any."

Frieda looked at the money in her hand and then at Abby's face.

"You mean I can spend this for food and coal and warm clothes? Are you sure? I thought Americans hated us and that all the Allies were trying to make us starve. I didn't know that any foreigners could be so good and kind. I didn't know . . . "

The magnificence of the gift was too much for Frieda to bear. She didn't want to cry in front of the strange lady and she held out her hand abruptly to say goodbye. Abby went over to the bed.

"Goodbye, Hans. You'll get better soon, won't you?" The child looked up at her and smiled and Abby turned to go.

"Fräulein," Frieda exclaimed, "I have never thanked you for coming. I am so bewildered. Thank you very much, it is too wonderful." Tears poured down Frieda's cheeks and she flung her arms around Abby's neck.

February 1920

Frieda stood at the top of the steep stair case waiting for Hans who walked very slowly, his thin, misshapen legs toiling up the steps. If only they could live where there were no stairs, but she knew it was better to put the money into coal and food and warm clothes than to pay more for a room. Long ago, when she had been a child she was able to run up and down stairs all day long without ever getting tired. A boy of ten ought to be able to run and shout and play but it took all of Hans' strength to get to school and then, later in the day, to drag one foot up after the other to reach the top where he had to sit down, exhausted.

Always when it was time for him to come home from school Frieda came and waited for him. Suppose he should stumble and fall, suppose his heart should stop beating? There were so many things that might happen to Hans and if anything did even the promise of Papa's expected return could not make up to her for the loss of the little brother. Hans was much better because with the money she had been able to buy coal which kept them warm. But even with money she could not buy the kind of food he ought to have. He needed good bread, not this sour stuff which was all she could get and which was not at all the kind Papa used to make. He needed a great deal of milk and butter and eggs. But she had kept him warm and the food she could buy with the money was better than nothing. There was very little food to be bought in Germany that winter, even if one were a millionaire.

She wondered whether Papa would have gone away if he had known that war would be like this. That August morning so long ago had been full of excitement and even gaiety. After all, Papa was going to fight for the Fatherland which was a glorious thing to do but no one had dreamed that Germany would be defeated and the Kaiser sent into exile. Everybody had gone without food so that the army could have plenty but all these years of sacrifice had brought nothing but starvation. Now that the war was said to be over there wasn't any difference, except that food was more difficult to get than ever. Unless someone brought good flour and sugar and milk into Germany nobody would be able to keep alive much longer.

After all this long time, Hans reached the top step and sat down beside Frieda. He was too tired to speak and she put her arm around him, holding him close against her, stroking his hot, damp forehead. She tried not to look at his crooked, clumsy legs but they were in front of her where she could not miss them, crooked because he did not have proper food.

"Come, Hansi, it's cold for you sitting here. There's a fire burning in our room." She half carried him to the bed where she took off his thick, heavy boots which weighed down his legs but kept his feet warm and dry. "I shan't let you go to school any more. It's too far and you get so tired."

"But Frieda! I can't stop going to school now. Just think, they told us the most wonderful thing today! We're going to get a meal every day, right there. They will bring it to us."

"A meal, Hansi? Where will they get the food? Even with money with which to buy, there is nothing to be had."

"I don't know, but it is the truth. A doctor came into our room and made us take off our shirts while he tapped our chests. He put his ear close to where my heart is and I did all the things he told me, Frieda. He asked me about my legs and how long they had been like this, but I really couldn't remember. I was glad I had worn my good shirt today."

"Yes, but what about the meal?"

"Somebody sat by the doctor and wrote things down in a little book. I thought that was all but when school was over the teacher told us to bring cups and spoons when we came back on Monday because there would be food for us. What do you suppose they will have, Frieda?"

"Didn't she tell you where the food was coming from? Don't you know anything more?"

"What was the name of the lady who brought us the money? She came from some Society."

"Quaker? Fräulein Worthington, you mean? Was she there?"

"No, but it is the Quakers who bring the food. There was a lady there who was very strange and couldn't talk to us very well. I thought perhaps she was slow and stupid like Eric. He can't talk properly."

"Hans, how stupid of you! The lady was American and doesn't know German. Was she a Quaker?"

"Yes, maybe. She had a funny thing on her sleeve which looked like a star, but it was red and black. I thought stars were always gold."

"I believe Fräulein Worthington went back to America and told them that there was nothing to eat in Germany. Don't you suppose she tried to buy food and couldn't, Hansi?"

"The big boys in school say that everybody in America hates us and hopes that we'll die. If they've been mean to us so long why would they stop now? Do you think Fräulein Worthington has so much influence in her country that it would send things over for us? Maybe she is really an angel and she has told God how hungry we are so God is sending the food. You've always said that if I prayed God would hear sometime, even if He didn't seem to right away. Don't you suppose this food has come because I've prayed to get well and look after you, Frieda?"

"Yes, it must be God. Maybe He told the Quakers to come. I'm going to school with you on Monday and find out." Suddenly big tears began to roll down the little boy's cheeks.

"Don't come, Frieda," he whimpered, "please don't come. You see the teacher said that only children between six and fourteen could have the meals and you're too old because you're eighteen. Frieda, I won't go back because I don't want to have things that you can't have."

"Don't be a goose. If you go to school and have food and grow strong, your legs will grow straight again and your cough will go away. I don't need to eat as much as you do because I'm stronger than you are. Don't you suppose the teacher will need somebody to help her because she can't do it all by herself? I could help and if I could it would make all the difference in the world. Oh, Hansi, if we can go to school together, you can have the food and I can be the one to give it to you!"

May 1920

Frieda was confused by so much conversation that she could not understand and she felt a little frightened although the people looked kind. She had learned a few

English words, like "roll" and "cocoa" and "flour" and she was used to hearing German spoken with peculiar accents and funny mistakes. She had even told Fräulein Worthington what Hans had said about the lady in school who was stupid because she could not talk. But Hans had never seen many foreigners.

Frieda was waiting for Fräulein Worthington who had asked her to come to this Committee Meeting. "If you are so interested in what we are doing please come and see the Quakers for yourself," Fräulein had said but she was late and Frieda looked out of the window at the trees along the Dorotheenstrasse, trees that had been bare and black the first time she had come there to ask Herr Scattergood if she might help in the child-feeding. The trees weren't bare any longer and the leaves were spreading over the branches like a lace garment. The terrible winter was over and it was not necessary to burn the precious lumps of coal in order to keep warm. Because of the warm sunshine and the good food at school, Hans was getting stronger. There was color in his cheeks and he did not cough very much. She remembered the spring two years ago in 1918 when everyone thought that the war would be over soon because news came into Berlin that the German soldiers were pushing back the Allies. Before long they would be in Paris and everyone knew that Germany was going to win. The push was a false one and the war dragged along until Germany was defeated. The Armistice had made no difference, nor had the Peace Treaty in 1919. As far as Germany was concerned the war had never stopped.

She remembered now the question she had asked Herr Scattergood. "How did you know that we were in need of food?"

"We knew," he had told her, "because in the summer of

1919 three Americans and four English people came into
your country as soon as the Peace Treaty had been signed.
They investigated and found that conditions were very
serious. Then Mr. Herbert Hoover, the head of the American Relief Administration, wrote to us in November and
told us that German children needed food and he asked
the American Quakers to come and feed these children. In
December four people came here from France to return
the wages to families of German prisoners. Everybody
who came to Germany told us the same story. That is
why we came."

She remembered, too, how he had answered her question, "How was it that you wanted to bring us help? Did
you not call us Huns?"

"Calling a person a Hun, Fräulein Heinrich, does not
remove the fact that he may hunger and thirst and have
need of clothes. Some of us in America loved your country in spite of the war. Your country was no more in the
wrong, perhaps, than my own."

Frieda felt a hand on her arm and looked up to see Abby
standing beside her.

"Ah, Fräulein, I have been waiting for you."

"I am glad you have come and sorry that I have kept
you waiting. The meeting is just about to begin."

"I cannot understand English and it is discouraging."

"Never mind. I will write down in German as well
as I can, what they say. We will sit near the back."

The room grew still as the men and women took their
seats and bowed their heads. Frieda watched Fräulein
Worthington who had bowed her head and covered her
eyes with her hand. Was this Church? There was no
Pastor and it was not Sunday and Fräulein had said it
was only a committee. Frieda felt a panic. If she had only

known it was to be a church service she would have worn her other dress. A woman rose and spoke several sentences of which Frieda understood only one word, "God." A man said something but there was nothing to understand. Then everybody sat up straight and there was a subdued murmur of voices.

"They always begin these meetings with a little time of worship," Abby whispered to Frieda. "I forgot to tell you before we sat down. Anyone who wants to may speak but sometimes we just sit in silence. That was Fräulein Norment who prayed and Richard Cary who spoke." Frieda recognized Herr Scattergood who was conducting the meeting and she watched his short fingers as he clasped his hands. She looked at all the people and tried to imagine what work they were doing. It was very hard for her to realize that they had come across the sea in order to feed children whom they did not know.

There was a great deal of talking which she did not understand and although first one person and then another spoke, Herr Scattergood never was flustered or confused, he never raised his voice and nobody seemed to be excited or angry. Abby wrote on the pad and pushed it over to Frieda:

"The map of Germany that you see in front is to show which cities have feeding centers for children and the pins indicate the number of feeding centers. There was discussion about the number of children who are being fed and the number who ought to be getting one meal a day. At the present time there are five hundred thousand children and nursing mothers who are getting food; the number is increasing all the time but perhaps during the summer it will decrease for a while. There are eighty cities which are feeding through three thousand centers."

Frieda looked at the map with new understanding. Each

pin meant a place where children were getting meals. There rose before her eyes a picture of Hans' school where she was helping, the long line of children waiting with their cups, the sweet, hot smell of the cocoa as it was poured into the cups, a fragrance which had tormented her at the beginning because she could not have any herself. On the days when there were rolls the air was filled with the smell of fresh bread and brought back to her mind the familiar bakery where Papa used to work. Nothing had ever reminded her of her childhood so much as these rolls when they were brought into the school room, still warm from the great ovens in the kitchens where they had been baked. If five hundred thousand children were eating a roll apiece that meant an enormous amount of flour, more than Papa had ever used in a day. She felt bewildered by the size of the relief work which the Quakers were doing. It had centered for her in Hans' school and the children there whom she knew, although she had been told that many schools were doing the same thing. She looked again at the network of red pins. All over the country cups were being filled with cocoa and little hands were grasping the soft, warm rolls.

"Now they are saying," Abby wrote again, "that it will be necessary to feed children younger than six years old. This will be difficult because they do not come to school. Fräulein Branson says that the older children need more food, too. Tuberculosis is spreading very fast. It is serious."

Abby rose to speak and Frieda was startled to hear foreign words coming from Fräulein Worthington's mouth but she was speaking more slowly and distinctly than the others who talked so fast that it was impossible to tell when one word ended and another began. Then she started to speak in German:

"I have brought with me today Frieda Heinrich, who is

helping in school number 15, where her younger brother is a student. It was her wish to know more about the Quakers and their child-feeding program. She heard of them for the first time when I went to see her with her father's photograph and the money he had earned. He was one of the German prisoners whom we employed in France." Frieda was embarrassed because everyone looked at her but Herr Scattergood rose and said:

"Fräulein Heinrich is very welcome and we hope she will come often." Tears came to Frieda's eyes. How could she stand up in front of these people? If only she had worn her other dress she might have felt less self-conscious but then she realized that nothing mattered except that these people had saved Hans' life and that she wanted to thank them. She rose from her seat, twisting her handkerchief between her thin fingers:

"Herr Scattergood and the kind Quakers, please excuse me that I cannot speak English," she began, "but I want to thank you, first for bringing me the money from my father so that I could buy coal and food for my little brother. If it had not been for that he would have died last Christmas. But even the money could not buy everything he needed so I want to thank you for bringing the flour and cocoa from America and for letting me help give it to the children where I am working.

"I have learned this afternoon how many children in Germany are eating meals which will help to make many crooked legs straight and to make weak lungs strong again. It is wonderful because there are many children who are worse than my brother. You have brought us these things which we needed very much but you have brought with them kindness and understanding and we needed these even more. Your country and mine were enemies so that we had been taught to hate your people. We were told that you did cruel things to little children. I have found that these were all lies. I told my little brother to pray God to make my mother get well and to bring back my father, but I didn't believe there was any God because He would never have let such terrible things happen to our Fatherland.

"Liebe Quäker, you have brought your ship loads and train loads of food but you have brought more than these, you have brought back our faith in God. It is for this that we are most grateful." Frieda sat down, trembling. It was the first time in her life that she had ever made a speech and she knew that every one had been watching her. Perhaps it had not been expected that she would have anything to say and Fräulein Wrothington would be annoyed. There was not a sound in the room after she sat down and at first she was frightened. She saw that the people had bowed their heads and were having another period of worship. She covered her own face with her hand and she knew, as though He were standing before her, that God was present in that room.

The committee continued, and Abby wrote:

"You spoke very well, Frieda, it was nice that you wanted to. They are talking about the future of the feeding. A letter from Wilbur Thomas, secretary in Philadelphia, says that Herr Hoover wants the Quakers to stay in Germany because the children must have food for another winter. Herr Thomas sent a cable to ask whether this will be possible and the committee has just said yes." That meant that next winter would not be so terrible because food would still be coming in from outside.

"Fräulein Kraus has just said," Abby wrote, "that she wants food sent to the health camps outside of the cities where children can be out of doors in the summer. The camps are there and all the equipment except the food.

It is as important as feeding in the schools. Several people say that they hope this will be done."

There was a great deal of talking which Frieda could not understand and she began to wonder how long it would be necessary for the Quakers to stay in Germany and give meals. Would conditions ever be right again and would it be possible for them to forget that there had ever been a war? Abby pushed the pad to Frieda:

"They have been talking about what you have said here today. It is easier to feed the children than to explain why we have come here and some people are suspicious because they think the Quakers are really trying to get something for themselves. It takes a long time for anyone to forget that the war is over and that there are no enemies any more. It is hard for us to interpret what we are doing because some of us do not speak German very well and the Germans who are translating what we say do not always say the right things because the Quaker message is not clear to them. It is important that this message should be very clear and that it should be given by those who understand what the Quakers are doing. Herr Evans has just said that it is part of our work to find people to do this who are sympathetic with the Quaker ideals. Anyone can serve food and hand in report cards."

Frieda's heart stopped beating for an instant. She was serving food and handing in cards now. Would it be possible that in a few more weeks she could understand this Quaker message well enough to go around and talk about it? It was frightening to think of standing in front of a big room of children or of grown-up people and talk to them but she could get used to it and she was beginning to understand a little what this Quaker message was, because it was not very difficult. "Whoever comes with food in his hand must have love in his heart and kindness in his face," she thought as the room grew still again. Every one shook hands and Frieda turned to Abby.

"What is this for? Is it good-bye?"

"This is the Quaker way of ending worship. I can't tell you just why it began but it is a symbol, perhaps of 'Grüss Gott' and 'Auf Wiedersehen,' a greeting and a farewell and at the same time sharing with one another something precious which has happened during the time of worship."

"You must tell me more about the Quakers, Fräulein Worthington."

January 1921

Frieda smiled as she entered the big schoolroom and saw the children eating at their desks. It was always the same, in every school, but the sight never grew monotonous because she would see a new group of children. She had started by being interested only in Hans, because he was her brother and the only person she had to love, but she loved all the children whom she saw and it was gratifying to see them improve week by week. These boys and girls were laughing as they ate and wriggling in their seats. The first time she had gone to Hans' school the children sat perfectly still without moving until the teacher told them to move. They were listless and tired. At recess no one ever ran or played but stood against the wall until it was time to go back to the schoolroom. The effect of hunger had crept through the bodies of the children so slowly that there had been no sudden change from health to sickness. The limbs and muscles had been numbed, gradually, by the lassitude which resulted from lack of nourishment. Flesh which had been firm became flabby and bones which had been strong and straight began to bend like putty.

She had seen a doctor bend a baby's legs just as though there were no bones in them.

Frieda walked around the room while the children were still eating and compared them with the hundreds of others she had seen. Under the shabby dresses the stomachs did not look so distended and the girls were sitting up straighter. The boys' chests did not seem quite so thin as they had once, and their eyes were less sunken. Their faces were beginning to show a little color. The recovery was gradual but it was coming. It was still hard to tell whether some of the boys and girls were six years old or ten.

The teacher introduced Frieda:

"Fräulein Heinrich comes from the Quakers to tell you about the 'Quäkerspeisung.'" Everyone clapped and Frieda remembered the first time she had been introduced when the children did not clap, but just smiled because it took less effort.

"Do you like the 'Quäkerspeisung'?" she asked.

"Oh, yes!" they shouted.

"Where did the flour and cocoa come from?"

"America!"

"Why did the Quakers come to Germany?"

"They knew we were hungry."

"Yes," Frieda continued, "they knew we were hungry but so did other people. We used to hate the Americans because we were told that they were a cruel nation but they hated Germany because they had been told we were a cruel nation and that it was our fault the world had a war. They fought our fathers and our brothers for four years and when that was over it wasn't very likely that they would begin to send food to children who were hungry. Lots of them didn't realize that we had nothing to eat so we must forgive them.

"But there were some American and English men who refused to fight in the war because they believed that it is wrong to kill people no matter where they live or what they have done. These were Quakers and a few others who believed as they did. When the war started they told their Governments that they wouldn't fight because Christ had taught that war was wrong and that love was the greatest thing in the world. The Governments wanted every man to fight and wanted to put the Quakers into prison, but a Committee was started to give the Quakers something else to do and the Governments approved of the plan, after a long time.

"We thought we were fortunate because there was no fighting in Germany and we didn't care what happened to France. But it was terrible for the French people whose houses and villages were destroyed and who had to run away until the danger was over. When they came back there was nothing left at all.

"The Quakers came over to France to build houses and to make new gardens. They weren't afraid of danger and there was a lot then because when they first came the war was going on. They heard that there was sickness and hunger in Russia and Poland so some of the Quakers went to those countries. In 1919 they found out that there was no food in Germany and although we believed that everybody hated us, it wasn't true. They brought food over here and began to feed children like you and mothers with little babies in February of 1920. Your bodies need certain things to make them grow but Germany didn't have any of those things. The Quakers found out from doctors and nurses what you needed and it is important to see whether you are growing taller and stronger and whether those who have been ill are getting well.

"You call this meal the 'Quäkerspeisung' and perhaps

you will associate, for the rest of your life, the word Quaker with a good meal. That will be very fine. But that is not enough. Have you ever thought how you would eat your meal without a cup and spoon? You must have an instrument with which to eat your food before you can begin your meal. The Quaker has been the *instrument*, and you must think about him as well as the nice rolls and soup and cocoa. He knew that you were hungry but he knew that the Germans had been beaten in the war and that we were unhappy about that. He knew that people did not like us and that we were bitter and discouraged. He knew that what the German people needed the most was to have some of the foreign countries care about them.

"Suppose your mothers kept saying to you, 'I like you,' or 'I love you,' but they didn't do anything else. They never kissed you or played with you and never tried to do anything for you. You wouldn't believe that they really cared what happened to you. The Quakers knew that they couldn't come over here where people were hungry and just say, 'We like you.' No one would really know whether that was true or not. In order to show that the Quakers meant what they were saying they brought the food in their hands to signify what they felt in their hearts. Food is only half of what they brought and the other half is friendship.

"There are thousands of schools like this one where children can have a meal. How many friends the Quakers have! So many that it is hard to count them. In fifteen years from now the youngest boys and girls will be grown up, twenty-one years old, and by that time the war will be forgotten and the whole world will be friendly again. As long as you live you will remember that the Quakers from across the sea have loved you and have shown their love by sending flour and sugar and milk to you when you needed them. We must show our gratitude to them in some way besides writing letters to Philadelphia. If we grow up to be fine, courageous men and women we can be living examples of the Quaker message by carrying love in our hearts."

Material for this chapter has been taken from reports and accounts written of the German child-feeding, and from a conversation with Dr. Hertha Kraus.

CHAPTER VIII

POLAND

IN May 1919 a group of three Friends, J. Thompson Eliott and A. Ruth Fry from England, and Dr. Walter Stephens, from America, took the difficult journey to Poland when "communication had only just been reopened by a weekly diplomatic train from Paris, to obtain seats on which was a matter of high privilege." [1] In August of that same year a Polish Unit was sent from London to carry on a disinfecting program in southwest Poland at Zawiercie.

At first glance one might say that Poland and Russia were facing identical problems and they were, in regard to the need for food and for checking typhus. People were dying by thousands. But the situation was different. In Russia the Unit, during the years from 1916 to 1918, had been dealing with refugees who had escaped from Poland into Russia where they wandered for several years. In Poland the Unit found that these refugees had returned to their homes where there was, literally, no stone left upon another. The peasants had been driven out of Poland as early as 1915 when the German invasion started the great march of refugees, many of whom went as far as Siberia and Turkestan as well as to the nearer territory of Russia. Armies had been crossing back and forth over these villages causing such desolation and destruction that the returning peasants could find nothing recognizable. No familiar landmark had been left.

[1] Fry, A. Ruth, *A Quaker Adventure*, p. 249.

Having returned to their native plot of land there was nothing for these homeless refugees to do but settle down in a dug-out and get along as well as they could. The dug-out provided a certain amount of shelter and there was no material with which to build a house. Many of these returned citizens were orphan children who had survived the terrible journey after their parents had died by the roadside, bequeathing only a document on which was written the title to a small piece of land in far off Poland. The Chinese farmer in *The Good Earth,* exiled in the south during the famine, clung to his few precious acres in the north no more passionately than did these Polish peasants, exiled in Russia and Siberia, having no possessions except the title to a piece of earth which it seemed unlikely they should ever see again.

They brought nothing back except typhus which spread with such appalling rapidity that authorities feared it would reach all the countries of Europe. The first job which the Quakers had was to organize housecleaning programs which were so strenuous that when an article of furniture or of wearing apparel could not be scrubbed nor washed it was burned. Much of the furniture, when there was any, could not endure the treatment which it received from the Friends. Heavy pieces had never been moved but members of the Quaker Unit moved them to scrub the wall behind and the floor below. In cases of this sort, the wardrobe collapsed.

The housecleaning was not confined to buildings alone but to the people as well. Public baths were started for the children whose clothes were taken from them and washed, the children were washed, hair included, and given a clean garment and a cake of soap, the latter as a suggestion that bathing could be done frequently at home. The Polish peasants did not always take kindly to this intensive program of washing nor to the strong odors of disinfectant which accompanied the housecleaning, but they began to co-operate more willingly when they learned that dirt caused lice and lice caused the dread typhus.

The Red Cross and the American Relief Administration were both working in Poland bringing food and clothing to children and the Friends Unit co-operated with them. One of the greatest needs was for milk and as there was no food at all to give the cows it was essential to import fodder from abroad. In 1920 William R. Fogg was appointed head of the Polish Unit. He was responsible for the scheme to import cotton-seed meal from the United States, "a food very rich in protein value, found by experiment to increase the yield of milk from one and a half to three liters per diem, when carefully used. A great deal of propaganda work was necessary to make people realize the urgent necessity of increasing the milk supply if the Polish children were to grow up healthy, and to make the many parties to the scheme agree to take their share, but finally the following plan was set in motion, of which one great benefit was the number of people who were induced to co-operate and to work together altruistically.

"About £6000 was spent on 630 tons of cotton-seed meal . . . for which the Polish Government gave free transport from Danzig. It was then distributed to farmers in the neighborhood of the big towns. . . . The farmers paid for this meal in the resultant milk for which they were debited at wholesale price. In the case of Warsaw, a big co-operative society volunteered, free of charge, to collect this milk from the producers and to distribute it to institutions in the city, chosen by the Society of Friends, where it was used for the good of the children. Where it was possible the distribution was made in connection with the American Red

Cross welfare centers." [2] This was a three-fold service as it improved the cow, the milk and the child.

One of the most important pieces of work was the rehabilitation of the land which had grown up to birch trees too small to be of use as lumber but large enough to have sent deep roots into the soil so that it took a great deal of labor to restore the land to its former agricultural uses. Barbed wire had been forced into the ground by shells so that where the land was clear of trees and an attempt could be made to plough, the barbed wire broke the plough. There were no horses and Friends purchased tractors, cultivators, implements of all kinds, and seeds and set to work at the difficult task of preparing the land for use again after its years of ill-treatment and neglect.

In the autumn of 1921 the Unit was granted the loan of 1100 army horses with harness for the purpose of developing their agricultural program. "During the winter they were lent out to the peasants in various districts, but this did not prove very satisfactory and in the early spring they were recalled and formed into 'columns' of twenty to thirty horses, each under the care of a 'horse controller' . . . The work was very arduous and under hard conditions. It was not to be wondered at that only comparatively few Poles of the right type were willing to undertake it, as they could so easily get better work . . . In the spring of 1922 the Polish War Office arranged to sell the horses and harness to the Mission." Seeds and tools were distributed and "there was a certain beautiful symbolism in the work of reconstruction being carried on by Polish Army horses and German trench spades, co-operating this time instead of working against each other as before." [3]

[2] *Op. cit.*, p. 296.
[3] *Op. cit.*, pp. 276–279.

It was impossible to build houses without material for them, and timber forests were too far away for the peasants to haul the wood into the villages. During the winter of 1923 and the spring of 1924 the Unit used these horses for hauling timber; they provided saws and saw mills so that reconstruction of the villages could be started.

In 1925 the Quaker relief work was closed and it was "planned to provide an institution for the training of orphan boys in agriculture and to provide a home for a few of the younger orphans, both boys and girls. The estate of Kolpin on the river Bug near Brest-Litovsk was leased for a period of twelve years and equipped for the purposes intended. After the institution was put into working order it was turned over to the Agricultural Department of the Government." [4]

[4] Jones, Lester M., *Quakers in Action*, pp. 118–119.

"Lord, Thou has hastened to retrieve, to heal,
  To feed, to bind, to clothe, to quench the brand,
To prop the ruin, to bless and to anneal;
Hast sped Thy ships by sea, Thy trains by land,
Shed pity and tears:—our shattered fingers feel
Thy mediate and intelligible hand."

ALICE MEYNELL

CHAPTER IX

KEEPING TYPHUS OUT OF EUROPE

THE following is a conversation which was carried on by Rufus M. Jones and Wilbur K. Thomas from America with Harrison Barrow and Fred Rowntree from England during a train journey in 1921 from Warsaw, Poland to Zurich in Switzerland which country was the destination of the two American Friends. The English Friends were travelling through without stop to England. The journey involved crossing frontiers between Poland and Czechoslovakia, between Czechoslovakia and Austria and between Austria and Switzerland. Their purpose had been to visit the work in the different centers in Europe. The incidents at the borders are based on actual facts.

"What are we coming to next? We must be getting into Austria. Haven't we crossed the border from Czechoslovakia?" The train slowed down as it came into a long, dark station and the four travellers craned their necks to read the name, hidden completely in the gloom. Before they could make out where they were an officer appeared at the door of their compartment and spoke in German:

"Where have you come from and where are you going? Show me your passports." These were produced and Wilbur Thomas replied,

"This gentleman and I are going to Switzerland. The two Englishmen are going to London. We have come from Warsaw."

"Ah," the official was impressed. "Will the English gentlemen please bring their luggage to the customs."

"Well, the joke's on you again," laughed Rufus Jones as
Fred Rowntree and Harrison Barrow, none too pleasantly,
pulled their bags down from the racks. "This is the second
time they've had to go out and we haven't budged once."

"I don't know what the officials have against the British
but they don't seem to miss a chance to make trouble. I
thought the red and black star on our sleeves would make
some difference in Austria. This evidently is the Austrian
border we've reached."

"This is the silliest thing I ever saw," panted Harrison
Barrow as he pushed his bag into the rack again. "They
didn't want a thing except to make themselves important.
Blow these customs! They didn't look at our bags when we
opened them. The next time we're asked to do this and you're
not," he nodded to the two Americans who were still gloating
over their escape, "I shall say that you are carrying dangerous weapons and must be searched."

"I've never wanted to be an American before now,"
admitted Fred Rowntree as he sank exhausted into his seat,
"but the American citizenship seems to carry with it a
peculiar freedom which I am willing to confess seems highly
desirable."

"I cannot understand," Harrison Barrow continued, "what
it is that a British subject is suspected of carrying which an
American citizen is known not to carry. Most confusing."

"We have a long way to go to the next border, Friends. I
hope we may be favored to continue our journey in great
peace! We shall leave you soon after we cross into Switzerland."

"Well, Rufus, we'll try and not let this be a personal
grievance sufficient to cause another one of your 'separa-

tions.' Or even to start hostilities between Great Britain and the United States!" The train moved slowly out of the station into the brilliant sunshine.

"I must say," remarked Wilbur Thomas, "that it is a relief to be out of that flat Poland. It's the flattest place I ever did see."

"Surely, Wilbur, thee can't say that after coming from the state of Kansas. There isn't anything to beat it in my mind. I find it a relief to be out of the depressing area where typhus is a pestilence and you have to keep watching for lice all the time." Rufus Jones scratched his neck thoughtfully.

"I feel as Rufus does," said Fred Rowntree. "The members of the Unit in Poland have taken their lives in their hands and are working with the utmost devotion but it has been depressing to me to think of their hardships and the dangers to which they must become accustomed."

"This trip of ours has been a revelation to me," continued Rufus Jones. "We've been to Germany, Austria and Poland. If we had been ordinary tourists I expect we would have returned saying that conditions in Berlin and Vienna were on the way to recovery. The hotel food was good enough and a tourist judges entirely by what he finds in hotels, and thinks there is plenty for everyone. One of the most terrible things about these two countries, Germany and Austria, has been the privacy of the suffering. Unless you look for it you don't find it and you have to climb stairs and see the people in their rooms. They're proud and have kept up appearances in an amazing way. You see them on the street and you wouldn't realize that they hadn't had anything to eat for two or three days or that in the poor, cold rooms were other members of the family who could not come out because there was only one dress or one pair of trousers which could be worn. In spite of the fact that a million children are being fed every day in Germany I came away from there with the feeling of individual suffering.

"It was quite different in Poland. There aren't any homes for the peasants to hide in and keep their misery private. They're swarming over the earth, wandering in a mass. I've come away from there with a picture in my mind of thousands of people walking aimlessly, living in mass formation. Like the Children of Israel trying to reach the Promised Land. But there wasn't any country flowing with milk and honey for the Poles when they got back to their villages after their travels in Russia. Just birch trees and barbed wire and shell holes. I couldn't believe that those acres of land where the trees were at least three feet tall had been potato fields and villages. Now in Maine, it would have taken longer than it did in Poland for a pasture to come up to alders."

"Oh, of course, if we're talking about Maine," laughed Wilbur Thomas, "the potatoes would have kept on seeding themselves and digging themselves by spontaneous energy received from the pure genius of Maine soil. I don't believe you two English Friends know that Rufus was born in God's state, the state of Maine!"

"As far as that goes, Wilbur, being born in Maine is highly preferable to being born in Kansas!"

"What does thee think is the outstanding piece of work which we have seen during our visit to the centers, barring Russia, of course, which we haven't seen?"

"Is thee addressing me, Harrison?" asked Rufus Jones. "To my mind nothing that the American Friends Service Committee has undertaken or is likely to undertake is so significant or so important as a gesture of friendship or in the number of persons who are actually benefitted, as the

WILBUR K. THOMAS

German child-feeding. You can't feed a million children in a country which has so recently been looked upon as an enemy without attracting a good deal of attention.

"When I visited the work in France during the winter of 1918 and 1919 I believed that the destruction which I saw was the worst which was conceivable. I should have said then that the men and women who were trying, in the face of great danger, to build up villages and smooth over shell-torn fields, and, as at the Châlons Maternity, give a safe place for little babies to be born into, were making an outstanding contribution to the world in the name of the Society of Friends.

"Nothing I have visited since the beginning of our overseas reconstruction work has seemed so staggering as the attempt our Polish Unit is making to clear the land of typhus. We've coped with destroyed areas and starving refugees and large scale child-feeding but the scourge of typhus is another story. It's like living in London during the Black Death. How the Unit has managed to fight this disease is as miraculous a story as those of the combat against yellow fever. Just a handful of devoted men and women trying to clean up a country in the face of danger is a wonderful thing.

"When we are talking about the work in Europe I think we must take into account the fact that one of the most important factors has always been the close co-operation between your Committee in London and ours in Philadelphia. We've been a united Society of Friends in this task, except for a period in Russia and in Germany. It has been a cause of great regret to me that due to our affiliation with Mr. Hoover's Administration we have been forced to work as a separate Unit."

"I wish," said Fred Rowntree, "that we could have been

in Poland during the first anti-louse compaign! Those 'blue columns' [1] in their blue hoods and overalls, rubber boots and gloves must have been similar to the militant suffragettes! They seem to have gone at their job with a fervor that was disconcerting to the poor old peasants who must have watched these columns advancing on them with a good deal of terror and dismay. Peasants have never been noted for their enthusiasm for water, either down the throat or over the body. It must have been a sight to watch them take a bath for the first time."

"I imagine they found several layers of clothes, in the process, which they thought they had lost!" Every one laughed at Rufus Jones' remark.

"They must have had to open their windows in order to get rid of the smell of carbolic acid! Poland and Russia have not been noted for their liking for fresh air. But the smell of dirt nearly knocked the Unit down when it first arrived. The stench and filth and the sight of so many bodies crawling with lice was almost more than some of the workers could stand."

"Thee knows, Wilbur," interrupted Rufus Jones, "why the air in France is so pure. It's because the windows are never opened! Ask any of the French Unit who lived with the peasants during the threshing season."

"Mavis Hay wrote back last year to the London Committee," said Harrison Barrow, "that some of the peasants were much disappointed about the anti-louse mixture for the hair because they thought it would make the hair curl. Amusing idea! How can people have lice and not mind?" He squirmed against the back of the compartment and examined a spot on the back of his hand.

"Is it moving, Harrison? Take my advice and don't eat poppy seed rolls if thee can help it. Wilbur and I had some

[1] The name given to the workers who were disinfecting.

in Warsaw and we enjoyed them until we found the poppy seeds were moving. The most stationary objects aren't to be trusted."

"Not one of you has mentioned what to me seems the most touching tribute to our work anywhere," Wilbur Thomas said. "Gertrude Powick's grave in Poland has impressed me more than any other single thing I've seen and I believe it shows the effect of what the Service Committee and the War Victims' Relief Committee have tried to do more than all our million meals a day or our gestures of friendship."

"She was a member of the French Mission, wasn't she?"

"Yes," Wilbur Thomas continued, "She went from France to Poland where she soon became ill with typhus and died. The Catholic priest was very much upset that she could not be buried in the Catholic cemetery because she was a Protestant and would not, therefore, be able to lie in consecrated ground. The fact that a Catholic priest should care so much for what became of the body of a Protestant woman from a foreign country seems to me to tell in a striking way what her influence in the community had been.

"Her grave was dug adjoining the cemetery, on the other side of the fence but the morning after the funeral it was found that the fence had been taken down and altered so that it enclosed her little plot and she was within consecrated ground."

"That is a touching story, Wilbur, and it's funny I hadn't heard it before. It all goes to show the truth of what I have always maintained that fences of denominationalism are never as firmly placed as we sometimes think they are.

"Another thing which is very significant about our Polish work," continued Rufus Jones, "is the way it developed due to the letter sent by the deacon from Hostynne Village to Amelia Farbiszewski. Imagine a man who had been a refugee in Buzuluk and known the Quakers there, writing to Amelia in care of the Quakers, America, because he could not remember her address. He sent the letter in the autumn of 1919 but he must have left Russia in the summer of 1918 when there was such an exodus from the Buzuluk district. One would never have expected that any of these refugees could have returned but their endurance and perseverance are wonderful. Their dogged and unceasing attempt to get back to their own plot of ground in spite of insuperable difficulties makes it doubly pathetic that they came back, in most instances, to find nothing left."

"The French peasants were just like that," Wilbur Thomas said. "No matter how safe they might be from air raids in some district to which our workers had evacuated them, they wanted to get back to their own land."

"What I like especially about the Polish deacon," Rufus Jones went on with his story, "is the child-like trust that the Quakers would receive the letter. It was sent out in blind faith asking for a telegram in reply which would say that the Quakers would send help. In four years' time, since the beginning of the American Friends Service Committee, we have made sufficient impression on the people of Europe for them to turn to us in the time of need."

"It's hardly correct to limit the period of time to four years, Rufus. After all, English Friends have been on the continent since 1914."

"Well, that is true, Harrison. Americans can't take all the credit to themselves and I am glad thee reminded me. However, the time element isn't so important as the fact that doors have opened in a remarkable way. Does thee remember, Wilbur, how we discussed what to do with our organization when the work in France should be finished? How amazingly service has been given us in Germany, Poland, Austria and Serbia! What seems to me so important is that as we give food to the hungry and houses to the homeless, we bind up the broken-hearted and give food for the spirit as well. We aren't trying to make proselytes. After all, making converts to Quakerism isn't our motive, but if a man or a woman can clean out a typhus-infested house or provide food to rachitic children and do it because they are impelled by a love which makes it possible for them to endure hardships, they are preaching with the deeds which their hands and feet perform just as much as though they were making a sermon, and I believe this method is far more effective.

"Giving out seeds to be planted, increasing the milk supply by bringing in food for the cows, helping women to sell their embroideries—these are things which have all been done to the glory of God and the men and women who have helped accomplish them are organs, they are God's right hands."

"That's all very fine, Rufus. What's to be our function when this type of relief work comes to an end, as it will, we all hope? Do we end up as a second-rate missionary society, living on the glory of our past achievements, with no message for the future?"

"No, Fred, I do not believe that is our fate. We'll not make our past an excuse for what we may be doing in the present, years from now. Doors have opened for wider service and I believe they will continue to open. When this period of relief is over I feel sure some new tasks will be found, perhaps of an entirely different kind, through which we can try to interpret the ideals of the Society of Friends. New generations are always coming on, in search of new adventure. Part of our function must be to provide these boys and girls and men and women with thrilling tasks which are not only worth doing but which increase the spiritual creative forces of those who do them."

"As far as I am concerned," Harrison Barrow said, "this trip has been a wonderful experience for me. Unless one can visit these countries and see for oneself what has been taking place, one can have no real conception of what the Society of Friends is trying to do. Our visit has been brief and hurried but it has been well worth every minute we have spent."

"I think the rest of us fully unite with thy remarks, Harrison."

*   *   *   *   *

It was nearly evening when the train crossed the Austrian border and halted at Zurich, the first station in Switzerland.

"We've had a peaceful and pleasant discussion, Friends, but I am looking forward with some anticipation to see what happens to our American travellers at this border. If they don't have to open their bags . . ." Fred Rowntree was interrupted by the entrance of the official. He asked to see the passports.

"Where have you come from?" he enquired.

"We have all come from Warsaw," Rufus Jones answered in French. "This gentleman and I are staying in Switzerland. These two are going to London." There was a tense silence as they waited to see what would happen.

"Ah, indeed. Will the gentlemen who stay in Switzerland please follow me?"

"Tough luck, old chaps! The stars and stripes couldn't save you this time. It does you no end of good to stretch your legs for a bit!" Wilbur Thomas and Rufus Jones followed the official into a dark, remote corner of the station. He beckoned to Wilbur Thomas to go into a room from which the latter emerged in a few minutes.

"I can't make out what he wants, Rufus. He doesn't want to see my bags. He acts as though he wanted me to take off my coat."

"I'll find out for thee, Wilbur."

"What is it that you want?" he asked in French.

"I have asked him to take off his shirt, Monsieur. Every person who has been in Poland and enters Switzerland must be searched for lice!"

"He wants thee to take off thy shirt, Wilbur, so that he can hunt for lice!"

"But that's nonsense!"

"Never mind, they're trying to keep typhus out of Europe and this is the only method. Won't those two Englishmen gloat when we tell them! I shouldn't be surprised, though, if the officials on the other side of the Channel make them take a Lysol bath."

Chapter X

"THE PAST IS SECURE"

ONE might have expected that the office at Twenty South Twelfth Street would have been too absorbed with its fields of service in Europe to be interested in other problems. One of the most remarkable features of this particular office has been that, although it was organized for a purpose—to meet the immediate crisis of 1917—it has never pursued a one track interest. It has been adaptable to conditions and changes and it has been flexible without losing its strength.

For seven years, from 1917 to 1924, members of the office staff organized Units and sent them to France, Russia, Germany, Poland and Austria. A small Unit was sent to Serbia where a hospital was started at Petch and one representative went to Mexico. Reconstruction work was carried along on a large scale which involved an expenditure of millions of dollars in the attempt to restore the destruction caused by the World War.

Even before the Armistice was signed or the last workers had left France, the future of the American Friends Service Committee was being discussed in committee meetings and in private conversations. If the need for relief was over the Service Committee would either have to come to an end or change its entire field of service. It had reached the dividing line between an emergency committee or a permanent organization.

On September 25, 1924, a meeting of the Service Committee was held to which a large number of concerned members of the Society of Friends were asked to come. This was to decide the future of the office at Twenty South Twelfth Street and Rufus M. Jones presented to this meeting a statement which he had drawn up especially for the occasion.

"For somewhat over seven years this Committee has been laboring to relieve human suffering, to open avenues of service for our Young Friends and to interpret Christ's way of life to the world today. God has enabled us to accomplish far more than our hearts dreamed of in those agonizing days when we began our work. We have often felt, I am sure, a strange sense of awe as we have seen the way the hand of God has led us forth and opened doors before us. The past is secure.

"It is extremely important that we should make no mistake about our future course. We should not go on unless we are sure that we have a vital mission to perform nor unless we can speak and act for the corporate membership of the Society of Friends. I do not want to see us go out and *hunt* for tasks to keep our machinery going; but if there are tasks lying clearly at our door—God-given tasks which we can do better than anybody else can—let us then once more say, 'Yes, send us to the work, and anoint us for it.' . . .

"The matters which seem to me urgent are these:

"(1) Message work for the continent of Europe. This has sprung naturally out of our relief work, and we *must* carry it on. It involves an interpretation of our Quaker spirit and way of life, both for the countries abroad and for ours here at home.

"(2) Home Service, too, seems to be a growing thing,[1] and it would look as though we had a real duty to perform for our Young Friends here.

[1] This section had been appointed April 29, 1920.

"Beyond those two things, now well under way, I see two more which call for united action of American Friends. The first is a concerted and well guided concern for better interracial relationship, a new spirit of understanding and fellowship between different racial groups, particularly, of course, Negroes, Japanese and Italians. This work ought to be done, not by conferences and resolutions, not by starting new institutions or managing old ones, but by quietly forming new contacts, bringing peoples together in friendly groups and practising the spirit and ideals of our way of life . . .

"The second most important thing is the work of interpreting our ideals, especially our peace ideals and spirit to our own membership, and to those who are near and kindred to us in spirit. America has not learned the lesson of war nor has our own Society learned it. We are still thin and superficial in these deepest issues of life.

"Our Quaker peace work . . . needs organization and guidance. It needs spiritual illumination and leadership. We ought to have a peace section of our Service Committee, work that should grip and absorb us as the German child-feeding has done . . . One of the most important of all the features of this peace-making work would be the business of uniting and unifying our own membership. This work calls not only for a secretary and a cabinet, but most of all for a delegation of devoted persons who can tour the country in small groups, and do this cementing, fusing work in person—in demonstration of the spirit and power.

"Thankful as we are to God for what He has done through us during the seven years, we must be deeply conscious of our weakness and our limitations. I am positively disturbed to find how little, as a body, we are awake to our mission in the world. I can hardly bear to think what would be the effect if the Service Committee should end its work and disband, and leave the sections to drift along without any central leadership. I believe, instead, that we should gird ourselves for a forward step, into which we should put the same energy and spirit that met the crisis of 1917." [2]

There was, at this same committee meeting, another statement which emphasized even more vigorously the need for the Service Committee to turn its attention to affairs nearer home.

"We shall not be able to solve the problems in Europe or Mexico until we are able to solve our own problems. We cannot hope to solve the Russian problems while we are sending machine guns to West Virginia; we cannot expect peace until we bring about more of that condition among ourselves. Friends should become a demonstration or an experiment station." [3]

Even before this time several Friends had been especially concerned to devote more time to work among the Negroes. A group of Young Friends was impressed with the need for peace education also.

At the meeting of the American Friends Service Committee on October 22, 1924, "it was proposed that the work of the American Friends Service Committee should be arranged in quite clearly defined but closely related sections:

"(1) *European Section:* To deal with the problems arising out of our work in Europe, and to co-operate further with English Friends.

"(2) *Interracial Service Section:* To give primary consideration to such questions as the relationship of the people of the United States with the Chinese, Japanese, Latin Americans, Negroes and Jewish people.

"(3) *Peace Section:* To encourage the formation of active

[2] Taken from the Minutes of the American Friends Service Committee, September 25, 1924.
[3] Statement by Ernest N. Votaw. Taken from the same Minutes.

peace committees in those yearly meetings that do not have active committees, and to form a nucleus for concerted action by all Friends upon special occasions . . .

"(4) *Home Service Section:* To continue the work already under way and to enlarge it to include other phases of work . . ."

This new program was not definitely organized until May 28, 1925, and its inauguration marked the beginning of a new era in the office at Twenty South Twelfth Street. "The past was secure" and an effort was begun to find new jobs and a new challenge for the Young Friends growing up in the post-war period. Many of them felt that they had missed something because they had not been able to serve in France, or Germany, or Russia, or Austria, or Poland. There is always a glamor connected with far away places and it is less romantic to help under-privileged children in the same city in which one lives, or spend a summer in the hot Middle West "peddling peace." So it seemed at the first glance, but subsequent chapters will show with what eagerness the new generation has taken hold of the new adventures.

CHAPTER XI

FOREIGN SERVICE SECTION

ALTHOUGH the Foreign Service Section came into existence in March 1925 it was not at all a new Committee. In 1917 the American Friends Service Committee had been created in order to do relief work abroad. As this work developed and it was found that actual relief was not the only contribution which Friends could give to Europe, Edith Pye and Hilda Clark, both members of London Yearly Meeting, came to America on a visit in 1921 and shared their concern that there should be a committee formed to foster religious work in Europe. This was organized in January 1922 and changed its name to the Message Committee in June of that same year. "It has been decided to send a letter to Friends teaching in the German Departments of Friends' colleges and universities informing them of the opportunity of taking positions as English Instructors in French, Austrian, Polish and German schools and universities as a part of our message work to bring about a greater degree of understanding between the countries . . . The committee decided that all questions of relief, work for the middle class, co-operation with relief work as it is carried on by English Friends, student relief, etc., be referred to the Message Committee for action after the child-feeding work is closed on July 31, 1922." [1]

[1] Minutes of American Friends Service Committee, June 1, 1922.

133

The Orient

It was an ordinary thing, by 1925, for men and women to be going out through the gates of Twenty South Twelfth Street for service on the continent of Europe. Even for those who stayed at home the work abroad had been made vivid. But China and Japan seemed very far away. Tom Jones, the first Field Secretary for the Service Committee, left the office in the latter part of 1917 to engage in mission work with Friends in Tokyo. There were groups of Friends in West China at Chengtu, in Nanking, and Canton, but there was little contact among them, or with them from the outside world. China was a mysterious and a remote land which was brought suddenly to the attention of concerned people by the reports of the terrifying incidents of communist shootings in Shanghai, Hankow and Canton in May and June, 1925.

In November of that year Lloyd Balderston sailed for China to spend four months as a representative of the Service Committee in order to find out what opportunities it might have for work in that country and he recommended after his return that the Service Committee should assist in sending Kagawa, then at the beginning of his great career, from Japan to China as an interpreter of good will; that it should help support the plan for the erection of a Friendship, model village across the river from Shanghai; that there should be a press bureau service for China, and that Henry T. Hodgkin, at that time one of the Executive Secretaries of the National Christian Council in China, should be encouraged to give all of his time to international service.

In 1926, Rufus M. Jones was asked by the Y.M.C.A. to visit China on the occasion of the celebration of the fortieth anniversary of its introduction to that country and in addition to many speaking engagements for this organization he travelled on behalf of the Service Committee, visiting

Friends in Japan, China, Ceylon, India and the Near East.
Thomas Q. Harrison, who had been travelling in the United
States for the Peace Section, made a trip around the world
in 1926 and 1927. These visits helped to bring the Orient
closer to Friends in the United States.

In September 1928 Hugh and Elizabeth Borton sailed for
Japan as joint representatives of the Mission Board of Arch
Street Yearly Meeting in Philadelphia and the Service Com-
mittee. They remained for three years. In 1929 Carolena M.
Wood who, with Elbert Russell had visited Nicaragua in 1927
and 1928, went to the Philippine Islands, joining in 1930 a
deputation of five English Friends and Gilbert Bowles, an
American Friend and missionary in Japan. These seven
Friends travelled throughout China, going as far as Chengtu
in West China, to visit Friends in that country and to experience some of the conditions under which they were living.
Rufus M. Jones returned to the Orient in 1932 as a member
of the Commission of Appraisal of Foreign Missions.

There have not been so many contacts with India. In
April 1929 Harry and Rebecca Timbres, former members of
the Units in both Poland and Russia, accepted an invitation
from Rabindranath Tagore, given through Charles F. Andrews, to serve as doctor and nurse in public health work in
and around Tagore's ashram, Santiniketan, Bengal. Tagore
visited England and America, accompanied by Harry
Timbres in the latter part of 1930, after which they returned
to India until illness forced the Timbres to leave in 1934.
Word has come that Harry Timbres died of typhus in Russia, May 12, 1937, where he had a post as doctor under
the Soviet Government.

France

When the last members of the French Unit came home in
1920 the contact between the office in Philadelphia and the

work in France which had concluded was continued by sending two young women each year as aides in the Châlons Maternity Hospital. As this hospital was a step-child of the Service Committee the relationship remained a close one by means of these young women who gained, not only a valuable nursing experience under the guidance of Mademoiselle Merle, but an enthusiasm for and a knowledge of the French language, customs and temperament. When the Hostel in Geneva was opened in the summer of 1927 some of the aides divided their year between Châlons-sur-Marne and Geneva.

There was no center in Paris until June 1924 when Alfred and Grace Lowry moved into 20 Avenue Victoria. From its very beginning the Paris center has been interested especially in the study of penology and prison reform. "The efforts for pressing reforms in the women's prisons of Paris, to which Gerda Kappenburg devoted all her time, have at last been crowned with success. A committee has been formed of which the Dean of the Faculty of Law, Monsieur Barthelemy, is Honorary President and Monsieur Donnedieu de Vabre, Professor of Criminology, actual President . . . The scheme of reform worked out at the instance of Gerda Kappenburg and afterwards, in the course of several personal interviews, submitted to the Minister for Justice, Pierre Laval, seems to have met with complete success . . . It is proposed to close gradually the prison of St. Lazare, a reform solicited in vain for the past hundred years, and to separate first offenders from habitual criminals." [2]

Phebe Borghesio, until her recent death, was a tireless visitor among women prisoners, bringing them much comfort and courage. In 1927 Henri Van Etten was appointed a probation officer and began giving a series of five minute weekly radio talks on penal questions. His influence and in-

[2] Ninth Annual Report of the American Friends Service Committee, June 1, 1925–May 31, 1926.

terest in this field of service has increased until he has become an outstanding figure in the cause of French prison reform.

Friends' Centers in European capitals have been places for social gatherings, for lectures and for worship. University students have found the Paris center a stimulating headquarters where they were not only free to discuss but were encouraged to bring their intellectual and spiritual questions for mutual consideration. A monthly magazine, *L'Echo des Amis,* has been issued regularly and has a wide circulation. In three years' time the rooms at 20 Avenue Victoria had become too crowded and inadequate so that the center moved to more spacious quarters at 12 Rue Guy de la Brosse. Alfred Lowry and his wife left the center in 1929 and their place was taken by Effie McAfee who continued in that position until 1933 when Mahlon and Vivian Harvey were appointed.

In 1931 the Paris Center started a program of relief for German children in Berlin, sending a small group of French workers and sums of French money to Berlin to supply one meal a day for fifty children during the winter, but in the spring of 1933 it was no longer possible to carry this work on in Germany and it was continued in Paris by Germaine Melon, a member of the newly established French Yearly Meeting. She "organized a kindergarten and club-room run by German refugees for their own members. The Entr'aide, or mutual help organization, has also helped to provide heat and food in the cold, unfurnished barracks offered by the French Government, where refugees have been herded, without work or hope, and a trained social worker has been hired to teach crafts."[3] Members of the center staff have succeeded in helping many of these German refugees who cannot return to their homes to find employment in other countries. It was estimated in 1936 that there were more than

[3] Annual Report for 1933.

two thousand of these people in Paris, four hundred of whom have been assisted by the Entr'aide.

French Friends were organized as a Monthly Meeting, holding the powers of a Quarterly Meeting, directly dependent under London Yearly Meeting. By December 1932 they proposed their wish to form a Yearly Meeting of their own and this was established early in 1933, "in order that Quaker life in France may have the opportunity to develop along lines best fitted to that country." [4] In 1933 French Friends opened a center in Le Havre.

The war in Spain has increased the economic and political tension in France, giving new responsibilities to the Paris center in its effort to demonstrate a way of life which does away with hatred and destruction of life and property. New strength has been given to the small group of Friends by the visit of President William W. Comfort of Haverford College who has travelled in France during the spring of 1937, speaking on subjects relative to Quakerism and world reconciliation. Ten years ago the statement was made that "the Friends center in Paris is becoming more and more useful as a means of developing interest in social problems that affect the national life and as an agency for forwarding the spirit of international fellowship and good will." [5] This is true, to a far greater degree, at the present time.

Russia

Workers in Russia always had great difficulty in obtaining suitable headquarters in Moscow. Until August 1921 their hotel rooms served as offices for relief work and in the latter part of that year when additional members of the Unit were expected, a private house was rented for the purpose of

[4] Minutes of the American Friends Service Committee, Dec. 22, 1932.
[5] Annual Report for 1927-1928.

housing the workers, but no sooner had it been cleaned up and made habitable than it was taken away from them. When Anna Haines returned to Moscow in 1925 after finishing her nurse's training, she found Friends occupying a house at 15 Borisoglevski Perioolok, where they remained, using a fewer number of rooms as the work decreased, until 1931 when they were not allowed to renew the expired lease.

Although the first group of Americans which went to Russia in 1917 was not trained for any medical service, this lack of knowledge was made up, later, by the fact that nearly all the work done in Russia after the relief for famine sufferers was finished, was along medical lines.

"During 1925 and 1926 I was teaching nursing in Moscow in one of the institutions connected with the medical school of the University there. The first manual for nurses written in Russian was prepared with my assistance. Dr. Semashko, Commissar of Health at that time, granted permission for Friends to conduct a modern school of nursing in Moscow for which the Russian Government would provide buildings, hospital opportunities and living expenses of the students." [6] It was unfortunate that this never materialized, because of the inability to raise the necessary funds, for it had been felt "that by making a demonstration of public health work as carried on in America and England through a Nurses' Training School Friends could make a great contribution to the Russian people." [7]

Alice Davis and Nadia Danilevsky took a course of study in a Russian Nurses' Training School in Moscow which was completed in 1928. They hoped to be associated with the Tolstoy Memorial Hospital, which was then being built at Yasnaya Polyana, by the Soviet Government. When this plan was abandoned they became regularly appointed nurses

[6] Letter from Anna J. Haines, March 3, 1937.
[7] Annual Report, June 1, 1927–May 31, 1928.

in the Botinsky Hospital just outside of Moscow for the year
1929 and 1930, devoting their spare time to translating some
of Tolstoy's works into English as they believed this was a
valuable piece of international service.

Nancy Babb had a particular interest in anti-malarial
clinics in the Buzuluk and Totskoe areas and developed what
she calls "W.P.A." technique in an effort to train the people
in these districts to carry on their own clinics, supervised at
intervals when doctors and nurses came to visit. "These
women, Nancy Babb, at Totskoe, Alice Davis and Nadia
Danilevsky, in Sorochinskoe, have, in conjunction with the
national and local health authorities, established clinics,
continued to support a summer tuberculosis home, assisted
local physicians in general public health work, and helped
to establish and equip hospitals for the districts concerned." [8]

Nancy Babb, for whom no undertaking was too difficult
or too strenuous, secured enough money through the sale of
embroidered goods and linen made by the Totskoe peasants
and the actual thread itself, to erect and equip a hospital at
Totskoe. On its completion she turned the hospital over to
the Soviet Government and returned to the United States
in 1928 after nearly ten years of devoted service.

Dorice White from England was in charge of the Moscow
center at 15 Borisoglevski Perioolok and "maintained herself by teaching; but at the same time has given to travellers
visiting the center the same, individual, sympathetic help as
that of our other centers whose personnel is larger." [9] Dorice
White was the last worker to leave Russia in 1931.

Germany

At the close of the first period of child-feeding in 1922 Gilbert MacMaster remained in Berlin and played an important

[8] Annual Report, 1925–1926.
[9] Annual Report, 1928–1929.

part in the difficult service of message work, in an endeavor to interpret the ideals of the Society of Friends to the people of Germany. In 1924 when the child-feeding was handed to the German Central Committee for Foreign Relief a group of Friends remained with Gilbert MacMaster and made contacts with large numbers of people who called themselves "friends of the Friends." Quakerism appealed to the German more than to any other nationality on the continent. His interest in the Society of Friends was not entirely due to the wide-spread publicity which it received because of its large and dramatic piece of work but to the fact that the principles, the ideals and the way of worship had an emotional kinship with the German.

During the period of child-feeding a little group had been forming which in 1925 became the nucleus of the Yearly Meeting which was established that year and consisted of one hundred members. This number has more than doubled since that time.

"In Germany international centers are maintained in Berlin, Frankfurt and Nürnberg. These are under the care of an international secretariat, composed of representatives of the American Friends Service Committee, the Friends Service Council and members of the German group. In addition to these centers, organized co-operating groups, wholly under the care of the German people, are to be found in Breslau, Charlottenburg, Dresden, Elberfeld, Fürth i. Bayern, Hamburg, Hanover, Köln Königsberg i. Pr., Krefeld, Magdeburg, Riesa, Sonnefeld and Stuttgart. The office in Berlin at Prinz Louis Ferdinandstrasse 5, serves as headquarters. All local work is entirely in the hands of members of the German Yearly Meeting of Friends. All international activities center in the Berlin office . . .

"Work among the university students in Berlin has continued to be an outstanding feature of the international service. The larger social room has been used four evenings a week through the great part of the year, on Monday by the Polish student group; Tuesday by a group of music students; Wednesday by a French group and Friday by an English debating club. In addition to these organizations the rooms accommodated a student circle formed by theological students who attended the Stockholm conferences; the War Resisters' Union and the Peace Cartel have used the rooms occasionally.

"The center rooms in Frankfurt have been used for student groups, peace meetings, English clubs and special lectures on national and international subjects. The rooms in all three of the centers have been used also for Friends Meetings for worship and for other religious gatherings. The Frankfurt Center has organized a special Franco-German Committee to consider the problems that affect the relationships of France and Germany and it works in co-operation with the Paris Center. A Polish-German Youth Camp was held at Neuhauser in Upper Prussia in 1927 . . .

"The centers in Germany have also been very active in helping visitors, providing speakers on national and international subjects for interested German groups and co-operating with pacifist and international organizations. The German people have been taking an increasing amount of responsibility for Friendly work during the year." [10]

Gilbert MacMaster resigned as head of the Berlin Center in July 1930 but he took up residence in Bâle, Switzerland, so that he has been near enough to return to Germany from time to time and he has always kept in close touch with Friends there. He has devoted himself particularly to the question of the Minorities in Europe and in 1936 he was asked to "resume again his relation with the Service Committee under the direction of the Foreign Service Section,

[10] Annual Report, 1927–1928.

with the understanding that he attend the Minorities' Congress, follow the literature, and keep us in touch with the situations of special significance." [11] Richard and Mary Cary came to Berlin in Gilbert MacMaster's place and in 1931 Corder and Gwen Catchpool from England came also to the Center, remaining until 1936. Richard Cary died very suddenly in 1933 but after a short visit to America, Mary Cary returned to Berlin for several months. In February 1936 Albert and Anne Martin sailed for Germany and have carried the burden of the work during the last difficult months.

In facing the many problems in Germany today the Yearly Meeting is a strength and power to German Friends. The old Quaker Meeting House at Bad Pyrmont, dating back to the eighteenth century, was taken down and rebuilt on a new piece of ground in 1932 as the Yearly Meeting headquarters and two hundred persons met together in August of that year. In the summer of 1936 two hundred and twenty-six assembled at Bad Pyrmont. Nearby is located the "Rest Home," a guest house managed by English Friends and many German Friends and "friends of the Friends" have found this charming, quiet place a haven of refuge. At Bad Pyrmont is located the Quaker Verlag, a publishing house, where the monthly paper, *Der Quäker*, is printed.

Poland

"Poland's problems are inherent even in her geographical situation. The position of the country, in the very heart of Europe, and surrounded on every side by so-called enemies, makes, at the outset, the task of administration a hard one. These difficulties are enormously increased by the fact that the newly independent nation, composed of many discordant

[11] Minutes of the Foreign Service Section, December 29, 1936.

elements, and still sore with the memories of long endured oppression, is almost ignorant of statecraft and must, by necessity, work experimentally . . .

"The present Quaker work has a background with a record of timber-hauling, house-building, ploughing, seed distribution, anti-typhus work and other forms of material help, which both the war-crippled peasants and a grateful Government have much appreciated." A "piece of permanent service is the Peasant Industries scheme. This has developed directly out of that part of the work of the Relief Mission which organized embroidery and hand-weaving amongst the poor peasant women, first of all as a means of providing the barest necessities of life and afterwards as spare time employment during the winter months. Weaving and embroidery are traditional crafts amongst the peasants of East Poland . . .

"The work began in one small village in the autumn of 1921" after the arrival of Florence Barrow from England as head of the Polish Unit. "The work is now carried on in more than sixty villages and upwards of sixteen hundred women and girls are now engaged in it . . . The finished articles are sold in Warsaw, Geneva, Paris, London, Philadelphia and elsewhere.

"The Peasant Industries is conducted on strictly business lines. It is a business proposition and all expenses are met out of the profit of the concern . . . The work at Kolpin Agricultural School and the Peasant Industries are both at present under the care and control of the Committee of Care for the Eastern Borders, a Government organization.

"Another group of Quaker activities centers around the office of the Goodwill Center at Widok 26, Warsaw. The premises consist of ten rooms on the ground floor of a one storied building conveniently situated close to the Central

Warsaw station. The reading room . . . contains a small
library of general and Quaker literature . . . Three evenings
a week it is thrown open to students and others who have
some knowledge of the English language and are interested
in American and British affairs . . . The meetings of the
Committee for International Friendship are held here
also . . .

"At the Danzig Conference the study of Polish and German culture was regarded as a useful means of promoting
friendship and mutual understanding between the two nations and something has been done in this way. A Polish
Study Group has been formed by the Berlin Students' Club
and members of that group are in correspondence with the
International Friendship group in Warsaw . . . In this way
the internationalism of the mind is being developed." [12]

Wilmer Young, one of the first workers to go to France
and later head of the French Mission after the resignation
of Charles J. Rhoads from the Paris office, with his wife, became head of the work in Poland in the summer of 1924 remaining there for a year until in the summer of 1925 Henry
Harris, an English Friend, came to Warsaw. He was joined
by his wife, Margaret, in 1926 and they were real Quaker
ambassadors in a rather lonely field until they left in 1928.
It was extremely difficult to find anyone who could stay in
Poland for any length of time and it seemed better to close
the center when the lease at Widok 26 expired in 1930. The
Orphanage was liquidated in the autumn of 1929 and the
Peasant Industries was carried on by two Polish women.
But although there is no foreign representative now in Poland there are several devoted Polish men and women who
endeavor to carry on by themselves the ideals of the Society
of Friends.

[12] Letter from Henry Harris in the Annual Report, 1925–1926.

Austria

"The problems to be faced in Vienna were, of necessity, not merely those of restoration. Austria-Hungary was a thing of the past . . . and a *modus vivendi* for a mangled Austria (with six instead of fifty million people) had to be found . . . Tiny Austria was cut off by hatred and tariff barriers from the succession states . . . Her size was about one-sixth of her former territory, but in point of view of fertile land it was only about one-tenth . . . Her former coal supplies were in Czechoslovakia, her grain supplies were in Hungary and she had no money to pay for them. These economic difficulties were multiplied many times by the racial antipathies and opposition fostered by the war, and by the peace treaties. Vienna was like a pathetic head whose body had been cut away from it." [18]

Relief work in Austria started as the result of a visit made in Vienna in May 1919 by an English Friend, Dr. Hilda Clark. Feeding and health work were carried on in a way similar to that in Germany, although on no such enormous scale and with a smaller personnel. It was, primarily, an English undertaking, although Frederick Kuh, an American member of the French Mission, came to Vienna in August 1919, and the Service Committee sent money and a small personnel for Austrian relief. Two hundred and ninety cows were brought into the country to increase the very inadequate milk supply and, as was done in Poland several years later, the cows were sold to farmers and dairymen who paid for them by delivering certain quantities of milk each day to the Friends' depots, or food centers. Tons of hay and linseed oil cake were imported in addition for the half-starved cattle which had survived.

[18] Fry, A. Ruth, *A Quaker Adventure*, p. 194.

Fuel for heating houses was almost impossible to obtain and the Viennese were allowed to cut wood in the Wienerwald, several miles outside of the city. Children and old people trudged out to cut what they could carry home on their backs, or, if they were fortunate enough to possess such a thing, in small carts. There was no soap, except a substitute product, made of earth, and very little milk. If possible, conditions were more terrible than in Germany. Babies were wrapped in paper which chafed their skin. There was no soap with which to wash them, so that skin diseases and irritations developed, as did rickets and tuberculosis.

Arrangements were made with English families and a large number of Austrian children were sent to England in 1919 and 1920 where they were cared for with great kindness and with good, nourishing food.

Relief work in Vienna has been housed, from the very beginning, in a palace, or town house, at Singerstrasse 16, built about two hundred years ago for a noble Austrian family. The entrance is very impressive with four great columns upholding the head and trunk of enormous stone figures of baroque architecture. The office rooms are on the second floor which is reached by climbing sixty-eight steps of a spiral staircase, formerly used by the servants of the establishment, but once inside the door at the top of the steps one enters a spacious area which contains seven rooms and a kitchen and adjoining these is the Hostel with five rooms, two kitchens and a storeroom. The Hostel was first opened for guests in May 1924 and has in thirteen years' time, until May 1937, entertained 1143 persons, of twenty-three different nationalities. Elsie Turner from England was the first hostess and Elizabeth Horsnaill succeeded to this position. The Hostel has rendered an invaluable service to visitors who have gained by living in close contact with the center a sympathetic and intelligent understanding of the problems of Europe.[14]

Headley Horsnaill was the English secretary in the office at Singerstrasse 16 when Emma Cadbury came as American secretary in March 1924. Special attention was being given to relief for old people by Lily Bugbird and to land settlements by Mrs. Atherton-Smith. It had been found that housing conditions in Vienna were seriously inadequate and that "the need for food led first to the parcelling out of un-used land to the poor as 'allotment gardens' . . . As the housing shortage increased allotment holders began to build huts on their plots to sleep in during the summer."[15] A demonstration for more permanent homes interested the government to give both state and municipal aid with the result that a tract of land was secured and small houses were erected by the families themselves. The Friends raised $60,000 to assist this undertaking and ran canteen kitchens for the supply of food to the workers on Saturday afternoons.[16] This experiment in housing helped to give an impetus to the interest which resulted in an expansion of the rehousing work of the Socialist Government in Vienna. The large apartment houses for workers which have been erected in Vienna have attracted the attention of people all over the world, who are interested in housing projects.

One of the most important pieces of service which the Quaker Mission in Vienna rendered was the three-year anti-tuberculosis campaign from 1924–1927, made possible by a fund turned over by the Central Relief Society of New York City for this purpose. Young women were trained in the anti-tuberculosis department of Dr. Pirquet's hospital in Vienna, after which they travelled among schools in the

[14] Statistics about the Hostel sent by Emma Cadbury and Elizabeth Horsnaill.
[15] Jones, Lester M., *Quakers in Action*, p. 104.
[16] *Op. cit.*, pp. 104, 105.

provinces, giving lectures and demonstrations. They were called Wanderlehrerinnen and remained a sufficient length of time in one place to accomplish a great amount of good.

It was natural that the two clubs of Austrian young people, formerly the children who had been sent to England in 1919 and 1920, should be housed, eventually, at Singerstrasse 16. These young people had much in common, especially their knowledge of English which they did not want to lose, and Friends Centers have always been especially hospitable to young people.

"There were small groups of boys and small groups of girls coming, the one, two evenings in the week, the other three, and wanting a little English or some simple games . . . There was an occasional mixed party of rather hectic character caused partly by a very evident lack of community feeling and partly by a lack of training in what is considered fair in games. These things comprised the club routine in 1928 . . .

"That this should be a club, partly educational and partly recreational with a deeper purpose in the building of character rather than in any more defined religious leading, seemed so far clear, but at the moment it was many little clubs rather than one . . . The answer to the heading 'what have we in the Center to give?' seems . . . much less a question of what are our own creeds and philosophies, than a question of how can we find the way to evoke growth in others." [17]

During the five years' leadership of Christine Clement-Brown, from England, the Joint Club was developed from these groups which has become a vital activity in the Center.

The Forum is another club consisting of about four hundred students or former students now engaged in professions.

[17] Clement-Brown, Christine, *Building and Discovery*, An Account of Five Years' Club Work at the Vienna Friends Center, 1928–1933.

Like the Joint Club, the Forum came into existence because its members had been in England. Baronin Friederika Appel, known to those acquainted with the Center as Riki Teller, has conducted the Forum for twelve years. In 1932 several members visited England during the summer and in 1933 she brought eight members to America.

The Forum "has become an influential body which meets eight times a month, in groups according to major interests. The Friends Center is one of the few places, and the Forum one of the few groups in Vienna, where Jews may meet on a basis of friendly intercourse and footing of equality with other Austrians. The Friends' International Service Union, started by Austrians who desired closer association with Friends, and the Adult School bring together regularly other groups of eager-minded people." [18]

A Meeting for Worship is held in the Center every Sunday morning to which come an average number of fifteen to twenty people. On the first and third Sundays of the month a study circle is held before Meeting for discussion of religious topics. There is a Quaker group of sixteen Austrian members which holds a Monthly Meeting for business and a group of "Young Friends" which meets weekly. "With one or two exceptions they are not Quakers, but friends of the Quakers, yet we value highly all that is noble and good in their principles and try to work according to these principles . . . The aim which we placed foremost in our work this year was that there should prevail in our little fellowship a spirit of sincerity, of solidarity, of oneness and of true friendship. We are a circle which has joined together in order to concern itself in common work for the understanding of present day problems." [19] One of the most difficult

[18] *Creative Experience in International Relations*, American Friends Service Committee, 1936.

[19] Report of Vienna Center, January, February, March 1937.

problems before this group is that of compulsory military service. If the young men refuse to give this, they lose their jobs and have no means of support, as is true also in Germany. One such conscientious objector in Austria was sentenced to three months' imprisonment with hard labor.

In November 1925, because of a report brought back to Vienna by Sherwood Eddy, Emma Cadbury, with Frederick Hankinson and Gilbert MacMaster, visited Bulgaria, just after "the Greeks had made a raid over the border and destroyed the possessions of several villages. The incident might have led to a war between Bulgaria and Greece, but the matter was arranged peacefully by the League of Nations." [20] These three Friends returned, after a thorough investigation of conditions and Ilse Lange, who had organized kitchens for American Friends during child-feeding in Germany, was given three months' leave by the German Government to go to Bulgaria. Nancy Lauder-Brunton went with her and they arrived in Sofia in April 1926, remaining until July. But the relief went on until May 1927 with funds given for Bulgaria from the center in Berlin and with money and five nurses sent by the German Red Cross.

With Rufus M. Jones and his family, Emma Cadbury visited Salonica, Greece, in November 1929. A Friends' Center had been opened by English Friends on the grounds of the American Farm School and it had assisted Greek refugees to settle on Macedonian land. Weaving and rug-making had been organized for the women, while two boy-scout masters carried on an intensive anti-malarial campaign, draining swamps wherever they could. This center had been closed in the spring of 1929.

In 1931 Emma Cadbury and Alice Nike returned to Bulgaria where they found that the tobacco and silk crops had not been good so that there were many families in great

[20] Letter from Nancy Lauder-Brunton, July 13, 1926.

need. The grape vines had been killed by a blight and it was necessary to replant them with vines from America which were not affected by this blight. "Our special concern in Sofia was the holding of a meeting for worship, as no one has succeeded in doing this so far as we know . . . There were fifteen besides Alice Nike and myself . . . I tried to explain to them our ideal of worship and suggested that we begin by a short meeting after which we should be glad to answer questions. However, the questions began almost at once." [21] There was only one Friend in Sofia at that time and five at Salonica.

There were two civil wars in Austria in 1934, the first in February between the Social-Democrat forces and the Dollfuss Government. The second was a National-Socialist uprising in July. Both of these caused a great deal of bitterness and suffering. Social-Democrats were put in prisons and concentration camps, many were killed, reported missing, or had gone into hiding so that families were left destitute. "With the approval of the Government, Friends have administered aid to some nine thousand of such families in Vienna and the provinces, the funds, amounting to $800,000, having been supplied mainly by the International Federation of Trades Unions and the International Co-operative Alliance, supplemented by contributions from other Swiss, Belgian and English sources." [22]

Austrian volunteer workers have carried on this relief since 1934 so that while this work has had its headquarters at Singerstrasse 16, much of the responsibility has been taken from Emma Cadbury and Headley Horsnaill.

The most recent undertaking has been the Work Camp at Marienthal where eighteen hundred spinning, mill and

[21] Report of Emma Cadbury, April 1931.
[22] *Creative Experience in International Relations*, American Friends Service Committee, 1936.

textile workers were unemployed because the factory had been closed in 1929. English Friends received "a request from Emma Cadbury very early in 1935 for a team to help start unemployed allotments . . . and we launched the idea at Cambridge University. We expected with luck to get six people to go. Owing to the splendid work of Mary Campbell and Hugh Doncaster we got sixty-six in 1935 and over seventy last year and hope for a hundred in 1937. The plans at the Vienna end were all made by Emma Cadbury and the Vienna group. We merely supplied the students. I think the outstanding contribution of the Quaker group in Vienna is the turning of the wholly romantic, unpractical Austrian good-will into practical channels like this." [23]

"It is difficult to assess the value of the camp. There is an increase in the standard of living, there is a real increase in mutual understanding of the conditions and problems of the two countries, there is the important fact that peace has been seen as a more concrete thing.

"One of the men said to me before I left, 'You know, before you came, we thought of England as a little country a long way off with lots of colonies and therefore very rich with no poverty and no unemployment. We did not want to fight but had there been a war we should have done so. Now we know that England has all the problems that we have, and that it is your home, we could not fight against you.' " [24]

Geneva

"Friends have a wonderful opportunity not only to establish a Friendly center in Geneva, but also to bring some influence to bear upon the men from the various nations who

[23] Letter from John S. Hoyland, April 20, 1937.
[24] Letter from L. Hugh Doncaster, April 21, 1937.

are at present connected with the League of Nations' activities." [25]

English friends, however, had started work in Geneva much earlier. A Swiss woman, Madelaine Savary, interested in Friends, opened her home in June 1920 for a meeting for worship and later became a Friend herself. Herbert and Ethel Jones who were living in Geneva felt the importance of having a center in that city and an arrangement was made that the Friends Service Council in London should pay rent for a room to be used for this purpose if money could be procured to furnish it. This latter was done through the gift of a Mrs. Fryer whose son had been killed while climbing in the Alps. A room was found at 5 Place de la Taconnerie and opened September 1923. Ethel Mather was the first regular secretary of the center, sent out from the Friends Service Council in October 1924.

Margaret Lester, an American spending the winter of 1925 and 1926 in Geneva, took Ethel Mather's place when she had to leave because of ill health in the autumn of 1925. Margaret Lester was influential in arranging monthly meetings for representatives of the many international groups having headquarters in Geneva. "A group of women who are interested in sewing for the Châlons Maternity Hospital and for some of the most needy in Geneva, meet once a week in the Friends headquarters. Afternoon tea is served to all who come and efforts are made to get in touch with worthwhile people." [26] Wilfred and Mary Conard, with their daughter, spent several weeks in Geneva during that same winter, and were helpful in the growth of the small Friends Meeting.

Bertram and Irene Pickard, English Friends, came to the

[25] Minutes of the American Friends Service Committee, November 20, 1924.

[26] Minutes of the American Friends Service Committee, July 22, 1926.

center in June 1926. Bertram Pickard immediately began gathering news material for Friends' papers in all parts of the world and he has developed a journalistic service to some eighty newspapers as well as a group of English dailies and an American Press Service. Students and visitors come to Geneva in search of information of all sorts for lectures, theses and historical research. The center has made contacts for them with the people whom they wished to see and has given help in countless ways.

The monthly meetings inaugurated by Margaret Lester have been continued. There are nearly seventy international organizations in Geneva and the Quaker center is entirely responsible for the monthly dinner which brings them all together. Socials and discussion groups are a regular part of the center's program.

The Geneva Center has never attempted to give out relief and in this way it differs from the centers in other European capitals which were created for that purpose but Bertram Pickard has given an immense amount of help in solving problems of the other centers and straightening out tangles resulting from the constant stream of refugees and stateless individuals who have been passing through Paris, Berlin and Vienna during the last years. Some of the cases which have seemed insoluble he has brought before the League of Nations.

Although the League's existence was threatened in 1932 by the Sino-Japanese conflict and its influence brought to a temporary end by the conflict between Italy and Ethiopia, Geneva has remained an important international city and it attracts nearly as many visitors as it did before. It is impossible to overestimate the value of such a center.

The Friends Meeting is one of the most important parts of the center activities. There is a small nucleus of devoted Friends of various nationalities and there are a number of visitors who attend, a greater number than would be found in other Friends Meetings on the continent.

The Student Hostel was started in the summer of 1927 as a joint undertaking by the Friends Service Council and the American Friends Service Committee because of a concern expressed by Irene Pickard that there was no suitable place for students to live. It was the first international student house in Geneva and its two main purposes were "to encourage young Friends to come to Geneva for first-hand study and experience of international affairs and to draw together under one roof young men and women of different nationalities and religions and to provide a homelike circle in which mutual understanding and friendship might grow up among them." [27]

The Hostel began in a furnished house on Chemin Krieg, Alexander and Edith Wilson from England serving as wardens and for the first year there were five American students, two German, two French, two Swiss and one English.[28] For the next two years Irene Pickard served as warden and in 1930 Mabel Ridpath, a member of the American Unit in France and of Iowa Yearly Meeting with her small daughter, Elizabeth, took her place. The Hostel moved to 18 Avenue Bertrand in 1933 where there was a large garden and more adequate accommodations.

In November 1927 Clement and Grace Biddle established the Geneva Study Scholarship for teachers of history in Friends Colleges and secondary schools and this has enabled a small group of men and women to have the privilege of spending a year studying in Geneva.

In August of 1937 the Center and the Meeting will leave their familiar home at 5 Place de la Taconnerie and move into a floor of the old Palais des Nations, the first head-

[27] Martin, Marjorie, *The Quaker Student Hostel.*
[28] Annual Report, 1927–1928.

quarters of the League of Nations. Two floors of this building were offered to the Friends; the Center and Meeting will occupy one and the Hostel will occupy the other so that for the first time both Hostel and Center will be housed together under the same roof. After this removal takes place, Mabel Ridpath expects to resign as warden and return to the United States, and her place will be taken by Anne Forsythe.

"I was informed that this mass was human beings in as great misery as they could be, and live, that I was mixed with them, and that henceforth I might not consider myself as a distinct or separate being . . .

"I saw this habitation to be safe,—to be inwardly quiet when there were great stirrings and commotions in the world . . ."

The Journal of John Woolman

CHAPTER XII

YEARLY MEETING

THE inside of the meeting house seemed very cool and quiet after the glare of the sunlight and the buzz of conversation out of doors. Friends had come from all parts of Germany to attend the tenth session of the German Yearly Meeting at Bad Pyrmont. There were visitors from abroad, too, many of them coming on purpose to be present at the tenth anniversary. Among them was Abby Worthington.

As she sat beside Fräulein Worthington, Frieda remembered the first time the two of them had sat together at the committee meeting in 1920. That was fifteen years ago and how much had happened since that time! Frieda tried to forget, during the first deep hush of the gathered meeting, what had happened since, but how could one forget when on her other side was sitting Hans' friend, Willie Solomon, his closely cropped head held in his two thin hands, and across the aisle were two officials, inevitable attenders of every religious meeting? They would sit there during all the sessions, listening intently, making it necessary for Friends to speak with caution. How could one forget when any minute might come the news that she was required no longer in her position as social worker? Not, she knew, because she was no longer needed, or that the work could be dropped to advantage. No, those would not be the reasons. Her point of view was not acceptable to those in control, and she never knew when Hans might bring his influence upon them. She never knew from day to day what Hans might do to make life harder for her.

Sitting beside Willie reminded her so much of Hans that she could not put him out of her thoughts. The two boys had grown up together, been playmates in school and inseparable companions in the university to which, by scraping and saving from her small salary, Frieda had been able to send Hans. Josef Heinrich had not lived long after his return from France in 1920 and Frieda had been forced to support herself and her brother.

She had lived for him and had been proud to watch his development into a brilliant student, winning prizes at school, so that she was determined he must go on to the university. He must have all the things which had been taken from her because of the war. He must have a carefree, happy youth, with all the advantages of education and she saw with gratification that the years of poverty and hunger and illness rolled off the boy as though they had never existed. It was a good thing for him to forget. Willie and Hans were very much alike except in one thing. Willie kept remembering how much they had suffered.

In her spare time she went with the two boys to the Quaker Center in Berlin because she did not want to lose touch with the Friends and because she wanted the boys to grow better acquainted with an organization which had done so much for them. They attended lectures and discussion groups and Frieda herself spent a great deal of time helping in the office. They came to the meetings for worship on Sundays and after Frieda had thought about it a long time, she became a member of the Yearly Meeting. Everything at the Center stimulated her. Its intellectual and its religious life made up for what she had lost because she had grown up during the war. Her pinched, starved years were somewhat forgotten in the joy of her regular work and the contacts with the Friends.

The greatest joy of all was her pride in Hans. She loved Willie, too, but he was not her brother, nor was he so promising as Hans. He was slower and less aggressive and while he would be a good man, Hans would be a great one.

Gradually, as though a sickness were creeping through him, Hans had changed. He could not go to Meeting one Sunday morning because he had an engagement. He could not go to the lecture at the Center because he was too busy. He told her he did not wish to have Willie come to their home any more and she learned from Willie that there had been a quarrel between them. After a long time she remembered that Willie's father had been a Jew. Hans began to talk about things which sounded dreadful to her. He rushed off to meetings about which she knew nothing and he talked more and more about nationalism, and a pure Germany. When he denounced America for its part in the Treaty of Versailles she could keep silence no longer.

"Oh, Hans! Remember what America has done for us. It brought us food and saved our lives. You and Willie would have died. How can you talk so bitterly?"

"That was all very fine but they knew they were doing a good thing and they got a nice lot of glory out of it. I get sick of hearing you talk about the Quakers all the time. They're just a handful of people and they don't have any real understanding now of what Germany needs. Love and goodwill is just sentimental talk."

"You didn't use to think so, Hans. Why have you quarreled with Willie?"

"Don't talk about him to me, Frieda. I'll have nothing to do with anybody who isn't of pure German blood. He and I aren't interested in the same things any more, and he would do better to leave the country. He'll find there's nothing here for him to do. And you, too, Frieda, had better be careful what you say. Stop all your talk about international brotherhood and love. Germany has found something better than the Quakers ever brought even with their food. I've got a job in a munitions factory."

After that Hans hardly ever came home and he had become a stranger. If it had not been for her work and the Friends at the center Frieda thought she could not have endured her unhappiness. All the love and care and sacrifice she had given to her brother; all the fine hopes she had cherished for his great career were gone. He had become a munitions maker.

Frieda looked at Willie. She knew that he had lost his job as a teacher and could not get married and she knew that there was no future for him in Germany. Perhaps the Friends at the Center would find a place for him in America. They were looking for one but America had problems enough of her own without finding positions for German exiles. "Exile." It was a terrible word and yet, perhaps, she too might become an exile. Willie used to be gay and full of fun but there was no humor in his face now and he looked stern and tired and even old, she thought, yet he was only twenty-four.

"I must stop thinking about these things," Frieda said to herself. "This is a meeting for worship." She looked at Abby who had only just arrived. Surely Fräulein Worthington would be able to give her advice and comfort and she wondered how Fräulein Worthington could have so serene a face and look so young after all the many years of service she had given for the Quakers. It was so difficult to keep serene. That was why Frieda had come to Yearly Meeting, so that the memory of these few quiet days of inspiration and fellowship with Friends would help her bear the hard months that lay ahead. There was a stir beside Frieda and Abby rose to her feet.

"Dear Friends," she began, "I have been thinking of a little story by an English Friend, Violet Hodgkin; she tells of a Friends Meeting in America, many years ago, when it was dangerous for people to come together for worship. Even as danger was threatening that little group a man arose and said, 'The Beloved of the Lord shall dwell in safety by Him. He shall cover them all the day long . . . He shall cover thee with His feathers and under His wings shalt thou trust.'

"Some of us have travelled many miles to share this beautiful experience of worship here at Bad Pyrmont. It has been my privilege to spend some time this summer in visiting among the different centers. First of all I met with Friends in London and then I came on to Paris where I stayed with Germaine Melon and saw some of her work with the Entr'aide. It has been many years since I have been in France and I was reminded, vividly, of my first visit in 1917. From Paris I went to Geneva and stayed in the Hostel where I was able to catch a glimpse of the wonderful work which Bertram Pickard is doing in the international capital and I could feel what a home of joy that Hostel has become to the many students who have lived there. I was much impressed in Vienna by the work camp at Marienthal and the Hostel at Singerstrasse 16 is, again, a real home.

"Now I have come to Germany and I remember the dark days of 1920 when there was no food and the little children were ill, victims of war and the cruel aftermath, the blockade. As we helped to bring them back into health by aid of the material things which we brought we believed that a rich future lay before them. We believed many things were going to happen but sometimes we hope that they will come to pass more quickly than they do.

"I have come here after visiting among the other Quaker groups in Europe. Dear Friends, there are not many of us but we are bound together by invisible cords of love. We are all one, sharing the same ideals and the same belief in God, willing to go through much travail of spirit because of them.

"Those of us who come in from the outside can do less today than when we brought food and clothing, fifteen years ago. It is easier to restore bodies to health than to feed the kind of hunger from which you are suffering now. We can do little except remind you of the early Friends who endured many hardships because of their faith and this great cloud of witnesses compasses you about, even as do Friends all over the world.

"We have come to give you courage, to bring you a message of love. And great as is the comfort which I hope this sympathy from human hearts will bring, remember that there is one, even Christ Jesus, who knows the heart of each one of you, and who can speak to your condition better than anyone else.

"'The Beloved of the Lord shall dwell in safety by Him . . . He shall cover thee with His feathers and under His wings shalt thou trust.'"

The room grew still again as Abby sat down. Fräulein Worthington had said nothing, Frieda thought, to which the two officials could object. What had been said was so simple that they would think there was nothing in it. It was so simple that already Frieda felt calm and rested. She looked at Willie and saw that he too had been comforted; the stern, bitter look was gone from his face. Frieda moved slightly and brushed her arm against Abby's. Abby turned toward her and they smiled.

"And I was almost wishing," thought Frieda, "that the Quakers had never come because then Hans would have died long ago and the suffering would have been over. But that was a wicked wish. They have brought something even

more precious than Hans' love and it is better that I must
be tried by fire. May God make me strong enough to bear
it. May the Society of Friends in Germany keep its faith
and not let these difficulties overwhelm it. Can it be true
that the Beloved of the Lord shall dwell in safety?"

Chapter XIII

INTERRACIAL SECTION

IF the Service Committee could send hundreds of workers abroad and spend millions of dollars giving relief to French, Germans, Russians, Poles, Austrians and the Albanians, why could it not spend some money and thought on a subject nearer home, the relations between the colored and the white race?

There were several members of the Service Committee who felt very keenly that this interracial problem was one of the most vital "not only in the United States, but throughout the world. In the past five hundred years, most of the great wars have been fought between groups that belonged to the white races. Unless the growing feeling of hostility between races is checked, it is only a question of time until wars will be fought between races. Prompted, not by fear, but by the desire to make available for mankind the best that all races have to offer, the members of this section during its first year have endeavored to carry on such work as will bring about understanding, confidence and goodwill. In Philadelphia and New York, as well as in other large cities, Friends and others have been encouraged to make a decided effort to get acquainted with those who were like-minded, but of another race. Special 'get-acquainted dinners' have been arranged for Friends and foreign students and for leading American business men and women of the Negro race. This intercourse has resulted in a much better understanding between those who participated . . ."[1]

[1] Annual Report, 1925–1926.

During the year 1926 and 1927 an experiment was tried in bringing two Japanese students to America. The young woman attended Smith College and the young man attended Earlham where they took active parts in American college life. One reason for bringing Japanese students to the United States at that time was the fact that the Alien Immigration Act had been passed to exclude Orientals from entering the country and the Interracial Section wanted to do everything it could to foster friendly relations between the two countries. A Japanese Friend, Mr. Hasegawa, was asked to travel in different parts of the United States under the auspices of the Section so that interracial activities for the second year were concentrated almost entirely on the subject of Japan.

As the interracial work increased in importance it became necessary to have a secretary for the section and Helen R. Bryan, one of the assistant secretaries at Twenty South Twelfth Street, was asked to take this position which she kept until the summer of 1928.

In the autumn of 1927 a folder was sent out from Twenty South Twelfth Street: "The American Friends Service Committee presents Crystal Bird, colored, young, dynamic . . . Realizing the deep need in American life for a more intelligent understanding of the colored people, the Interracial Section . . . is presenting Crystal Bird, one of the most outstanding young leaders of the colored race . . . Her wide experience with both white and colored groups equips her in a remarkable way to interpret her people. She speaks with great vividness and with the utmost frankness, but without rancor or bitterness. She knows personally most of the people of achievement of her own racial group. Her appreciation of the music of her people is an experience of rare loveliness in itself. Her greatest aim is to bring to her audience the humanness of the Negro wherever he is found.

Hers is a dynamic personality, rich in reality, and in seeing and knowing Crystal Bird one's vision is cleared, one's sympathies are deepened and one experiences a new revelation of life."

No one who saw and heard Crystal Bird for the first time at the Service Committee meeting in September 1927 will ever forget the impression she made on the group as she outlined, in a few sentences, her plans for the winter. She visited schools and clubs, religious gatherings, meetings, conferences, and to all of them she interpreted simply and beautifully the needs of the colored race, the achievements of the colored race, and how both the white and colored races could be mutually helpful to each other. Nearly all the letters which came into the office, written in gratitude for the privilege of listening to Crystal Bird, spoke of her poise and her charm. Her manner of address predisposed one immediately to listen to what she had to say. She was young and dynamic and talented and charming. She was also a Negro. One remembers Crystal Bird's year with the Service Committee with particular gratitude.

Milton C. Davis acted as secretary for the Interracial Section until February 15, 1929, when it was decided to discontinue interracial activities as a specific part of the Service Committee. In the autumn of 1928 Helen R. Bryan had accepted the position of secretary of the Committee on Interests of the Colored Race of the Race Street Yearly Meeting. It was hoped that the similar committee of Arch Street Yearly Meeting would co-operate, which it eventually did and Helen Bryan became secretary of the Joint Committee which, while not supported financially by the Service Committee, is housed in the same building.

From July 1928 until April 1, 1931, the American Interracial Peace Committee had its headquarters in Twenty South Twelfth Street. It was developed under the leadership of Leslie Pinckney Hill and other well-known colored men and women and Alice Dunbar-Nelson, full time secretary, was added to the office staff. This was organized to foster peace work among Negroes, but the committee was discontinued in 1931. Since 1933 the Service Committee has co-operated with the Committee on Race Relations of the two Philadelphia Yearly Meetings in holding a Race Relations Institute. These have been at Swarthmore College until the summer of 1937 when the location has been changed to Cheyney State Teachers' College, Cheyney, Pennsylvania.

Chapter XIV

PEACE SECTION

"Will the church outlaw war or condone it as a necessary evil? The spectacle of Christian nations fighting each other has turned a great many thinking men and women in these nations, as well as the great majority of the non-Christian world, away from Christianity. The question that has concerned the Peace Section has been, therefore, 'What can be done to encourage people to think Peace?' Holding that war under any circumstances is out of harmony with the teachings of Jesus, emphasis has been placed on those things which tend to disarm the mind and bring nations to the point where they would be willing to have their disputes settled around the council table. To this end, support has been given to the League of Nations, World Court, and to such movements as tend to bring about a better understanding between nations."[1]

"If we were each asked to name the thing that we considered to be the greatest piece of work to be done in the world, we should reply without question, perhaps, that it was the abolition of war. The problem that confronts the Society of Friends, therefore, is one of encouraging Friends to work actively for the abolition of war in times of peace . . . A visit to the old battlefields very recently proved again how rapidly one forgets the war and its attendant horrors. One can only feel with others that it must not happen again, or say with Sherwood Eddy, 'We must not let the present

[1] Annual Report, 1925–1926.

generation pass until we have made war impossible.' The Peace Section came into existence because there was a very decided feeling that there was work that could be done by the united Society of Friends . . . A determined effort has been made not to overlap with existing organizations." [2]

A six-fold program was arranged which should, (1) work in Yearly Meetings, (2) work among colleges and college students, (3) send literature to Friends' papers and other magazines, (4) work with young people, (5) work with other churches, and (6) arrange for deputations of Friends to inter-visit.

Thomas Q. Harrison was travelling and speaking for the Fellowship of Youth for Peace and in October 1925 the Peace Section agreed to use him as a part time Field Secretary. He visited schools and colleges during the winter and spring, presenting the challenge of peace to students in various parts of the United States and it was expected to appoint him full time Field Secretary beginning in October 1926, but he sailed late in the summer on a trip around the world where he continued to address students in universities. After his return in 1927 he remained with the Peace Section for three months during the summer to carry on field work in the middle West.

During the first year of the Peace Section Edward W. Evans joined the staff of the Service Committee in order to devote his time to speaking on the subject of the United States' entrance into the World Court and Wilbur Thomas was working with the Committee on Militarism in Education which had its headquarters in New York. It was carrying on a campaign for the abolition of military training in schools and colleges in the United States.

In the summer of 1926 it was suggested that different

[2] Minutes of the American Friends Service Committee, December 2, 3, 1925.

groups of Young Friends should travel about, visiting in communities and holding meetings where they could speak on the subject of peace, but the scheme did not prove as successful as had been hoped because it was suggested too late in the season. Young Friends had arranged their summers already. However, two or three such "Caravans" did materialize. "Both of us, as well as our Yearly Meeting Peace Committee, feel that the work was very much worthwhile. We were received excellently everywhere, and had good order in all our meetings. Lots of young people attended which is an important fact. Such work should be done all through the south, in the small towns and out of the way places; the field is almost unlimited and an exceptionally needed one just now if we want to create public opinion for peace and against militarism." [3]

By February 1927 plans were being made to send out several Caravan teams for the following summer. "Just as early Quakerism was knit together in a unity of purpose by an active itinerant ministry, we are sending out speakers and representatives to Quaker centers throughout the country . . . The Caravan project for next summer is showing great promise. Application blanks have just gone out to the Friends' colleges and already we have assurances of at least five or six teams of two men each . . . The project involves the purchase of a small automobile for each team, the payment of $125 to each man for his expenses and $75 as compensation. The automobiles will be sold at the end of the summer. Each team is to travel in progressive circles, first arranging meetings and then filling the engagements." [4]

Twenty-one young men and women volunteered to spend their summer travelling with the Peace Caravans going into

[3] Minutes of the American Friends Service Committee, September 23, 1926.
[4] Minutes of the American Friends Service Committee, March 24, 1927.

the rural districts of California, Colorado, Nebraska, Iowa, Indiana, New York, New England and North Carolina, New Hampshire and Massachusetts.

On June first Ray Newton came into the office at Twenty South Twelfth Street as secretary for the Peace Section and his first job was sending these Caravan teams off for the summer, after a three day conference at Haverford College, June 18–21, which gave them a chance to meet together and to have a little training in methods of discussion before they were expected to address audiences. They were all college students, young and with little experience, other than college debates, in public speaking. This conference was an admirable preparation for them and these "twentieth century equivalents of the first publishers of truth" left Haverford in their second hand model T Fords, which were filled to the brim with literature on peace.

A sum had been given to provide medals for winners of Oratorical Peace Contests throughout the country and in December 1927 this project was being considered as a means to stimulate peace education among children and young people between the ages of nine and sixteen. During the winter of 1927 and 1928 Anna B. Griscom compiled a book entitled *Peace Crusaders*, a suitable collection of essays, stories and poems to be used in these contests. This was published in September 1928 and by the end of 1930 seven hundred of the contests had been held in all parts of the United States, nearly all of the declamations used being taken from *Peace Crusaders*. During 1928 special attention was given to the case of Rosika Schwimmer whose application in the courts of Illinois for citizenship in the United States had been denied because of her pacifistic principles and her objection to war.

In 1928 Amy E. Sharpless, a Caravaner in 1927, attended the World Youth Peace Congress at Eerde, Holland, and when she returned to the United States she asked the Service Committee to use her as a travelling speaker among colleges and universities. From October 1928 until June 1929 she visited forty colleges in New England, the middle west and the south, speaking to groups on peace and the Service Committee. She was financed by the Peace Section, the Philadelphia Young Friends and the National Student Federation of America.[5]

Eleven peace caravans were sent out in the summer of 1928. One of these was a Negro team. Funds were donated to send out two teams to speak on the cause of prohibition.

"The two Baltimore Yearly Meetings have been doing a considerable amount of peace publicity by supporting Lucy Meacham Thruston in her work of getting news releases on peace subjects into local county papers." On June first the Peace Section began to sponsor this journalistic venture "The Trend of World Affairs" which has increased in size and importance during the nine years through which Lucy Thruston has carried it on.

The most absorbing occupation of the Peace Section was its preparation for the peace caravans. A great deal of time was spent in interviewing possible candidates, for obtaining material for them to use and for planning short, preliminary conferences which could give them some training before they set forth on their ten weeks of intensive speaking. It became apparent that these conferences could be of greater value if they were longer.

Haverford College had offered its buildings and grounds in 1917 for the use of the first "Caravan" of one hundred young people to go out under the red and black star of the Service Committee. It was fitting that it should offer its buildings and grounds for a few days when the first Peace Caravaners

[5] Minutes of the American Friends Service Committee, May 24, 1928.

met together in 1927. In June 1930 the first Institute of International Relations was held at Haverford College. This new type of conference instantly became so popular and valuable that it has spread to all parts of the country and has attracted persons from all over the world.

"There are a great many people in the United States eager to help get rid of war and to carry on education, the purpose of which is to promote world co-operation. They would be more active and more effective if they were better informed, and if they had assistance in working out peace programs in their communities. To meet this need the American Friends Service Committee, during the past five years, has been establishing Institutes of International Relations in various parts of the country.

"An Institute is a good, short, inexpensive school, the board and tuition averaging from $25 to $35 for the period. In the past they have been set up especially for educators, teachers, ministers, Y.M.C.A. and Y.W.C.A. secretaries, club leaders responsible for educational programs, and others with some outreach among the oncoming generation . . . Institutes ought to be located at well and favorably known colleges and universities interested in the Institutes and in their type of service to their constituency, to co-operate financially in setting up the program and in recruiting students." [6]

The first Institute in 1930 was held, primarily, for the Peace Caravans and peace workers. In 1931 two separate Institutes were held at Haverford, the first one for ministers, editors, and peace workers, and the second, immediately following, for teachers. The attendance jumped from fifty who came the first year to nearly three hundred who came the second and a great many more attended public evening lectures. Planning for the Institutes became a full

[6] Statement concerning the Institutes.

time job in itself and on September 1, 1931, E. Raymond Wilson was added to the staff of the Peace Section as a travelling secretary.

Although the depression brought unemployment to a large number of people, it brought also a deepening of interest in world affairs. People who had not thought very much about international or economic problems began to believe that these problems mattered very much. The news of the Institutes at Haverford spread fast and there was a demand to have similar ones in other parts of the United States.

In 1932 the number was increased to three; Institutes were held at Haverford, at Wellesley College, Massachusetts, and at Northwestern University, Evanston, Illinois. The enrollment increased to four hundred and fifty. In 1933, in addition to the three of the previous year, one was started at Duke University, in North Carolina. The Haverford Institute was organized in co-operation with the Pennsylvania Federation of Labor and the Central Labor Union of Philadelphia, and was held primarily for labor leaders, and this was repeated in 1934. At the end of this year the value of the Institutes was recognized by an award of $3000 from the Woodrow Wilson Foundation. In 1934 an appropriation of $5000 was given by the Carnegie Corporation.

In January 1935 Raymond Wilson was appointed Dean of the Institutes, with an office on the Campus of Northwestern University while each Institute had its own Field Secretary.

During the summer of 1937 there will be ten Institutes, two of which,—Midwestern and Kansas, will give college credit for the period of attendance. The eighth annual Eastern Institute, formerly the one held at Haverford College, and in 1936 at Swarthmore, was at Cheyney State Teachers' College, to which the Emergency Peace Volunteers from the eastern half of the United States came for training before starting their summer's work. A similar course of training for the volunteers on the west coast will be given at the third annual Institute at Whittier College, California. Duke University will hold its fifth and Wellesley and Midwestern their sixth annual Institutes, although the latter has changed its location from Northwestern University to North Central College, Naperville, Illinois. Institutes will be held for the third year at Reed College, Portland, Oregon, at Mills College, California, and at Grinnell College, Iowa; for the second year at Bethel College, Kansas, and at Nashville, Tennessee. During 1934 and 1935 Institutes were held at Atlanta, Georgia.

It is difficult to estimate the far reaching effects of these Institutes which brought, in one summer, that of 1936, a total of 1496 registered attenders from forty-four states. Since 1930 two hundred and forty outstanding leaders have come from all parts of the world in order to spend a few weeks during the summer in what they consider a most effective way of sharing information. T. Z. Koo, the Chinese secretary of the World Student Christian Federation, is coming all the way from New Zealand to attend three of the 1937 Institutes.

It is not possible to quote an exact figure but it has been estimated that the total membership of the Institutes since their beginning in 1930 through 1936, has been forty-five hundred persons and this number does not include many thousands more who have attended the public lectures only.[7] These students have been drawn from all denominations as there is no desire to make the Institutes sectarian.

"This nation-wide project is made possible by the support and co-operation of many groups and individuals, including the Congregational Council for Social Action, the Emergency

[7] Statement made by E. Raymond Wilson.

Peace Campaign, the Friends' Peace Committee, the various universities and colleges where the programs are held, the active local committees at each place, the hundreds of people who contribute financially, the loyalty of former members, the vision of Ray Newton who organized and launched the various Institutes, and the energetic promotion on the part of the Institute secretaries." [8]

The only method of evaluating the worth of such an undertaking as an Institute of International Relations is to read what those who have participated in one have said.

"It has meant a great deal to me. I believe that its chief value is to clarify ideas and to help people find a method of coming to a conclusion in these very difficult situations. It gave information, inspiration for further work, encouragement and methods. To me it gave confidence that men can work out problems, though results must come slowly." [9]

Although no attempt was made to conduct the Institutes along Quaker lines, there was a request in 1936 to have a Friends meeting for worship every morning at Northwestern University. One leader remarked of the 1936 Emergency Peace Campaign volunteers training at the Grinnell Institute that they were the keenest group of young people he had ever met in his fifteen years' experience of conference leadership.

"When I came to the Midwestern Institute of International Relations four years ago,[10] I had an interest in world peace and a vague desire to do something about it. My interest in international affairs was crystallized and the things I have accomplished during the past three years have been due largely to the stimulus, the information and the inspiration received at the three Institutes which I have attended . . .

[8] E. Raymond Wilson, an article written for the Friends papers, July 27, 1936.
[9] The Midwestern Institute for 1934.
[10] 1932.

What I have done anyone can do. It is nothing startling nor unusual. I have simply worked with and through the materials and facilities with which I normally had contact." [11]

The development and growth of these Institutes did not decrease, in any way, the interest and enthusiasm for the peace caravans which began to benefit from their experience at the Institutes during their period of training and from the fact that the caravans were no longer in the experimental stage but had acquired a definite place for themselves. In 1933 three caravaners tried the experiment of acting as counselors in Y.M.C.A. camps, their purpose being to arrange programs which would encourage discussion on peace topics and which would have effective results in peace education.

Every effort was made to present the cause of peace to the public and in 1933 the Peace Section entered another journalistic venture besides the one carried on by Lucy Meacham Thruston. "The Nofrontier News Service was organized in October as a co-operative undertaking between the Peace Section and Devere Allen, Editor of *The World Tomorrow*. It is an independent news agency serving the cause of world peace and operating with professional standards of accuracy and literary appeal. It compiles material from one hundred and fifty correspondents in all parts of the world and about eight hundred papers and publications received regularly by the editor. Bi-weekly news releases are supplied to editors of the religious and labor press, rural weekly newspapers and small city dailies in this country. In the first two months of operation editors of papers with a total circulation of over a million readers have paid the nominal subscription price for these services. *World Events*, a pocket periodical for students of international affairs, is issued bi-weekly from October to June. Eighteen hundred

[11] Statement made by an Institute member.

subscriptions were received during its first three months of existence. Nofrontier News Service also sends out special articles to editors; conducts research on peace questions for writers, speakers and institutions; furnishes illustrations for articles on international questions and acts as a rental agency for lantern slides and lectures." [12]

In three years' time the material supplied by the Nofrontier News Service has found a much wider public since it has been estimated that over ten million persons subscribe to the papers in which this material is published. *World Events* is sent to a subscription list of twenty-two thousand.

In the autumn of 1935 a deep concern arose in the Peace Section "with regard to the need for increased power and effectiveness of the Peace Movement in our country at this time. There are a number of significant developments going on which call for increased alertness . . . Chief among these are the increased military tension between nations; the greatly extended appropriations for Army and Navy in our own country; the universal re-armaments throughout the world, . . . the imperial ambitions of Japan [13] and the obvious deep-seated feeling of mis-treatment and frustration on the part of Germany and Italy today. We, as Friends, cannot find adequate expression for our convictions through movements which simply assure American isolation or which attempt to restrain offending nations by economic or military sanctions. It is urgent that religious groups discover and make vivid to our country in every way possible the sacrificial steps which might be taken to remove . . . occasions for war." [14]

A conference was held at Buck Hill Falls early in De-

---

[12] Annual Report, 1933.
[13] As shown by the military leaders.
[14] Minutes of the Board of Directors, November 6, 1935.

cember and at this gathering the Emergency Peace Campaign was organized as an autonomous movement, to be an intensive, wide-spread, two-year campaign, sponsored by various peace groups. Ray Newton was to remain secretary of the Peace Section but the Service Committee gave him liberty to be the Executive Director of the Emergency Peace Campaign for the two-year period. Harry Emerson Fosdick has served as chairman.

The Campaign was launched publicly at a meeting in Philadelphia on April 21, 1936, at which Sir George Lansbury and Kirby Page addressed a large audience and a paper, written by Mrs. Roosevelt, was read by Hannah Clothier Hull. During the following weeks a series of peace meetings was held in 300 cities. Local peace committees have been organized in 1200 cities. Altogether 38,000 meetings have been held and 450 religious and educational leaders have participated. During the summer nearly 250 college men and women served as Peace Volunteers, an undertaking almost identical with the original peace caravaners, and this program will be repeated in the summer of 1937.

"I live in virtue of that life and power which does away with the occasion for all war."

The Journal of George Fox

CHAPTER XV

PEDDLING PEACE

"To whom it may concern: The bearers of this letter, Richard Green and James Kite,[1] are duly appointed representatives of the American Friends Service Committee and are serving as volunteer peace workers in the interest of peace and international good will during the summer of 1927. Any kindness or courtesy which you may extend to them will be deeply appreciated."

Here are given the weekly reports of these two caravaners Dick and Jim, travelling in the middle west in their second hand model T Ford, Ophelia Bumps.

June 26, 1927

Dear Afserco, which, being interpreted, is American Friends Service Committee.

You will be wanting to hear of the progress of Jim, Dick and Ophelia Bumps since this trio left Haverford bound for the great open spaces. Everything O.K. with the steady, reliable men of this party, but Ophelia does not seem to be caring much for the trip. She is worse than a horse smelling his stable afar off. When she gets the scent of a garage she rushes for it, and there she sits, perfectly content. A little home body, if I know my machinery. One shouldn't look a gift horse in the mouth, but I believe a little looking in Ophelia's engine before we started would have shown that the emergency brake wasn't attached to the rod, that the

[1] Names are fictitious.

187

rim of the spare tire was bent and would not fit on the wheel; and while no one could have foreseen that we would have a blow out two hours after we left Haverford, the fact remained that we had to buy a new tire because the spare would not go on. The next day we picked up a nail in the new tire. Today we have been resting while Ophelia has recovered from burning out a bearing. This happened because we found, too late, that the oil wasn't flowing properly. We have run out of gas only once. After this first week I think we'll get the hang of things and be all right but we've spent nearly all the money we had to start with and we're behind on our schedule because of the delays. I guess it couldn't be helped but we've had to go on slim rations to save our money till we can get to our destination.

We've had plenty of leisure, however, in which to try and digest all that we heard at Haverford and to plan what we are going to say when we start our speeches. It was a great experience to be with the whole bunch of caravaners for four days and to discuss with everybody the salient points of peace. Even though we've had some debating experience in college, something tells me that we're going to get into tight spots where nothing in the way of past debates, or speeches, or anything will be of much help. We've been taking turns reading aloud, against the roar and thunder of Ophelia's complaints, some of the literature you gave us and which we didn't have time to look at before.

I think we're pretty well up on the costs of past, present and future wars, peace treaties, and so forth, but there will be those audiences which won't believe a word we say. It seems hard to think that people will believe we are lying! Anyhow, it was a real inspiration to be with the other teams and see such an enthusiastic group of boys and girls, going off to spend their summer peddling peace. It's a challenge to all young people, I should think, because it's about the most worthwhile thing anybody can do right now. It's ten years, almost, since the Armistice and we're a long way from peace yet.

I'm writing this while Jim is trying to hurry up the garage man. He's about finished Ophelia's oil shampoo and I just hope she'll be satisfied with this and not want a permanent wave by next week. Sorry to report so much trouble and hope the next letter will sound more cheerful. We are really anxious to get started on our work and our ardor hasn't been dampened too much by Ophelia's behavior. I hope the girls aren't having such a time with their cars.

We don't mean to sound mercenary, but we're pretty short of cash and would appreciate the sight of a check or money order, or anything in the line of shekels, as soon as you can spare it. Jim has just come along to say we can start in another fifteen minutes. We'll keep our fingers crossed and hope for the best! Jim, Dick and Ophelia.

July 3

Dear Afserco,

Joyfully received money order yesterday after it had been forwarded. Enclosed please find receipt-certificate for same. An influential Quaker signed the order as witness and furnished personal identification, so we realized its cash value without any trouble. We were just about to start dish-washing in a restaurant for our food. Two nights without dinner seemed to indicate something was necessary. Ophelia doing better. Will write more later.

July 10

Dear Afserco,

We are making rather a successful tour, if busyness has value as a barometer of success. When we are not speaking, we are driving to the next speech, arranging for the next speech, or eating and sleeping. Calling on interested people for arranging meetings or follow-up work in a community takes quite a bit of time. Church groups of various denominations, Kiwanis clubs, W.C.T.U.s, Lake camps and conferences and other organizations have co-operated splendidly, and our average is nearly two meetings a day besides the personal contacts that we make through calls. The responses from our audiences have been gratifying and royal entertainment plentiful, much more so than we ever expected. This has been the case even in places where the only point of contact was our common interest in peace. In one city, for instance, Jim addressed the Kiwanis Club and has prospects for a Union service and other meetings, all through a minister who was interested in peace.

We have finished calling here and are now en route at thirty miles per hour over fresh gravel. Occasionally we deign to race railroad trains on a track beside us and you can imagine how fast we, or rather the train, are going. We manage to hit a bump now and then but have proved to be marksmen too poor to hit a hen. Meetings are coming so thick and fast that we have to divide our party of two to provide enough speakers.

Please excuse the break. It's noon of the next day. Jim had a splendid meeting with Marion Friends yesterday as I did with Anderson Friends. We discussed at Christian Endeavor the questions on war that Kirby Page suggests and had a live response. Met many people here. Just got back from the finest speech in my career at the Kiwanis. Please don't mind if I blow a little. I was followed by a banker who referred several times to my fifteen minute speech. He was talking about the development and romance of American business.

I told them how the lions didn't eat Daniel because they would have had to make an after dinner speech and I mentioned my greater predicament of having to make my peace talk directly to the Army and Navy, pointing out thus indirectly the fallacy of preparedness. I spoke of the evils that had been justified in their times, as slavery, dueling, inquisition, etc., and how we were now far enough away from the war to see its evils. After hoping that our soldiers had not died in vain in a war to end war, I showed a few possibilities of war ten years from now and tried to paint a picture of that next war, compared with which the last one was a baby.

While they were shuddering at this, I referred to the twenty-two billion dollars' worth of the inter-dependence and entanglement that the United States has, and the powder line around the world that a little war might touch off. Then I told them that business had found the secret of competitive co-operation, using such examples as the recent organization of New York clothing manufacturers and their election of a Columbia professor as head. Then I spoke of the Canadian-American co-operation and the Christ of the Andes as examples, showed how America, with half the world's gold, would be the deciding factor for peace, as she had been in ending the war, and appealed to them as Kiwanians to "build" for international peace and friendship, ending in this wise: "Give us millions of persons in this and other countries who will think, talk and work for peace, and statesmen and diplomats, as if by a miracle, will find some way to abolish war." The applause was enthusiastic and members afterwards took pains to express their appreciation of what had been said. Am feeling fine, Dick.

July 17

Dear Afserco,

Just a post card to say that as we sat in a restaurant last night someone remarked that Dr. Smith was planning

to hear the lecture that evening. We asked the subject and
this man went out to look at the sign on the telephone pole.
He announced, "World Peace". Wife in rear said, "Why
don't they let them fight and be done with it!" "Quaker it
says," he continued. "Quaker?" she asked, "Oh, Lord!" And
so it goes. Incidentally a wind blew up and not a soul appeared. Ate breakfast with pastor. Fried chicken. Jim and
Dick.

July 24

Dear Afserco,

My last communication was brief, I am afraid, and I'll
try and do better this time. Jim is changing a tire right
now. I changed the last one. Gravel roads seem to be full
of nails. They must be indigenous.

You'll enjoy this episode. We were scouting around for a
Union prayer meeting and finally found it. A Baptist minister, who used to live in Oskaloosa, knew Friends there, and
Presto! He told us they were having tent meetings every
night this week but he said they had no speaker for tonight
and would be glad to see us. So we went out to the tent.

Apparently this family goes around putting up a tent and
trusting to the Lord for the speakers as well as the money.
They looked at us dubiously and we said we were talking
peace. *They* said they were preaching Christ. That's all
the same thing in the end, we explained, at which they
looked very much surprised and admitted that it was a
new idea. Suddenly the woman said, "You boys pray, don't
you?" This caught us a bit unawares, but Jim said, "Oh,
yes, certainly." "Let's pray then," said she so we knelt
on the ground and prayed by the wooden benches. The
woman prayed that she might know whether we were really
sent by the Lord and would say things that were acceptable.
After prayer the woman said earnestly, "Boys who can pray

like that are all right. You are sent by the Lord." So, that was that, any way you look at it. Jim did the speaking and I played the organ and we all swatted mosquitoes. Afterwards every one who came up shook hands and murmured, "The Lord bless you, brother."

Did you know that I am strongly recommended for the Methodist ministry? In a church announcement the other day, these words appeared: "Sermon by Rev. Richard Green" and again, later in the bulletin, "Rev. Richard Green preaches at eleven o'clock. Hear him." Because of this mistake, that church Bulletin, which circulates rather widely among the Methodist ministers of this part of the state, has led the Methodist pastors to call me Reverend and Brother. After my "sermon" both the minister and the visiting pastor told me I was missing my calling by not being a Methodist minister. The best thing happened in the evening when a former Chautauqua manager spoke highly of my meeting and strongly advised me to go into Chautauqua work! Since it is hard to decide between that platform and the pulpit, I think I shall remain with the A.F.S.C.

The anticipation that other audiences might prove more receptive than Friends seems to have proved to be true. Perhaps it is because other audiences have not heard the peace message so often that they are bored hearing it again. The office's prompt response, by the way, to every need, whether it be for slides, song books, literature or cash, has been very heartening.

We are often greeted with the remark, when we announce that we are talking about peace, "Christ came not to bring peace but a sword." We cap that with the whole armor of God and the sword of the spirit!

Are Jim and I wrong in our method? We feel that the religious and abstract, perhaps sentimental side of the peace question, has been the one mainly stressed. We are interested in showing people that economic, imperialistic, political and militaristic causes of war, as well as the spirit of misunderstanding and prejudice, must have practical solutions. We stress the Outlawry treaty and urge people to work for that and against our militaristic policy in the shape of the Big Navy Bill, military training and imperialism. Of course we do stress the Christian attitude against war, but we find that most people's idea of Christianity is spiritual redemption. We completely remodel our speeches every other meeting or so, discovering that if they aren't rather new and interesting to us, they aren't interesting to anyone else, either. To be continued. Dick.

August 11

Dear Afserco,

You have been wondering why you did not hear from this trio but Jim, Dick and Ophelia have been pretty busy, and our labors in this section seem to have been not all in vain. We are inclined to count the past month a success. Folks have told us that they had not been thinking along peace lines till they heard us; that they had never considered the problem in the light of our approach; that they were glad to know that others were thinking as they did on the question. Our arguments seem to have reassured a good many on their stand for peace and we hope that seed blown in doubtful quarters will bring forth unexpected bloom. We have had our ups and downs. All great men do, but we consider ourselves as lucky as Lindbergh as we glide in Ophelia Bumps from community to community, circulating "pink parlor propaganda" by foot and by Ford.

In the last forty days (and forty nights, to retain the language of the Flood) we have conducted or contributed to threescore and ten meetings, an average of one and eight-tenths meetings per diem. Eight meetings in one day, four each, is our record. Our schedule included, along with miscellaneous meetings, seventeen camp fire programs, eleven church services, eight prayer meetings, five Christian Endeavors, seven W.C.T.U.s, four noon-day luncheon clubs, five groups of church women, ten meetings at three conferences of young people and an address at a Methodist-Protestant Camp Meeting Tabernacle. These meetings have been well attended and people everywhere seem to be interested in a discussion of the problem.

We have found people, as we expected to find them, who insisted that past wars were justifiable, that present wars were necessary and that future wars were inevitable. The idea of another way than war to settle disputes, just as we cook with gas and electricity rather than burn down the house to roast the pig, rather staggers some people. They had always looked at the question from the point of view of glorious battles and "But 'twas a famous victory." The abolition of international anarchy is a new idea to them. It is largely a matter of education after all. "The usual seems justifiable, the habitual the inevitable."

Many admit that "the war of 1846 was frankly political and rotten, a war of conquest to extend slavery. Yet what would we have been had we not whipped the Mexicans and stolen their territory just the same as we did with the Red Indians?" These are quotations from an editorial in the July 14th *Liberty Magazine,* but bespeak well the attitude of a great many. "Every war has its evils which are indefensible. No one can judge the good or evil of war until memory of personal loss and suffering has faded." After describing the possibility of the next war we ask whether it would be justified, even though past wars might have been.

The final argument is, of course, that war is inevitable as long as human nature remains the same. "We hope against wars, and know that they will come. They are bad in many ways (Where, I ask people, are they good?) but of one thing we are certain, and that is, when they do come, it is better to win them than to lose them. Follow the lead of the pacifists in this country and the next war will come, just as it always has. It will even come ahead of time, if our rivals know us to be weak. And when it comes, we'll get a terrible beating from which, as a nation, we may never recover. Look at Austria today." [2] They all say, "Well, I feel safer with a shotgun up over the door." People are rather surprised when it is suggested that aggressive good-will from her neighbors might have kept Germany out of the world war.

This "inevitable" idea permeated the argument of a medical practitioner and Rotarian who "arranged" our first refusal for a meeting, who was anxious to fight when expedient or necessary, who furnished an hour of entertainment for me as his opinions were expressed in the secrecy of his office. I took each blow and turned each gently, yet neither opinion was changed in the finals. I, seeking diligently for the truth, was kindly advised, among other things, that as a student from a Quaker college, I was "indelibly marked" as a dangerous suspect; that the American Legion and D.A.R. had known we were coming long before we arrived, and they were going to make sure what we would say if we spoke in their town. Of course, he explained, it was not our fault; we just inherited the stain against that institution as we inherit sin from Adam; our opinions were not our own (he didn't say whose opinions his were), we just automatically absorbed them from our environment in that "hotbed of pacifism." He pointed out that we, innocently, were taking advantage of those demanding protection for their

[2] One can scarcely refrain from making the observation ten years after these remarks were written and twenty years after the United States entered the war that even winning the war does not have many compensations.

country in thus parading our peace arguments (not our own), splendid in theory, but suicide in practice, before a fickle public. He said he could not conscientiously aid us in getting engagements, for he frankly feared our influence on the fickle, impracticable public. The Sunday School hour passed swiftly.

We have discovered women, both maid and married, who share the "inevitable" idea. One camp directress, who was much interested in this "Thirty Million Dollar Peace Propaganda" (don't know where she got her figures), said that she was a Bolshevist and didn't believe as the rest of us did. She claimed, as others do, that our stuff was good in theory, but less plausible in practice, that the present stage of civilization (that makes such terrible wars possible), is not ready yet to get along without warfare, that Christ came too soon, the world was not ready. She, said to be the leading lady seller of insurance in a large city, preferred to "keep a shotgun over the door."

After promoting pugilism with the Rotarian-practitioner, we ate dinner in the home of an ex-soldier, who reminded us that most of the noise from the Legion came from soldiers who saw no actual warfare, and he told us that those who really fought are not anxious to fight in another war. That same evening his opinion was corroborated by another ex-soldier. On the same day the opinion of the militarist was out-weighed, two to one. After a Union meeting a Legion chaplain came up and told us to keep on, that he could see nothing objectionable in what we said and he invited us to take his church in a couple of Sundays. Yours, Dick.

August 19

Dear Afserco,

The receipt of the last green slip a couple of days ago reminds us forcibly that we have only two more weeks left.

Then no more peace, i.e. active, Service Committee work for a while. Our chief disappointment as we look back over our schedule is that we have not been able to cover more ground in our limited ten weeks.

A college professor spoke to us about our remarkable repertoire of subjects and titles, and we had to remind him, that, like other great speakers, it was all the same line with a little more emphasis on the points suggested by the requested title. I, for instance, in my increased experience, have evolved an ingenious outline that resembles Gaul with its three divisions and has more flexibility than a garter snake. It must be kept fresh and forceful by constant rearrangement and revision, by continual alteration of the illustrative, argumentative or appellative materials. Here we have an outline that can furnish a speech lasting from ten minutes to an hour and a half.

We are wondering how much time we can devote to peace and Service Committee work during the college year. As Sunday School workers, college students, Y.M.C.A. employees and A.F.S.C. enthusiasts we are frankly on the fence. But we are looking forward to college again after the strain of a busy summer. We have off hours there, at least, while on this little tour we are working all the time! We have been able to iron out many of the wrinkles that were present during the first weeks. This sort of work is more enjoyable than selling even automobiles. We have actually accumulated some ideas and put ingenious schemes into practice. This team would like to sign up again for next year. We are looking forward to seeing how our college work and activities will go next semester with all this additional wisdom. We have certainly enjoyed it all, thick with thin, and are thankful for the opportunities and experiences which it has brought. We hope that our summer's work will be a definite contribution toward the cause. Jim, Dick and Ophelia.

August 31,

Dear Afserco,

Home, sweet home! That's where we are now and we hold the last official, caravan meeting tonight. I want to send in one last letter, which is not official. Ophelia Bumps has been kept on the move most of the summer and we feel that our time has been well spent. Many people have been appreciative, admitting that we were the first to present the problem of peace as such, and that they had never looked at the problem from our angle of approach.

Some one, about ten years ago, predicted that "high powered" advertising methods would make the service of the salesman unnecessary but we have found that no matter how good your stuff may be there must be that personal contact to register with the public.

It is difficult to evaluate these experiences to me personally. Various new friends make the name of a town mean more than a mere dot on the map. I find myself seeking out articles of an international or economic import, a thing not likely last year. After some of the interviews and addresses we made this summer we feel ready to try the Congressional rostrum! It is interesting to compare those first speeches, which weren't bad, with our later ones, and to note our development as we gained confidence, evolved a broader viewpoint and got our material really in hand.

We've had a delightful vacation, freed from the boredom of having nothing to do. At the end of a profitable summer I want to express my gratitude, so far as words can express it, for the opportunities afforded by the Committee in permitting me to work under its auspices. All the caravaners, certainly, will use their time and influence through the winter. When one gets a conviction, he cannot stop. Very sincerely yours, Dick.[8]

[8] The letters used in this chapter are actual letters, with the exception of the first one which has been compiled from several. I have made a few changes so that the letters have not been quoted verbatim. They were written by William Webb, George Peacock, Mary Roberts and Robert Gronewald.

Chapter XVI

HOME SERVICE SECTION

"We have been deeply moved at this time as we have listened to accounts of the closing of the Mission in France . . . Our thoughts go out . . . and embrace all the members of this Mission, all the workers who have gone overseas under our care to engage in this ministry and service. The roll is a long one, including men and women from all parts of our country, most of whom are now back once more at the home tasks and duties. To all these, whether in America or scattered in other lands in continued service, we send a message of love and affection, of appreciation and gratitude, and we unite in the hope that all those who have worn the star may find new openings for ever increasing service to mankind." [1]

Chronologically, the chapter on the Home Service Section should follow immediately after the chapter on work in France. Plans for the formation of the new committee on Home Service dove-tail, in the Minutes for 1920, with the final reports of service in France. Young men and women who had been too young to join the Reconstruction Units were eager to give some form of service. "Howard H. Brinton, who has been out on college deputation work, told of his contacts with students in six of the Friends' colleges. He reported that there was considerable interest on the part of the young people in the future of the Service Committee work and that as soon as we could outline some definite plans he felt that a number of them would respond to the

[1] Minute sent to returned workers in France, April 29, 1920.

call. The Executive Board was directed to appoint a *Committee on Home Service Work*, such committee to have the same liberties and privileges as any other sub-committee of the American Friends Service Committee." [2]

On paper, it was as simple as just recorded. Young Friends were eager for occupations. If it could not be in France, then it must be nearer home. The new generation was a restless one. The Victorian era was gone forever and with the 1920s came the mad period of activity, when business was booming, when life, like the jazz which symbolized it, was speeded up to a degree not known before. No young person was content to sit at home and wait for something to happen. He wanted excitement and outlet for his energies; he wanted to be in the great vortex, set in motion by the war and which accumulated too powerful a swirl to be stopped by the Armistice. The young person who missed the war did not miss the contagion in the atmosphere. "I don't know where I'm going, but I'm on my way," is the modern version of "Wherefore wouldst thou run, seeing that thou hast no tidings?" "Nevertheless, let me run!"

The Home Service Section was created for the new generation, so that they might have tidings and run, so that they might be on their way and have some intimations of direction. Although it would seem the logical thing to put this chapter far earlier in the book it has been put in this position because the Home Service Section, which evolved from the desire of a few college students to have definite connections with the Service Committee, has developed into the most important piece of work which the Committee is undertaking at the present time,—the Social-Industrial Section, the rehabilitation of the coal fields.

[2] Minutes of the American Friends Service Committee, March 25, 1920.

This has come, step by step, from the desire of the few college students, first reported by Howard H. Brinton in March 1920.

"Wilbur K. Thomas reported that the Home Service Committee was now functioning and that there was every prospect of making this department a very large part of the work of the American Friends Service Committee . . . Workers were engaged in Home Service work as follows: Pauline Ratliff, Fairmount, Indiana, engaged in community service work at Sandy Spring, Maryland; Ralph E. Levis, a returned reconstruction worker now teaching in the Indian School at Tunesassa, New York; James A. Hull, Stafford, Kansas, a returned reconstruction worker, now teaching manual training in the Kansas State Reformatory . . . Helen J. Ellis, a junior at Earlham College, has volunteered for work at Sleighton Farm during the summer." [3]

Just as this new field of service was starting in the United States attention was being concentrated on child-feeding in Germany. There was no Home Service secretary and Wilbur Thomas had very little time to give for the location of volunteer jobs for inexperienced workers. The personnel for Germany consisted of only forty men and women, who, because of the difficulties of their tasks, had to be persons of maturity and experience. It was an entirely different field from that of France, and young college students could not be encouraged to go to Germany.

One finds little mention of the new Committee on Home Service in the Minutes during 1920 and 1921 when child-feeding in Germany and the famine in Russia occupied the attention of the Service Committee but there are reports scattered here and there, punctuating the problems in Germany, Poland, Russia and Austria, which state that

[3] Minutes of the American Friends Service Committee, May 27, 1920.

students have been placed in institutions for the summer, or that Wilbur Thomas has interviewed young people in colleges. When the Service Committee was re-organized at the meeting in September 1924 and the plans took concrete shape in the spring of 1925, the Home Service Committee merely changed its name to the Home Service Section. It had been in existence for five years.

"The object of the Home Service Section is to encourage young people, both within and without the Society of Friends, 'to render service of national importance in times of peace.' It is in direct opposition to the idea that patriotism or loyalty to one's country can be expressed only in time of war.

"During the year, a personal appeal to volunteer for this type of work has been made to practically every member of the senior and junior classes in all the Friends' colleges, and to Friends in non-Friends' colleges. Many have responded to the idea but have been unable to take up the work on account of financial obligations. A number of young people have volunteered, however, and have been placed in suitable positions. Practically all such work is confined to some form of social service work, as we have not been able to find openings in strictly governmental service." [4] During that year there were thirty-one young men and women in various institutions such as Berea College, Kentucky, Hindman Settlement School, Kentucky, Friendsville Academy, Tennessee, Pine Mountain Settlement School, Kentucky, Calhoun Colored School, Alabama, Sleighton Farm School, Pennsylvania, Western Community House, Philadelphia, Government School in the Philippines, Santa Julia Industrial School in Mexico, Frontier College, Toronto, and other places of similar occupations.

The Home Service Section had been struggling for ex-

[4] Annual Report, 1925–1926.

istence during its first years of competition with the relief work in Europe but with the advent in 1924 of Margaret E. Jones, as assistant secretary in the office, and devoting nearly all her time to the Home Service Section, this particular field of work came into its own. It was she who visited among the colleges, trying to enlist young Friends and non-Friends to volunteer for jobs and it was she who corresponded with the heads of the many institutions who were anxious to secure young workers.

"The Home Service Section endeavors to encourage and to open up the way whereby those young people who, in time of war would refuse military service, can show their loyalty to their fellow citizens. The real conscientious objector is the last person in the world to shun social responsibility. For a number of years the Service Committee has been trying to work out plans whereby young men and women could give one year of service to the Federal Government. So far nothing has come of these efforts, as practically all of the government work is under Civil Service, and none of the departments, such as the Department of the Interior, has funds available to pay for a supervisor of volunteers . . .

"We have opened up opportunities in social service work. The problem of the delinquent boy or girl, recreational activities in congested districts, the study of educational opportunities for Negroes and Indians and foreigners, are problems that affect the public welfare." [5]

In the summer of 1927 an experiment was tried in a slightly different field. A student-in-industry group was formed with the expectation that a large number of students would volunteer to secure jobs for themselves in factories and mills, working on the same terms and under the same conditions as the regular industrial workers. Only

[5] Annual Report, 1927–1928.

eight students applied and they had such great difficulty in securing jobs that much time was used up before they began their work. Some of them interviewed forty places before they were taken as employees. It was unfortunate that so small a number of persons tried this first-hand method of understanding the life of the laboring class, but for the eight it was an illuminating and valuable experience. In 1929 came the crash which changed the entire industrial and business world so that the new decade, 1930, began on a different level from the comparatively carefree adventurous one of the 1920s.

Margaret E. Jones resigned from the Service Committee in the summer of 1928 although she returned during the winter of 1929 to give two days a week in the office at Twenty South Twelfth Street. Her place was not filled until September 1930 when Elizabeth Marsh came to the office and on her fell much of the heavy work of the child feeding and relief work in the coal fields in 1931.

The number of applicants for summer jobs increased, and, incidentally with the hard times, so did the number of applicants for remunerative jobs which grew more and more difficult to find. In the summer of 1932 there were four hundred and fifty applications and only sixty-four people received positions. Fifteen of these workers met together for a few days at Pendle Hill, the new Quaker School of Religious and Graduate Study just finishing its first year, in Wallingford, Pennsylvania. This gathering for the volunteer workers was similar to the first conference at Haverford for the training of the Peace Caravaners. It proved to be such a valuable experience for those who attended that in 1933 another conference was held at Pendle Hill to which all fifty-one of the summer workers came. Two small groups of these workers were sent into Boone County, Kentucky, and Letcher County, West Virginia, where the

Service Committee had been carrying on relief programs. Each group lived together in the midst of the regular community, where they had plenty of opportunity to see and discuss social and industrial problems at first hand. "During the summer of 1936 sixty-eight volunteer workers served in twenty institutions located in eleven states . . . They worked in detention homes, migrant work centers, health camps, settlement houses, camps for under-privileged children, Indian reservations, mining towns, Negro schools, reform schools and rural communities. With few exceptions, the workers were placed so that they might be accessible for group meetings during the summer . . ."[6] Fifty-five of the sixty-eight workers attended a conference at Pendle Hill before they separated for their different positions. "The conference hoped to achieve among the workers: first, a sense of fellowship with each other and with the American Friends Service Committee; second, a more workable philosophy concerning the present social order and trends toward change; and third, an understanding of the conditions under which summer volunteers must work, giving consideration to the techniques of group work."[7] Thirty summer volunteer workers attended the Pendle Hill Conference in 1937.

A new development grew out of the experiment tried in the summer of 1933. The experience of the two groups who had lived in Boone County, Kentucky, and Letcher County, West Virginia, had been so valuable that it was decided to repeat this in a slightly altered program, which would be undertaken by the Peace and Home Service Sections, with help from the Coal Section.

In the middle of April two workers went to Greensburg, in Westmoreland County, Pennsylvania, and made prelim-

[6] Annual Report, 1936.
[7] Annual Report, 1936.

inary arrangements for the organization of a "work camp" to which a group of young men and women were to come in the summer, paying their own expenses for the privilege of installing a water supply for the use of the Westmoreland homestead. There was a discussion on the subject of a special uniform for the campers. Such a uniform had not been worn since the Reconstruction Unit returned from France and, although the decision was made that the campers might wear old clothes which were suitable for their jobs, a certain uniformity was attained since the boys wore nothing except shorts, shoes and socks.

The camp began June 25, 1934, almost immediately after the Workers' Conference at Pendle Hill. Wilmer and Mildred Young, who had served in France and Poland, and who have now gone to the Delta Co-operative Farm in Mississippi where they are living among the share-croppers of that community and making an intensive study of that situation, were the directors of the first work camp at Greensburg. There were fifty-six campers, forty-two men and fourteen women.

This camp was an experiment in giving an opportunity for young people to obtain first-hand knowledge of difficult social and industrial problems in conflict areas by working in the communities, to explore the possibilities of social change by non-violent technique and to perform some worth-while job of social significance during the summer. In spite of the fact that the workers paid their own way and had strenuous day-laborers' jobs, young people responded to such an opportunity with so much enthusiasm that four camps were organized in the summer of 1935. A camp for younger boys, under the auspices of the Service Committee and the Friends Schools was held at Greensburg, where the campers graded and leveled the ground for the community center. "The campers at Neffs, Ohio, constructed a much-needed community pool, did relief work in one of the valleys following a serious flood, built playground equipment and conducted a library project in bookbinding. They studied the problems of the coal industry by having discussions led by operators, union officials, and miners; visited mines, attended union meetings and observed arbitration proceedings . . . There were two camps in Philadelphia, one at Kensington in a hosiery textile community where the work project consisted in the grading and leveling of a playground near the Carl Mackley Apartments and the study program dealt with the application of the non-violent technique to the industrial problems of organized labor, especially the hosiery workers. The Bedford Center Service Camp was in a congested Italian-Negro district, which offered unusual possibilities to study and observe the complicated social and industrial problems in an interracial section. The campers cleaned, repaired and remodelled some houses belonging to the Bedford Center and now used as homes and workrooms." [8] The total number of campers was eighty-four.

There were two junior work camps in 1936, one for boys on the Cumberland Homestead in the Tennessee Valley area where they constructed a grist mill for the homestead community and one for girls at the Indian School, Tunesassa, at Quaker Bridge, New York, where they renovated the school buildings.

The five regular camps were well scattered over the country. In the Tennessee Valley, the Clinch River Camp, near Tazwell, "constructed a fish-rearing pool as part of a Tennessee Valley Authority project for stocking Norris Lake. The TVA provided the materials and technical skill and the evenings were spent in the discussion of TVA problems, such as flood and erosion control and the so-called 'power

[8] Annual Report, 1935, with some slight changes.

yardstick'; government attempts to stimulate and regulate industrial and economic life; problems of the coal industry and those of the co-operative movement." [9]

The two Philadelphia Camps at Kensington and the Bedford Center continued the projects started in 1935. A camp was held at the Big Jim Mission, near Norman, Oklahoma, and the workers built a dam that was much needed for erosion control. An effort was made at this and at the junior camp at Tunesassa to study the problems of the Indian. "The seventh camp was held at Dillonvale, in the eastern Ohio coal fields. Here the students, under the leadership of Stanley and Marie Hamilton, transformed what had been an unsightly city dump heap into a well-equipped community playground. Living within thirty miles of Wheeling, West Virginia, provided opportunity for practical study and experience of the problems of both the steel and coal industries." [9] There were 190 campers.

The plans for 1937 include laying a water system and assisting in the development of a new community for displaced miners in the Fayette County homestead; building a work-shop, a road and clearing land for the Delta Co-operative Community; the renovation of several houses at the Friends Neighborhood Guild in Philadelphia; two projects which have been worked out in co-operation with the TVA, one a junior camp for high school age boys and one adult camp; painting and renovating the buildings at Tunesassa and building a community center for the Indians, in co-operation with groups from the Church of the Brethren and the Mennonites. "In the light of their historic convictions on pacifism, the camp will consider the present organization and attitudes of the three religious groups, the present world crisis and the policies which conscientious objectors should follow if the United States

[9] Annual Report, 1936.

becomes involved in another war. Serious attention will be given to government plans for conscription and industrial mobilization and future relations between the government and pacifists.

"This generation of students must face a world threatened by war, torn by class strife and thwarted by poverty in the midst of plenty. They can be defeated by the thought of entering such a world or they can be challenged by it to start, during their student days, the building of a better one . . . Laboring with one's hands makes it possible, as nothing else can, to understand realistically the problems of the working class. Class barriers tend to disappear in the fellowship of hard, physical labor. A new appreciation of the intrinsic value of human personality is born. Work camps are laboratories in which problems of human relations and basic motivations may be experienced." [10]

The Home Service Section became part of the larger Social-Industrial Section which was formed on June 5, 1935. This new section includes the Coal Committee which was formed at the beginning of the child-feeding in the coal area in 1931, the Economic Commission which began in February 1934 at the suggestion of the Social Order Committees of the two Philadelphia Yearly Meetings, the Work Camps and the Home Service Section. The Social Order Section was to be a committee which might take action in projects already under way and those which might come in the future. Homer Morris was made secretary of the entire section. In 1935 Elizabeth Marsh resigned, after her marriage, and Ruth Outland, first holder of the Mary R. G. Williams Fellowship for Ram Allah, Palestine, took her place, as personnel secretary for the Home Service Volunteer Workers. W. Elmore Jackson is secretary of the Work Camps.

[10] Folder on the Volunteer Work Camps, summer of 1937.

Chapter XVII

THE SERVICE COMMITTEE ENTERS
THE FIELD OF INDUSTRY

1

It is necessary to remember that the depression which became universal after 1929 had already affected the coal industry. Immediately after the war, in 1920, there was a period of economic depression in the coal fields of West Virginia, and, in addition to the decrease in the demand for and the output of coal, there was keen competition between the union and non-union mines which resulted in the closing down, to a large extent, of the former because they could not compete with the reduced wages of the non-union workers. Union organizers tried to hold meetings for the purpose of urging all miners to join the union, while operators paid sheriffs to terrorize and exclude union organizers.

By 1922 the situation had become serious and the Service Committee, through its sub-committee of Home Service, sent Walter H. Abel, editor of the *Friends' Intelligencer*, and Drew Pearson, instructor of Economics at the University of Pennsylvania, to investigate in the West Virginia coal fields. They found that the relief fund, a sum composed of Union Strike Dues, was nearly exhausted because the strike had lasted for such a long time; that an unofficial Miners' Relief Fund, raised through the efforts of an editor of a Charleston Labor paper, was rapidly decreasing; that a West Virginia Miners' Relief Committee, an unofficial, but partisan group, had been giving what funds it was able to raise, and that the Red Cross had planned to inaugurate a miners' relief program, but, after taking a stand on the side of the operators, the Red Cross had withdrawn from the field. There were no funds in the state being given for relief and children of both union and non-union miners were suffering.

As a result of this investigation, a small group of workers was sent by the Service Committee to West Virginia in July 1922. One meal a day was given to seven hundred and fifty children for two months until the mines were opened in September. Although the feeding came to an end, clothes were distributed until the following February. Important as was the relief which they gave an even more important service was their co-operation with local agencies and personnel by which means they were able to interpret the needs of the miners to the local public.[1]

2

"In 1924, at the insistence of Secretary of Commerce, Hoover, the coal operators of Pennsylvania and Ohio signed contracts with the United Mine Workers of America at Jacksonville, Florida. This 'Jacksonville Agreement,' providing a fixed scale of wages, $7.50 a day, was to expire April 1, 1927. In 1925, the Consolidated Coal Company and the Pittsburgh Coal Company were faced by ten economic problems:

(1) The soft coal industry was capable of producing more than twice as much coal as the nation needed.

(2) There were two miners for every job in the entire industry.

(3) There was reduced coal consumption because of the increasing mechanical efficiency of power plants.

---

[1] Material for this section taken from *Quakers in Action,* pp. 186–193.

(4) The cost of labor which constitutes 75% of the total cost per ton in the production of coal.

(5) New machinery in the coal industry which increases production and decreases need for labor.

(6) Capital charges on machinery, high taxes and royalties which increase the burden of indirect costs of the coal companies.

(7) West Virginia and Alabama mines operating on a non-union basis which makes wage cutting a feature in competitive price cutting.

(8) Some railroads give reduced freight rates to non-union mines.

(9) Lower taxes on southern coal properties.

(10) Mines which have seams far underground cost more to operate than those which have seams near the surface.

They broke their agreement with the union whereupon their employees struck and in April 1927, when the agreement expired, the remaining coal operators refused to renew it at the old wage rates. As a result the union workers throughout the soft coal districts of Pennsylvania and Ohio went on strike, and, although available statistics are very conflicting, it appears that at least 80,000 men are out, making a total of over 400,000 people affected . . .

"At each mining camp visited were found from sixty to three hundred families living in barracks, long, low frame buildings erected in mid-winter by the miners themselves from lumber donated by the national organization. There is practically no sanitation, two or three faucets of running water and two or three out-houses comprise the average camp accommodations . . . In front of the doorsteps run narrow board walks, the only secure footing in a sea of mud. In such places as these thousands of families have been living since early December when they were evicted

from their houses by the coal companies . . . Several of the
closed mines . . . present the tragic picture of families living in the rude barracks while the houses they occupied
formerly, with windows and doors boarded up, are within
a stone's throw. From vantage points the barracks are
guarded by the famous Coal and Iron Police, officers of the
law, hired and paid by the coal companies, as permitted by
Pennsylvania statutes.

"Peaceful picketing, because of its effect on the morale
of the strikers and its influence on the strike-breakers, is
one of the most powerful strike weapons of the union. In
most places visited . . . pickets were allowed to assemble
in groups of not more than three to accost strike-breakers,
. . . kept under close scrutiny by officers of the law. At
Rossiter, however, a court injunction is in effect which totally enjoins the picketing of every description. This . . .
is indicative of the partisan attitude of the courts of
this district which throughout the strike have, on the whole,
supported the operators . . .

"In many instances where mines are operating, the strike-
breakers and their families are just as badly off as the
strikers. They are crowded into company houses and where
those houses are too near the roadside or are for other
reasons considered by company officials unsuitable for occupation by the strike-breakers, they are living in converted
stables and garages . . . The strike-breakers are largely
of the poor 'drifter' class who have come to the strike
area from regions of unemployment. A large proportion
of them are colored." [2]

"The relation of the miner to his job is not so much that

<hr />

[2] Report of a Joint Committee sent to Pittsburgh area, March 1928,
by the Metropolitan Federation of Unitarian Young People's Societies
and the Metropolitan District Universalist Young People's Christian
Union. Margaret E. Jones refers to it in a letter of May 19, 1928,
as a "fair report of the situation."

'mining gets into his blood' as that nothing else gets there. It is a blind-alley occupation which does not lead to other industrial contacts. The miner not only works in an isolated room, but the whole camp in which he lives is isolated from the industrial world. The miner is in an occupational rut from which he can extricate himself, even in normal times, only with the greatest difficulty. His mining experience is no asset to him as an industrial worker. In fact his work habits in the mine tend to be a definite handicap. He does not fit easily into this rigorous, lock-step, boss-controlled factory organization. The expression, 'Once a miner, always a miner,' does not signify so much the passionate devotion a miner feels towards his job, as it expresses the limited occupational opportunities open to a man once he has become a miner. The miner, in trying to get a new job, experiences somewhat the same difficulties as an ex-convict. The miner's attitude of independence and non-co-operativeness has been so thoroughly advertised that employers discriminate against him when hiring a new man. One of the unemployed miners interviewed said bitterly, 'I had a good job promised me until the boss found out I'd been a coal digger and then he wouldn't take me on.'

"It is little wonder, therefore, that the miner clings tenaciously to his trade, and does not often venture far from the tipple to find a new job. His experience has led him to believe that he can make a better living in the mines than in any other place." [3]

While nearly all industries were booming in the decade of the 1920s, this was not the condition of the bituminous, or soft coal, industry except for a brief period in 1926 when the general strike in England and strikes in the an-

[3] Morris, Homer L., *Plight of the Bituminous Coal Miner*, pp. 68, 69.

thracite coal area of the United States produced an abnormal situation. Conditions in the coal industry were bad before 1929 and the advent of the depression only made worse a situation which was already bad. Gradual shutting down of mills and factories, and the doubling up of families in order to save expenses, reduced, by a large degree, the demand for coal. In 1922 conditions were beginning to be serious. By 1928 they were a great deal worse and by 1931 it was obvious that there would have to be radical changes if anyone connected with the production of coal was to survive.

In February 1928 Sophia Dulles, Edith Coale and Edith Hall arrived in Barnsboro, Pennsylvania, to make a survey in that area. After their investigation they recommended that the Service Committee should concentrate its efforts on feeding school children and this program began a month later, in March, and continued until the end of the school year. During this period nearly a thousand children were given a supplementary lunch of milk and graham crackers.

When the feeding came to an end the workers remained during the summer to distribute shoes and clothing for which there was desperate need. Shoes were purchased but the clothing consisted, for the most part, of second-hand garments sent by interested people to the store-room at 1515 Cherry Street, Philadelphia. Here it was unpacked, sorted, listed, repacked and sent to the field by Elizabeth Marot who gave thirteen years of service in the store-room from 1919 until 1932.

The small group of workers did all they could to remedy the situation by visiting mine operators, superintendents and owners. They talked with miners' unions and the miners themselves. They made every effort to be completely neutral and non-partisan, saying always that they were not on one side or the other, but were concerned to better the condition of the children who were in need of food and clothing.

The presence of persons who were sympathetic and unbiased in that atmosphere of hatred and bitterness had a salubrious and heartening effect.

A small attempt at health work was made during the summer when two third-year medical students, Helen Potts and Dorothy Dunning, carried on a program of health and social work. Grace W. Brown did a remarkable piece of service with the co-operation of an oculist, Dr. Calvin Rush, in fitting sixteen children with glasses.

At Christmas time 1928 the work in Barnsboro was completed.

3

"There are two possible approaches to the Marion situation and the industrial problem in general on the part of those who desire some action. The first is the approach of believers in unionization of the workers. To this group I belong. But I can conceive that men and women of good will, not committed, as I am, to the proposition that the organization of the workers is a necessary step in democracy, may yet recognize the tragic situation that arises when there is no industrial Red Cross to do, in the industrial struggle, anything like what the Friends Service Committee did during and after the international war in Europe. If there are strikes like those in Marion, North Carolina, strikes which are marked by massacre due to the panic-stricken incompetence, if not the cruelty, of the sheriff, and those strikes end in defeat of the workers simply because of hunger, the result only adds to the sum total of human bitterness and the outlook for the peaceful adjustment of our difficulty in the future is made less bright.

"It is for this reason that I should like to see some plan worked out for the American Friends Service Committee to give aid in acute industrial struggles where relief funds run short . . ." [4]

On July 11, 1929, seven hundred workers in a textile mill at Marion, North Carolina, struck because twenty union members had been discharged because they wanted the right to belong to the union; a ten hour day instead of a twenty hour, twenty minute day shift and an eleven hour, twenty minute night shift, and a weekly wage of $12.10 instead of an average wage of $11. One month later a neighboring yarn mill, at Clinchfield, went on strike, adding a thousand persons to the list of strikers. On September 11 the strike was settled, the workers having achieved a five hour reduction on the work week, but twelve of the most active union members were not re-employed. On the following day the president of the Marion mill broke the agreement by refusing to take back ninety-two of the workers and taking in a hundred and twenty-five "scabs" in their places.

Between that time and October 2 there was a continual struggle to make the president live up to his agreement and at one o'clock on the morning of October 2, the night force walked out, leaving seventy-five pickets outside the mill to inform the day shift that a strike was on. When they arrived the sheriff ordered them to scatter and fired tear gas into the crowd. As far as can be ascertained, the sheriff and his deputies then opened fire on the hysterical, blinded mob, killing four men and wounding thirteen, of whom two died later. The strikers were unarmed and it was later proved that they had been shot in the back.

On the following day, forty strikers were arrested for resistance, conspiracy and rebellion, on the charge of the sheriff, issued after his arrest from which he was bailed out by the president of the mill.

[4] Statement made by Norman Thomas.

An eye witness of the events of October 2 and 3 wrote, "I am convinced that when the record of this tragedy is known, it will be unparalleled in the history of industrial disputes in America. There has never been such a brutal, and uncalled for crime committed against workers . . . The whole South must be organized into a strong labor movement if the present intolerable labor conditions are to be improved. And southern workers must not be shot when they do come out on strike." [5]

James Myers, Industrial Secretary of the Commission on the Church and Social Service of the Federal Council of the Churches of Christ of America, visited Marion immediately after the second strike and found the conditions so appalling that he was convinced the people could not get through the coming winter without help. He found nearly a thousand people dependent for daily food on the Emergency Committee for Strikers' Relief and although he investigated the possibility of relief being given by local churches he found that it was impossible for any of them to be impartial. "The M.E. village pastor at Marion is referred to by the strikers as their 'worst enemy.' All pastors and church officials agreed that the best way for a church channel for impartial relief distribution which would include both strikers and their families and non-union families purely on the basis of need, would be to have the American Friends Service Committee take charge of such distribution . . . The Bishop and others added, 'The Friends have done that kind of work before, they know how and are equipped for it, and they would be the best way.' " [6]

The most important service that could be given was to

---

[5] Letter from Tom Tippett, October 9, 1929. Material for summary of events on and before October 2 supplied by his letters.

[6] Brief submitted to the American Friends Service Committee, "Need of Relief at Marion, North Carolina," by James Myers, October 18, 1929.

show the strikers that there were people in the world who harbored neither hate nor bitterness. An attempt to bring kindness and good feeling among these people who could think of nothing except revenge was as important a task as bringing food to the hungry families. Because the ministers were not allowed to be on the side of the strikers, religion had received a black eye and it was hoped that if religious groups in the United States could contribute to correcting this situation, it would build up respect, in the strikers' minds, for the Christian church.

At a special meeting of the Board of Directors and the Home Service Section held on October 17, James Myers presented his story of the situation and asked the Service Committee to take charge of distribution of relief in Marion while the Federal Council of Churches undertook to secure funds. At the meeting of the Service Committee on October 24 this project was discussed and it was decided to undertake it, after a representative had been sent down to go over the field. Frank D. Watson, Professor of Sociology at Haverford College, went to Marion for this purpose and wrote back: "It is a situation of pouring in the oil and wine for the victim left by the roadside. Ultimately the union must come. The spirit calling for it will never die but the present need is a labor of love for those wounded and bleeding in body and spirit in this first clash of the economic struggle." [7]

J. Lawrence Lippincott of Riverton, New Jersey, arrived in Marion on the 12th of November and Hugh Moore, pastor of the Friends Meeting, Winston-Salem, North Carolina, came later on the same day. Elmer Cope had gone to Marion as early as October 9th to distribute relief for the Emergency Relief Committee of New York. There was desperate need for a social worker and a nurse but

[7] Letter from Frank D. Watson, Marion, N.C., November 14, 1929.

it was not until December 2 that Winifred Wildman from Ohio and Ruth Biddle from Philadelphia were able to come. A trained nurse, Betty Fowler from North Carolina, came a week later.

The workers visited families and kept a careful case record of each one; they distributed clothing and they bought school books from a special fund of $100 for children who had none and who had been told by the teacher that they must bring books to school. A Christmas party was given when toys, candy and oranges were handed to every child. "There were two villages involved and these groups were handled separately, coming on alternating days or weeks for both food and clothing." An old store was turned over to the workers and each family came twice a week for rations,—flour, lard, all fat salt pork, dry beans and sweet potatoes. Rice, cabbage and beef were sometimes given, as were also sugar, soda, baking powder, soap, washing powder, matches and kerosene. Feed was given to those owning cows in return for which the owners gave butter and milk which were distributed to the families in the greatest need. Eagle Brand milk supplemented the insufficient supply of fresh milk. All of the work at the food commissary was done by the strikers themselves under the supervision of the social workers. It was impossible to make an adequate survey of the health conditions because the nurse was so busy taking care of immediate calls that she could do little else.

The total number of families cared for from November 1929 until August 1930 was 215; 177 from East Marion and 98 from Clinchfield. This made a total of 1041 persons.

It was expected to close the work by March 1st, 1930, but there were sufficient funds to carry the relief, on a reduced scale, until August. When the staff left in the middle of March, Hugh Moore returned from Winston-Salem for one day a week for a check-up on the accounts and to see that people were getting the help they needed.

"In a quiet, unassuming way the Quakers began their work, the distribution of relief . . . It was with suspicious minds we watched them. They were church people. It became known that Hugh Moore was a preacher. More suspicion . . . They have performed a humane service. What else? To a large degree they have restored our faith in the Christian ministry, in the churches. Ninety-eight per cent of us now believe that there are good Christians still living. The other two per cent wouldn't care whether the church or the devil was rendering the services so necessary to worldly existence and of vital importance to our life hereafter. I only write this letter that you may know from one in the midst of this situation, that regardless of what others may think or say, I know through the Federal Council of Churches and the American Friends Service Committee one thing has been accomplished. A people have been given a renewal of faith; a hope that was lost has been revived in the Christian ministry and the churches." [8]

[8] Quoted from a "Record of an Adventure in Industrial Understanding, the Relief Work in Marion, N.C., November 1929–August 1930" by the Federal Council of Churches and the American Friends Service Committee.

CHAPTER XVIII

RELIEF AND REHABILITATION IN
THE COAL FIELDS

IN the early spring of 1931 the Children's Bureau, whose Chief was Grace Abbott, was asked by President Hoover's Emergency Committee for Employment to investigate conditions of children of unemployed miners in counties of Alabama, Arkansas, Illinois, Indiana, Kansas, Kentucky, Missouri, Oklahoma, Pennsylvania, Tennessee and West Virginia. These were visited during 1931 and a report made by the investigators, giving a black account of the serious situation of these areas.[1]

Not long after this investigation had been started Grace Abbott attended a function at Bryn Mawr College and happened, by chance, to be seated at the luncheon next to Rufus Jones. During conversation on other topics, she mentioned the survey which her Children's Bureau had undertaken and told of the reports which were coming in. She turned to Rufus Jones and said, "Dr. Jones, I wish your Service Committee could do something to save the lives of my children."

On May 13, 1931, Grace Abbott and Fred C. Croxton, acting chairman of the President's Emergency Committee for Employment, came to a special meeting of the Board of Directors of the American Friends Service Committee and presented the situation of the coal fields to this group, asking them to direct relief. On May 27 Grace Abbott and Mr. Croxton accompanied Rufus M. Jones, Lucy Biddle Lewis and Henry Tatnall Brown on a visit to President Hoover to discuss the whole matter of relief work in the coal fields.

[1] "The Social Service Review," June 1932, Vol. VI, No. 2, p. 185.

"They explained to him that the Service Committee does not undertake relief work merely, that it does not exist for that purpose and that there must be combined with the relief work some other aspect of reconciliation or way of life or help to solve the breakdown of civilization at some critical point. This condition in the bituminous coal field does represent a collapse of civilization at a critical point. The proposal is that a few most critical points be picked out first and the work be extended from those points as funds and personnel permit . . .

"Mary Kelsey suggested that the work is not without precedent, since the work the English Friends have done in South Wales is quite similar. Henry Tatnall Brown wanted the Committee to face the idea that this is the biggest job that has ever been offered us. It is the coal problem of the world and the problem of decadent industries . . . Patrick Malin pointed out that we are asked not only to deal with a decadent industry but are asked to deal with it on the borderline of the South where industrial conflicts are intensified by racial conflicts . . . Clarence Pickett said that from the point of view of the office, the personnel is the most difficult part of the undertaking. It all depends on the spirit and quality of the people who go . . . Rufus Jones recalled the definite leading of the Spirit at the time Alfred Scattergood was chosen leader in the German child-feeding work, and said, 'I agree we cannot let go of it when we get in it, but I don't see how we can let go of the proposal before we get in it.' Hannah Clothier Hull has felt the burden of the proposal ever since it first came before the Board of Directors, because they were told at that meeting: 'There is no one else to do it.' Refusal to do it is saying that we cannot face the situation the world is in." [2]

[2] Minutes of the American Friends Service Committee, May 28, 1931.

A Coal Committee was appointed on the 4th of June and at a meeting of this committee five days later the following draft was drawn up, suggesting the principles for the proposed work of the Service Committee in the Bituminous Coal regions:

"(1) After studies of surveys which have been made already by various agencies in the regions involved, it will be our plan to send a delegation of perhaps two persons from the Service Committee, together with one of the surveyors from the Federal Children's Bureau, and their commission will be to pick out two or three of the most needy locations where we can begin relief work.

(2) We shall ask for a clear understanding with:
   a. The Children's Bureau
   b. The President's Unemployment Commission
   c. The Governor and Department of Public Welfare in the states in which we work.

The object of clearing with these agencies shall be to define our relationships with them and to fix clearly the authority that is vested in the Committee. Although co-operating with all agencies involved we shall wish to be free to operate as the need of the community may dictate.

(3) We shall attempt to make in the two or three centers, demonstrations which we hope may be suggestive of constructive steps to be taken in such situations by state agencies, county agencies, coal operators, or other groups that may wish to undertake rehabilitation work.

(4) We shall attempt to be unbiased in the treatment of local unions in their relations with one another, in the relation between organized labor and the operators, and in the relations of organized labor to forces of the state.

(5) Our aim shall be continually to rehabilitate the social and economic life of the miners, ex-miners and their families, either carrying out this function ourselves, or co-operating

with other agencies better equipped to meet the rehabilitation needs.

(6) We ought not to be thought of as attempting in a summary fashion to reconstruct the whole coal industry. Our policy will be to emphasize relief and rehabilitation work in a comparatively limited number of centers, hoping that we may indicate thereby, to some extent, lines along which rehabilitation may be carried out, but expecting the example to be followed by many other agencies.

(7) If in the course of our work we discover situations which we feel need publicity and which indicate weak spots in our social order, we reserve the right to speak out concerning them." [3]

The minimum amount of time for the execution of such a program was suggested as two years. During the middle of June Clarence Pickett made a survey of counties in Kentucky and West Virginia and reported that he had found "intense suffering and the prospect of conditions that would lead to chaos during the coming winter. He was particularly impressed with the possibility of a clear-cut piece of child-feeding, together with rehabilitation that might be promptly organized and carried out in Monongalia County, West Virginia." [4]

On August 4, Clarence Pickett, Rufus M. Jones, Lucy Biddle Lewis, Henry T. Brown and Fred C. Croxton met with President Hoover and informed him that the Service Committee was willing to undertake this piece of work. At a committee meeting held on the following day a statement was authorized for the press:

"Various agencies concerned over the distressing conditions of the children in some localities of the soft coal mining regions of our country have summoned the American

[3] Taken from report of the Coal Committee, June 9, 1931.
[4] Minutes of the Board of Directors, July 1, 1931.

Friends Service Committee to take charge of child-relief in certain areas where the suffering is most acute . . . It is the hope and belief of the Service Committee that the coal mining states, counties and towns will share the burden of this relief and will co-operate with the Quakers in meeting the very serious need of the children and, in many instances, of whole families who are at present suffering by reason of the conditions which prevail in this great industry." [5]

Henry Tatnall Brown was appointed chairman of the new Coal Committee and Bernard G. Waring was made "coal chief" and director of the undertaking, which position he held until September 1932.

It had been hoped that the Red Cross would appropriate a large sum for this work and plans had been made on this supposition, but the Red Cross did not feel that this particular service lay within their province and for a while the Service Committee was afraid the new project would have to be abandoned for lack of funds. President Hoover was able, however, to secure a grant of $225,000 from the American Relief Administration Children's Fund, this grant to be "paid in ten monthly installments, under the condition that these funds are to be devoted to children's relief and applied solely to supplement the efforts of local agencies." [6]

In addition to the initial sum, the Service Committee received during the first year a total of $94,375 from Friends, and non-Friends and this amount includes gifts in kind.

"The Executive Secretary, Clarence Pickett, and Bernard G. Waring, together with Anna J. Haines and Mary Skinner, of the Children's Bureau, have entered into arrangements with county officials and various other social agencies in Monongalia County, West Virginia, so that our share of the

[5] Minutes of a Joint Meeting of the Board of Directors and the Coal Committee, August 5, 1931.
[6] Letter from Edgar Rickard, Vice-President of A.R.A., August 13, 1931.

responsibility involves feeding about a thousand children one meal a day through the public schools. This feeding will open on Wednesday, September 30, 1931." [7] A clothing committee was appointed of which Eleanor Stabler Clark was chairman and urgent requests were sent out to meetings and to individuals to send second-hand clothing to the store room at 1515 Cherry Street and to organize sewing groups for the making of new garments.

"The peak load, for the first year, was reached in April 1932 when approximately 40,000 school children were being furnished one substantial meal a day and in addition milk was being furnished to 7,697 pre-school children and 1,071 nursing and expectant mothers. Relief was given in 563 communities, divided into ten major districts in 41 counties located in the states of Pennsylvania, West Virginia, Maryland, Kentucky, Illinois and Tennessee. A field staff of 55 men and women workers, mostly volunteers who were paid expenses plus a small allowance of $10 a month, was secured . . .

"In each case where new districts were opened up the workers consulted first the county health officer, school trustees, local doctors, mine operators, school teachers, and in some cases, local welfare committees which were already in the field . . . In many cases, local authorities were loath to admit that distress existed. However, as the winter advanced, the services of the Service Committee were asked for more frequently in order to meet the increasing need. As a rule, local groups welcomed our workers and helped in every way with investigations and with the preparation for actual feeding. They made every effort to locate places for serving the meals and found people to cook them, they hunted out the best stores and built needed benches and tables. It would

[7] Minutes of the American Friends Service Committee, September 24, 1931.

not have been possible to carry on the work in the out-lying camps, far up in the hills and sometimes reached by incredibly bad roads, without the help and devotion of the local people, especially the teachers who gave untiringly of their time and strength." [8] Many of these individuals were under-nourished and weak from insufficient food and their aid was given to the Service Committee in spite of great physical handicaps.

Many of the families in the mining communities had been able to produce gardens for the summer and because the frost was late in coming, the gardens lasted longer than had been expected and the lack of food was less desperate in the autumn. But as the cold weather started, the need for food and clothes became imperative. The store-room could not send bales of clothing down fast enough, and although sewing groups started where women cut out and stitched hundreds of layettes, girls' dresses and boys' shirts, and yarn was knit into sweaters, and shoes and overalls were purchased, the demand for clothes never decreased. Charles and Maud Woodruff, who succeeded Elizabeth Marot in 1932, have packed and shipped, from that date until the present time, 150 tons of clothing for the coal fields.

The workers could not be on the field without recognizing instantly that relief was a small percentage of the real needs of the people. At least 100,000 men, probably twice that number, would never be called again into the mines, because of shrinkage in the coal market, the wide scale use of substitutes for coal and also because of the tremendous increase in the use of machinery instead of hand labor in the mines themselves. There were, however, 200,000 men working spasmodically, one or two days a week, never knowing from day to day whether they would be called. There was no

[8] Report of the Child Relief in the Bituminous Coal Fields, September 1931–August 1932.

occupation for them when they were not in the mines. There was no future for them, nor for their sons who would marry as soon as they could so that another generation would be born to grow up without a trade. This prospect depressed the Service Committee workers more than the filth, the illness, the poverty and the under-nourishment which were everywhere. Relief is one thing when it consists in feeding children until their parents can undertake the job again, but it is another thing when it will be needed to feed children and their children and their children.

Alice Davis, a former worker in Russia, and a volunteer in the coal fields, watched this situation until she could endure it no longer. "These men are up against a blank wall," she said. She went to the Extension Department of the University of West Virginia where she found a man who was interested in her problem and he volunteered to teach carpentry every Saturday morning for ten weeks to a group of ten men, two from five different mining camps. This program was started in January 1932.

A donation of $10,000 from the Elmhirst Fund, to be used for rehabilitation only, made it possible to buy equipment and materials and set up workshops in Crown Mine, Fort Grand and Canyon, all mining camps in the vicinity of Morgantown, West Virginia. Homer L. Morris, who had been appointed Field Director of the Coal Relief Section, heard of a man named Bud Godlove who lived in Wardensville, one hundred and fifty miles away. He was a chair-maker, having inherited the trade from three generations of Godloves, or "Gottlieb," as the name had been originally in Germany. Homer Morris brought him to the workshops where he set up the machinery and taught the men, not only the art of making chairs but also how to select the right kind of tree for the purpose while it was still standing in the woods, and how to cut it down and split it. After the tree was selected it had to be purchased from the owner. After it was cut down and split, trucks brought the wood to the shops and then Bud Godlove showed the men how to dry the hickory rungs and force them, after a sufficient period of seasoning, into partly green uprights. After this process, nothing except dynamite could make the chair rickety. He remained at Crown Mine for seven months.

In January 1933 the furniture business had outgrown the inadequate quarters and it was moved to an old junk shop along the Monongahela River in Morgantown and it remained in the junk shop until August 1935 when it was moved into a wood-working factory of the Government homestead at Arthurdale. From being known as just "Service Committee furniture" it graduated to a name and a trademark of its own, the Mountaineer Craftsmen Co-operative Association, or the M.C.C.A., and when, in January 1937, it became part of the Arthurdale Association in order to enlarge the industry and to co-ordinate co-operative activities being carried on in this new community, it kept its own trade-mark and has not, in any way, lost its identity.[9]

In the spring of 1933 Edith T. Maul, who had been working with Alice Davis and had been closely associated with the new project, brought a truck-load of furniture to exhibit and sell at Philadelphia Yearly Meeting. Later she went to New England and to the World's Fair in Chicago. This was the first appearance of the "Godlove" chairs and the small gate-leg tables which have, thanks to her irresistible salesmanship, become widely known and in great demand. $43,000 worth, in approximate figures, has been sold from 1933 through 1936. The M.C.C.A. are now making beautiful objects of pewter and iron with the result that in the spring

[9] Information concerning furniture and M.C.C.A. obtained from Edith T. Maul.

A New House on the Government Homestead at
Reedsville, West Virginia

M.C.C.A. Furniture

of 1937 a telegram was received from Horace Jayne, Director of the American Federation of Arts:

"Through grant of the Rockefeller Foundation, the American Federation of Arts has unusual opportunity to sponsor section at Paris Exposition devoted to American Arts and Crafts. Selected material must be in Paris by last week in April . . . Anxious to include your pair candlesticks and trust that in view of international importance of undertaking you will accept invitation . . ."

The reply was sent back by William Simkin: "We will be glad to have you include our candlesticks in the Paris Exposition . . ."

In April 1936 a permanent show room for the furniture was secured at 1504 Race Street, the Co-operative Center in Philadelphia.

William and Ruth Simkin went to Crown Mine in February 1932 where they made their residence in the mining camp, living in a vacated miner's house. They became an integral part of the community; he organized the rehabilitation project in the workshops while she helped in families where there was illness, nursing the sick, helping deliver babies,—a general adviser for all difficulties.

Mrs. Scott, secured through the Extension Department of the University, taught the women how to weave. Looms were set up after many difficulties and the women became greatly interested in this new occupation. University professors' wives helped to can and preserve vegetables and fruit which the families had raised in their gardens during the summer of 1932 and instead of the future being absolutely hopeless in this district, people were beginning to look forward a little and face the coming winter with more courage.

For two months in the summer of 1932 the relief work was closed and all the workers, except three who were experimenting with rehabilitation projects, left the field. But the need had grown no less and in the latter part of September the Governor of Kentucky asked the Service Committee to return and carry on a similar program for the next winter. The request was repeated by the state of West Virginia, both states offering funds which they could borrow from the Reconstruction Finance Corporation. In January 1933 the Service Committee was in sixteen counties of these two states doing child-feeding. In two counties of West Virginia it was in charge of the entire relief program.

A first attempt to start a health project began in two counties, Monongalia and Logan, West Virginia, in the autumn of 1932 when, in connection with the school lunches, tooth brushes, soap and towels were introduced as part of the routine, and the children were instructed in simple methods of hygiene. A few months later, in February 1933, through the co-operation of the Monongalia County Welfare Board, a volunteer nursing service was inaugurated. Many Morgantown nurses were unemployed and some of these were brought into the work of visiting homes and starting local health centers. Local doctors and dentists co-operated with the Morgantown Council of Social Agencies in removing tonsils and adenoids and extracting teeth asking, either no charge at all, or a fee sufficient to cover the cost of materials. The City Hospital took the tonsil cases for a sum which covered the cost of the laundry and anaesthetics. Children were fitted with glasses and special care was given to the starting of tuberculosis clinics. Winifred Way Wencke has been in charge of this service from its beginning and its value and place in the community was shown in 1935 by the fact that "a vote of confidence in the work of the Health Service was made in the spring by the action of the coal operators and the miners' union making a substantial contribution to it from a fund administered jointly by the two organizations." [10] In 1935 and 1936 the scope of the health work was greatly enlarged by the organization of a Maternal Health Clinic as part of the Friends Health Service. This was made possible by a contribution from Dr. Clarence Gamble of Philadelphia for the employment of a full-time nurse. "The Clinic is under the medical direction of Dr. Raymond Squier of the National Committee on Maternal Health. The Milbank Memorial Fund has made an appropriation to the National Committee on Maternal Health to finance the project. The Logan County Medical Association has endorsed the work of the Clinic and has co-operated fully in the program. As far as we know this is the first Maternal Health Clinic to be organized in the coal fields." [11] The nurse in charge has been Alice W. Beaman.

At a meeting of the Coal Committee on October 9, 1933, Clarence Pickett announced the plans for the winter of 1933–1934. They were called the "Five Point Program in the Coal Fields."

(1) To give a small amount of relief in Monongalia and Logan Counties, West Virginia; perhaps in a few other counties in that state and in Kentucky. This would be carried on with Federal funds. [12]

(2) To continue health work in Logan County under the supervision of Winifred Way Wencke who would establish a clinic and small hospital in the Poor Farm.

(3) To develop the craft work in Monongalia and Clearfield Counties into a training school for additional craft workers. Funds for this purpose had been given by the Federal Relief Administration.

(4) To develop a counselling and recreation service in operating the coal camps. An experiment in Letcher County

[10] Annual Report, 1935.
[11] Annual Report, 1936.
[12] All feeding stopped in June 1934.

during the summer had opened the way for further service in this field which was much needed as operators and newly formed unions were bewildered and anxious to have assistance.

(5) To develop educational and social programs in the subsistence homesteads which have been set up by the Government. This would include libraries and recreational equipment.

One of the unique contributions which has grown out of this program has been that given by the Friendly Advisers. Harold Marley and his family moved into Blue Diamond, Kentucky, on January 25, 1934, and Stanley Hamilton and his family moved into Shadyside, Ohio, on February 4, 1934.

"There is a wide range of educational needs and opportunities . . . The most intensive and best work can be done in small, informal groups, bearing as little resemblance to the traditional school room as possible. Along with the group there would seem to be a need for the use of mass methods in workers' education. The radio, motion pictures, posters, capable speakers for union groups are some means which might be used . . . The United Mine Workers' task has been an almost impossible one in the past year. The reorganization of old fields and the unionizing of fields where they had never dared to appear before has been done . . . It is and should be the task of the American Friends Service Committee to help district and local officers in any and every constructive task. A kindly word here and there or an explanation may smooth over a fancied wrong . . . It should be a part of our work to stimulate and help the unions in the promotion of helpful activities for the men, done in the name of the union, that the union may, thereby, become a greater constructive social force . . .

"Friendly relations must be maintained where possible with the operators in the district . . . In the eastern Ohio district there are at least three kinds of relations where conciliation and understanding are needed,—(1) racial and political divisions among the miners themselves; (2) differences between the miners and operators; (3) racial, social and other differences between the miners and other residents of the open towns . . .

"A worker in the field should help in any possible way with the functioning of and the promotion of any constructive activities of the established agencies. Where there is a lack of an agency . . . one should be started, no matter how small the beginning. In the eastern Ohio field there seems to be needed work along the following lines,—libraries, recreation, parental training and adult education, clinics for children, community and home gardens. There is no answer to such conditions as exist among the miners except a program of rehabilitation, possibly a combination of subsistence farming along with some craft training . . . In several of the mining communities . . . there are co-operative stores. A study of these should be made, as to their experience and success . . . The Service Committee should work with other agencies . . . to take the profit out of the liquor business. These observations and suggestions are made after a residence in this field of only two months." [18]

Two months later Stanley Hamilton wrote: "One devout Presbyterian lady has called in her minister to find out why we are really here. She thinks we must be up to something. The miners seem to accept us but the proprietary group think we must be here for no good reason. Some of them seem unable to understand frankness."

In January 1935 plans were well under way for the starting of the "People's University" in Shadyside and it was hoped to start classes on the 4th of February. "People's

[18] A paper entitled, "Some Problems in the Coal Fields as Seen by an American Friends Service Committee Worker."

University is the name chosen by the Bellaire-Shadyside
Committee on Adult Education which is developing the
plan. Sixteen possible courses and interest groups have been
announced and enrollments are being received . . . If the
committee works on the plan, all along the line, something
very good should come of it." Edwards and Marjory Dickinson arrived in Shadyside to be with the Hamiltons on the
21st of January and classes began on the 11th of February,
not on the 4th as had been hoped. They were held in any
place which was available,—private homes, basements,
churches, superintendents' offices. Some of the subjects were
dramatics, art-crafts, foods, current problems, English, knitting and sewing, contract bridge, municipal government,
parliamentary law, effective speaking, tinkering, music appreciation, wood working. A few classes were held at Neffs,
not far away, and the total enrollment for the first week was
311. By the end of 1936 the total attendance reached 512
in forty classes.

Eduard C. Lindeman, Professor of the New York School
of Social Work has written of the People's University:
"What I discovered was a philosophy and a method so
simple and so humble as to seem almost foreign to this age
of sensationalism and mass reform . . . In a sense rarely en-
countered in these days, these young people, the Dickinsons
and the Hamiltons, were investing their lives in a region and
a folk. They were no longer specialists or experts attempting
to meet the external needs of people; on the contrary, they
were human beings sharing the lives of the people . . . They
actually believed that they could help the miners and their
families, not by doing something for them but, rather, by
doing things with them."

In January 1933 an experiment was tried. A miner and
his family were transferred from the mining community
where they had been living to an allotment of twenty acres

of land in Bell County, Kentucky. The land was deeded to the man and the mortgage held by the American Friends Service Committee.

"In June 1933 [14] Congress passed an act providing for $25,000,000 to be used for the establishment of subsistence homesteads. Preceding that, the Service Committee had been trying out a few experiments in placing families on the land, and this had gained some publicity. I was called into conference with about thirty other people by the Secretary of the Interior, Hon. Harold L. Ickes, to discuss how this Act might be administered,—President Roosevelt having issued an executive order that the funds should be administered by Mr. Ickes.

"Shortly after that I was called to his office and asked whether I would assist in administering this Act under the leadership of Dr. M. L. Wilson, who was then the Administrator of the Wheat Plan for the Department of Agriculture. I agreed to give four days a week and was released by the Service Committee for that amount of time to help in laying such plans.[15] I first secured the services of Homer L. Morris and together we made a study of the worst spots in the bituminous coal areas where we might try out experiments in transplanting miners to the land in an effort to tie up small-scale production of vegetables and grain, chiefly for personal use, together with part-time employment in industry. It was hoped that we might get small industries to move out to these projects.

"I worked from August 1933 to August 1934 with the exception of two months when I was in Europe during the months of April and May and there I was under commission by the Government to investigate some of the work being

[14] This quotation is a statement written by Clarence E. Pickett.
[15] Elizabeth Marsh, assisted by Grace E. Rhoads, Jr., took over the majority of the tasks of the Executive Secretary at 20 South 12th Street.

done by the German, Austrian and British Governments.

"We established four communities of the type mentioned, on an experimental basis,—one in Westmoreland County, Pennsylvania; one in Preston County, near Morgantown, West Virginia; one in Randolph County, near Elkins, West Virginia; and one in Cumberland County, Tennessee,—all designed to drain off surplus mining populations in nearby communities and this experiment resulted in transplanting about a thousand families.

"One of the most important things that we undertook was the establishing of a special school at the experimental community at Arthurdale, West Virginia, in our attempt to make a school which would train the young people of the community to fit into the kind of environment which we are attempting to create. This meant raising a considerable sum from interested persons. The Government built a $125,000 plant and established the school, involving a budget of about $50,000. The school is still operating, although it is now almost entirely a West Virginia school with some supplementary funds from the outside. This project, particularly, has been greatly enriched by the interest of Eleanor Roosevelt who has taken a living and most helpful part in the support of the Service Committee."

The American Friends Service Committee has been so close to these Government Homesteads during their period of development that it is particularly important to stress the fact that the Service Committee has only one homestead of its own which has not gone beyond a very early stage of development.

In May 1936 Errol Peckham and his wife, who have been in the coal fields since 1931 and have been responsible for many of the rehabilitation projects which have been undertaken, moved to Republic, Pennsylvania, in Fayette County, twelve miles west of Uniontown, where they started garden plots for the miners' families. A month later, Carl Landis and his family moved to the mining camp of Orient where he does community work and continues as secretary of the Mennonite Peace Society. He was at one time pastor of the First Mennonite Church in Philadelphia. Levinus Painter, a Quaker pastor from Poplar Ridge, New York, has moved also into that area.

Two hundred acres of land in Fayette County, known as the Craft Farm, were bought in March 1937 with money contributed by various industrial firms and business men. A Trust, The Friends Service, Incorporated, has been established for the purpose of holding the title of the land apart from the American Friends Service Committee. David W. Day, with his wife and two small sons, have moved into the old farmhouse on the new tract of land and he has been made the manager of the Fayette County Rehabilitation Project of the American Friends Service Committee.

As this book goes to press [16] construction on the first unit of sixteen houses is just beginning. There is still some employment in the mines and it will take time before crews of men can be organized, many of whom will have to be taught the rudimentary beginnings of house building, although, on the other hand, because of the varying types of work in the mines, many of them are well equipped for this kind of labor. It is hoped that by March 1939 families will be able to move into their new homes.[17]

[16] July 1937.
[17] Material on Fayette County obtained by an interview with David W. Day.

"And the Lord God formed man of the dust of the ground, and breathed into his nostrils the breath of life; and man became a living soul." Genesis 2:7

"Jesus answered and said unto him, Verily, verily, I say unto thee, Except a man be born again, he cannot see the Kingdom of God. Nicodemus saith unto him, How can a man be born when he is old? . . . Jesus answered, Verily, verily, I say unto thee . . . That which is born of the flesh is flesh; and that which is born of the Spirit is spirit. Marvel not that I said unto thee, Ye must be born again." John 3: 3–7.

Chapter XIX

NOT ALWAYS A MINER

Sewing Meeting, November 1931

THE sun was streaming through the windows when Nancy Evans[1] came into the room at the Meeting House. The long tables, boards on trestles, had been set up and the sewing machines had been wheeled out to the middle of the room. Lucy Warner was busy already stitching green bias binding around a collar.

"You're bright and early, Mrs. Warner!" exclaimed Nancy. "I thought I'd be the first one here this morning."

"Well," Lucy Warner took her foot from the motor of the machine, "I got to thinking last night about those poor children down there in West Virginia till I couldn't sleep. Wasn't it a cold night! I never got warm at all and I had covers and a warm nightgown, but goodness! Down there they haven't anything. I thought I'd try and get a few of these dresses finished up today." She touched the motor and the machine whirred as the needle sped along the edge of the collar.

Nancy went over to one of the long tables and lifted the heavy bolt of green and red striped canton flannel. It felt soft and warm to her cold hands as she unrolled several yards, holding the bolt clumsily. Spreading the material smoothly on the table, she unfolded the brown paper patterns and began to pin them to the flannel. This done, she cut carefully around the edges of the paper.

---

[1] All names and persons fictitious. Material for this story has been taken from letters written by the workers.

Women came in and greeted one another, sitting down in groups after taking a garment from the pile of things which needed hand-work. There was an assortment of gray flannel boys' shirts, white flannel babies' nightgowns, green and red, blue and red striped flannel girls' dresses. At the other long table Hannah Dexter pulled gray flannel from a bolt and pinned brown paper patterns to it. She turned to Nancy.

"Doesn't this break your back? If these tables were a foot higher it would make all the difference."

"I know. I can hardly stand up straight for the rest of the day when I've been cutting out. We may be able to get the things cut out by machine in town. It would save a lot of time."

"How many things do you suppose we've made?" Hannah Dexter asked. "Of course giving only one morning a week isn't much and we haven't been working very long, but we've turned out quite a tidy pile." Nancy straightened up and took the pins out of her mouth.

"I guess I'm getting old. I believe I'd rather do hard work than lean down all the time! Elizabeth Marot and Eleanor Stabler Clark in at the store room at 15th and Cherry Streets told me the other day when I took some clothes in that they can't begin to get enough things to send down. They're getting letters all the time from the workers asking for more of everything, especially layettes and shoes. They say people have the quaintest ideas when it comes to second hand clothing. They received a box full of fancy evening dresses and some silver slippers. People send frilly bed jackets. They can't conceive what it's like down there. Well, I don't blame them, for I can't, myself." Nancy leaned over the table again and pinned her patterns on another length of flannel.

"I've had letters from some of the people down there,"

Nancy continued, "and read the reports that have come up about whole families without clothes, so that the children can't go to school, and babies that have nothing to be wrapped in when they are born, but it doesn't sound real. I went to a baby shower the other day and while I was looking at the pink sweaters and the hand embroidered dresses, I tried to think what it would be like to be expecting a baby and have nothing for it. This friend of mine said she'd been given so many things that there wouldn't be much left to buy for her baby. I wondered how she'd feel if all she had was a flannel nightgown like those over there, but they must seem wonderful if you haven't anything.

"I don't suppose one of us here can really picture what it's like in West Virginia. We sit here one morning a week and cut out, sew and knit because we've been told that clothes are needed and we think we're generous to devote one morning out of our busy lives. If we went down there and visited among some of these families I guess it would come home to us."

Lucy Warner came over to the tables, holding up three dresses.

"Aren't they nice?" she said. "I can't decide which I like better, the red binding or the green on the collars. The red brings out the red stripe, but suppose the child has red hair? Still, I suppose when you haven't any dress at all, it doesn't matter. It's hard for me to realize that there are people who haven't anything." Nancy straightened her back to look at the dresses which were perfectly plain, except for the collar with the bias binding.

"I'd like to see some of these girls when they get their dresses," Nancy said, "but I wish we could vary this pattern a bit and have different materials. I hate to think of a whole place where the girls of all ages go around in these dresses.

They'll look like an orphan asylum. I hope the packers in the store room mix these dresses up and send them to different counties. But yours look lovely and the binding brightens them up a lot."

On the other side of the room women were sewing on snaps, turning up hems, pulling out bastings; some were knitting, their nimble fingers weaving between the needles and the yarn.

"You certainly are a hand at knitting," Bertha Hammond remarked to her neighbor. "I never was much, myself, and I'd rather sew. Those children will look nice in your pretty sweaters. That maroon color is so handsome."

"Well, I'd rather knit than sew," Anna Smith replied, her fingers flying as she spoke. "There are those who can do one thing and those who can do another. I figure these children need sweaters as much as anything else. This flannel doesn't seem very heavy to me." She paused to rub the white material between her thumb and finger. "I don't believe it will hold up after it's been washed a few times and they're making a mistake to buy this cheap stuff. Why, Bertha Hammond, what's the use of putting feather stitching on that nightgown? There's no call to spend time fussing things up any. The plainer they are the quicker you can get them done. Babies down there aren't going to notice."

Bertha Hammond stuck her needle with its blue thread firmly into the hem of the nightgown and smoothed out the fuzzy flannel with her fat, stumpy hand.

"I suppose it is a waste of time," she admitted, "but doesn't it look pretty? I thought maybe a little bit of color would make some poor mother happy. Seems as though a new baby ought to have something a little special." Helen Parrott, sitting on Bertha Hammond's left, looked at the feather-stitching.

"Well, Bertha, you always were sentimental. This will

only encourage people to have more babies. Just so the
garments are neat and well made is all that matters. Takes
time enough as it is and I've half a mind that it's bad for
these people to get too much given to them anyhow. They
ought to be learning to look after themselves instead of getting to rely on charity." She yanked at her needle. "There
now, I've broken my thread again."

"Excuse me for noticing," Bertha Hammond spoke gently,
"but you've put two snaps of the same kind on that neck.
It won't hold together very well. As for their relying on
charity I guess they haven't anything else to do if things
are as I hear with no chance for the men to work in the
mines." Helen Parrott examined the neck of the nightgown.

"If that isn't just too annoying. Well, at least the women
can make dresses for their own children, I should think, if we
sent them the material."

Bessie Elliott clipped a green thread from the dress she
was hemming and turned to Lucy Warner who was putting
a new spool on her machine.

"You know, Mrs. Warner," she said, "I just look forward
to these mornings here at the Meeting House. They seem to
do me good. I didn't know very much about the Quakers
until my neighbor, Mrs. Dexter, started telling me one day
about the work they're doing down in the coal fields. I'd
been wondering what I could do to help those poor people
because I'd heard what a hard time they were having. Every
week I come here I learn something more and I'm so interested in the whole undertaking. It seems lovely for us to
get together and work with one another, because sewing
or knitting is something that we can all do. I love to think
of the homes we are helping and how happy the little girls
will be to get these pretty new dresses and how proud the
boys will be of their shirts. The mothers will be pleased with

these soft, fluffy nightgowns for their babies. It's been a real sacrament for me to join with you and I just wanted to tell you how much I enjoy coming." Lucy Warner sucked her thread and pushed it through the needle.

"It's certainly a pleasure to have you come, Mrs. Elliott. There are some who think it's a waste of time for us to be making the clothes when we might buy the material and let the women down there make them. Maybe that can be done, too, but I can tell you, it never hurts anybody to do something for somebody else and I think the work is as good for us as the clothes are for them." Nancy came over to the machine bringing a bundle of flannel pieces tied together with a long strip of the same material.

"Here's another dress, ready to be stitched," she said. Her back ached and she was hungry but she had forgotten her discomfort. Insistent and impelling was the one thought in her mind. "What good does it do for me to cut out dresses for children when I can't visualize them? Anybody can do this job. I've got to go down there and see these children and do something more constructive than this. I've got to go down there and see for myself."

Miner's Family, January 1932

"Maybelle, you shet up your face! If you don't quit your hollering I'll shove you out of doors. Your Ma's moaning and Ruby's crying and Levoy's coughing. There aint no call for you to be doing anything. Magnoly, you look after Maybelle. If John don't get up here pretty soon with Sadie Brand the baby'll come first. Ma's having a bad time." Will Beemis shook the little girl who sniffed and hiccoughed and wiped her eyes and nose with the back of her grubby hand.

"Come here, Baby," Magnoly said not unkindly, and with

a dirty, greasy rag she tried to augment the hand-wiping without visible signs of improvement. During the lull which followed Maybelle's howling, the sound of a hard, racking cough filled the airless room and a small boy, lying on a pile of rags in the corner, coughed until blood covered his mouth. Nellie Beemis and her oldest daughter, Ruby, were lying on the only bed in the room.

Nellie was in labor and during the intervals between her pains she was quiet but the intervals were so short that hardly a minute passed without her moans. Although the room was cold the sweat stood out on her forehead and rolled onto the dirty sheet which covered the mattress. Her fingers gripped and twisted the thin quilt which covered her and Ruby.

There were no intervals in Ruby's pain. It tore at her flesh every moment and the quilt only augmented her suffering. Without it she had fits of shivering. She tried to lie still for Ma's sake but the terrible anguish of her body kept her shifting and turning. Only that very morning, only an hour ago, when she was heating some water for Ma she had tipped over the kettle and poured the fiery liquid against her side and her leg before she could jump away. Before she could tear off the ragged dress which clung to her skin like sticking plaster, the pain had struck her like needles jabbing into her flesh. The skin had come off with her dress and there was nothing in the house to rub into the burned flesh, no butter, no cream, no ointment. Only a little bit of lard which wouldn't begin to cover the surface of the burn and which was all the rest of them had left for cooking. Screaming with pain, Ruby had flung herself down on the bed beside Ma. Magnoly tried to cover the burn with the part of Ruby's dress that wasn't wet, but Ruby couldn't stand anything touching it so Magnoly mopped up the water with it as best she could and tried to comfort John and

Levoy and Maybelle who had been frightened by the long patch of raw flesh, and the sound of Ruby's screams.

Will Beemis came over to the bed and stood beside it, looking at Ruby and Nellie. He was numb with the tragedy. It was bad enough to have no work and to have another baby coming, but now Ruby couldn't do anything to help and there wasn't anything to do for Ruby. Likely enough this burn was bad enough to kill her if it didn't get treated. He couldn't stay still. He wandered back to the window to look for John. Why didn't he come back with Sadie? He saw the sunlight on the water, far below in the valley. The clouds were almost golden with the sun on them and they blew around the edge of the mountains which formed a rim. He saw these things but they made no impression on him except to make him hate the place more than ever. Here was winter and the cold weather and nobody would get to their cabin. Even when Sadie did get there she wouldn't be much help. He slouched his shoulders under the straps of his overalls and turned away from the window.

It didn't seem right to have the baby born without some kind of outside help. When Ruby was born they had the company doctor and a woman to stay with Nellie. He didn't believe John would get back with Sadie in time, like as not he was off playing, having forgotten. Will looked at his other son. Nobody had wiped Levoy's mouth and the blood had dried as it trickled down the sides. His eyes were large and bright staring from their sockets. His cheeks were thin and drawn. Will knew that Levoy ought to be having fresh eggs and milk, but they'd eaten the last of the chickens, the tough old rooster, and the cow had died, long ago. Will knew well enough what was the matter with Levoy and that he needed fresh air and good food, but they couldn't have the windows open because there weren't enough covers. There wasn't any other room where they could put Levoy.

"My God, Pa. Can't you do something?" Nellie gasped out. He walked over to the bed.

"Is it real bad? John aint come back yet. You want me to go after Sadie? I kinda hate to leave you though I aint much good."

"Can't you and Magnoly take the baby? I just can't stand . . ." The pain seized her again and she lay speechless.

"Come here, Magnoly," Will beckoned to her. "You was here when Maybelle was born. You help Pa."

"Honest, I can't." She crouched in the corner, hiding her face with her hands. Will looked at her helplessly. After all, she was only thirteen. He went back to the bed but he didn't know what to do. Once the baby was born he could wash it, perhaps, and wrap it in an old dress of Maybelle's, but there wasn't any baby yet. Suddenly Magnoly jumped up.

"Somebody's coming, Pa." She ran to the window. "John's back with two strangers."

"Aint he brung Sadie?" Will was disturbed but Magnoly, thankful to see anybody, ran to the door and opened it. Then she ducked back into the corner beside Levoy but as she ran she bumped into Maybelle who had moved. The little girl fell flat on her face and began to scream nor would she be comforted by Magnoly who picked her up. John came into the cabin, followed by two women who were strangers.

"Aint it like I told you," he announced, "though I didn't reckon on Maybelle hollering. I'm glad to get them shoes off, they aint half big enough."

From the Workers' Point of View

It was beginning to get dark when Abby Worthington and Nancy Evans left the cabin. Down in the valley there were lights flickering. The air was cold and the two women sniffed it eagerly.

"Isn't it wonderful to breathe something fresh again? Did you ever smell anything like that cabin?"

"It isn't much worse than many others, Nancy."

"You know, Miss Worthington, what upset me most of all was that little boy lying in the corner through all the hub-bub. He never cried and never made a fuss and nobody ever paid any attention to him. He was so pathetically grateful when I washed his face that I could hardly bear it. My soul! What a place!"

"I know, but all the cabins are alike. Nearly every family has at least one child with T.B., and nearly every woman is just going to have a baby, or has just had one. There's never any food nor clothing. But it isn't often that you have to see such a terrible burn."

"Do you think she'll recover?"

"I think she will, Nancy. It's one of the worst burns I ever saw but as long as we got here so soon after it hap-pened and have been able to attend to it, there's a chance she'll be all right. But there's no hope for the little boy and even if we could get him into a hospital he's too far gone. Poor little thing, the quicker he goes the better. That John's a smart lad, the pick of the lot, I should say. Imagine a ten-year-old remembering that his teacher had talked about some people who could help."

"It's funny the way things happen, isn't it? Here we were, on our way up this holler anyhow when we met him. Did he think he could walk all the way to the town? Did you notice his shoes, Miss Worthington? They were much too small for him and he could hardly walk by the time we got to the cabin."

"Shoes, Nancy! They are the things we need the most. Children can't come to school in this weather without shoes.

MINERS' CABINS

Sometimes there is one pair in a family and the children take turns wearing them. Errol Peckham,[2] in Cambria County is trying to start a project for making them. He says he needs four thousand pair.

"Oh, the solution for all of this," Abby waved her hand to indicate the cabin in particular and the area in general, "is not relief so much as teaching men, like that one we've just left, new jobs so that they can support their own families. There are the old slogans, 'Once a miner, always a miner,' and 'you can't teach an old dog new tricks,' but these men aren't old and they have some pride left. Why shouldn't they learn to make shoes so that their children won't have to go barefoot in winter or wear rags tied around their feet? That man we saw this afternoon looked as though he'd been whipped, but suppose he had another job which paid him enough to support his family, I believe he'd be as good as anybody. What I can't bear, Nancy, are not the new-born babies that have to be wrapped in old rags, or the little boys with T.B.—I saw enough of that in Germany to grow accustomed to it, somewhat,—but the men are the ones who make my heart ache. You heard what he said when we left, 'I can tell you, lady, I'm mighty grateful. Guess we'd lost Ruby and the baby if it hadn't been for you.' I've got so I can tell whether a man could pull himself up if he were getting steady wages."

"What's going to give him steady wages? It doesn't seem as though miners were ever going to be needed again in such quantities and what's that mean for the future? If other jobs aren't created for them we'll be down here for years giving relief, won't we, Miss Worthington?"

"That's just it. Relief is necessary now. That's obvious enough from our experience this afternoon but we've got to spend most of our efforts in thinking up projects which

[2] Actual person.

will make the wage-earner of the family actually a wage-earner. That's the part of this job which interests me the most. There must be other things besides coal mines to which these men can turn their hands, which are used to tools. There must be other tools which they can use as well.

"America is going to get the most intensive social education that any country ever had from this experience. Right now, with everybody out of a job, it doesn't occur to the people that these men are never going to have jobs in the future when things pick up. John Jones may get back to his office in a few years, and forget the depression but Will Beemis isn't going back to the mines. What's that smart lad, John, going to do, or that pretty Ruby if she gets over her accident? What are the boys and girls growing up in cabins like this one going to get out of life? Not one thing. Not unless somebody, right now, begins to direct the miner's talents into other channels. There you are up against another problem. Who's going to pay for this kind of education? We're in a depression period when nobody has any money, people are scared over their own hard luck and won't listen to stories about someone else. Until we can get the whole country awake to this situation anything that we as Quakers do will be little more than a drop in the bucket. I get so discouraged, sometimes, when I think of all the things I want for these people that I wonder whether we'll ever get any of them.

"Take this family we've just seen. It's typical of thousands of families in coal mining districts. Think what it would mean to the Beemises to be back on their feet, to be self-supporting, equipped to bring children into a home that wants them instead of a new baby being one more unwanted mouth to feed. Then multiply what could be done to them by a hundred thousand. I can't think of anything more thrilling than accomplishing a task of this sort."

"You can't imagine, Miss Worthington, how little people

do understand what's happening down here. Perhaps you can but as you were one of the first to come into the field you didn't hear the talk about it. Nobody can conceive of a family like the Beemises. I came because I wanted to see for myself. Once you do see, it gets you. And, of course, what gets a novice like myself is the suffering of the children. You've seen so much of that that you can see through to the deeper tragedy right away. I get side-tracked by the dirt and poverty. That terrible bed and Ruby's burn and the poor little sick boy took up my entire attention. I realize now, after listening to you, that these results aren't as terrible as the reason which made them."

"Here we are back at the car. You're the smart one of this party as it was your idea to bring the flashlight. I thought we'd be back here in a short time. Why did they name that poor mite of a baby Claude? Wasn't the mother pathetic over her joy in having some clothes for him?"

"Did you notice, Miss Worthington, just as we were leaving, she discovered the nightgown had blue feather-stitching on it? You might have thought it was hand-made lace."

"We've got to have more layettes right away. They go like hot cakes. And we've got to start feeding up in that holler."

Meals for School Children, February 1932

"All right, Magnoly, it's your turn on the scales." Self-conscious and shy, Magnoly came forward and stepped on the scales. The teacher, Miss Bell, wrote down in a note book, "Magnoly Beemis, Age 13; height, five feet and one inch; weight eighty pounds." The child noticed Abby Worthington.

"Why, I remember you, Miss. You was up to our house

last month when Claude was born. The other lady has been up and brung me this new dress," she fondled the soft material.

"Don't you look nice?"

"Oh, I just love this dress. Aint this red stripe the prettiest thing, and this red around the neck? I aint never had a dress that was all mine. I git Ruby's things when there's anything left of them."

"How is Ruby?"

"She's getting on good. A nurse come up and fixed her leg all up. She come again the other day and took off the bandages and then put some more on. She acted like she was real pleased."

"All right, Magnoly. Who's next, Miss Bell?"

"Doville Brand." A sandy haired boy in overalls which were worn at the knees and across the seat came to the front of the room. He stumbled as he stepped on the scales and would have fallen if Abby hadn't caught him in her arms. He blushed with embarrassment.

"Doville Brand," the teacher wrote, "age 12; height, 55 inches; weight, 75 pounds." He stepped down and started to his seat.

"That's a nice looking shirt you have on, Doville," Abby said. He straightened up and grinned.

"It sure feels nice."

"John Beemis." None of the other children in the room responded as quickly as John. He was an up and coming youngster as he strode up the aisle. There was nothing awkward or clumsy about him. Abby looked at his feet and John smiled.

"These shoes is great," he told her. "I could walk miles, now." He might be alert and quick but his cheeks had no color in them and seemed pale in comparison with the maroon sweater which came around his neck.

"John Beemis, age 10; height 47 inches; weight, 50 pounds."

"All right, John, thank you."

Abby weighed the ten children in the room while Miss Bell wrote the figures in her book. They were still far below the normal weight. In three weeks of feeding they had gained very little. Five children were still absent with flu. One hardly ever came anyway, Miss Bell said, because she was too black and blue. Her father drank all the time and beat Aline whenever he could catch her. Abby made a note, "Investigate North family."

"Can't you do something about it?" Abby asked.

"Well, he's fair crazy about her when he's sober but when he's had a drop too much he's the devil. She ought to be taken away but nobody's had the nerve to try. He's a terror."

"These children aren't gaining fast enough. Five have gained a little, four are just where they were when we started and one has lost weight. I expected them to pick up faster than this."

"Well, I don't know, Miss Worthington. You know when a car runs out of gas it takes a whole gallon before you can get it going again. Same with these kids. It takes a lot of feeding to get them started gaining. Tommy has been out most of the time since the meals started. Had flu. No cause to worry about him losing, he'll be picking up. They all look a sight better to me with some decent clothes. I'd hardly know them for the same kids. We've got a good cook now, Doville's mother, Sadie Brand, started last week." Miss Bell addressed the school room:

"I guess lunch ought to be about ready. Whose turn is it to find out?"

"Mine!" A high, shrill little voice shouted and a thin hand waved violently.

"All right, Edith, you ask Mrs. Brand if she's ready."
Tense with excitement and the importance of her mission,
Edith walked into the hallway which served as kitchen,
pantry and cloak-room. There was a great kettle steaming
on the smelly oil stove, and on the table covered with an
oilcloth, faded from much scrubbing, were two plates of
thick brown bread sandwiches, and a pile of green celluloid
cups. A faint aroma of Lysol pervaded the atmosphere,
Lysol, flavored with kerosene and cocoa. To Edith the sight
of this improvised kitchen and the heavenly fragrance of
cocoa which filled her nostrils seemed so wonderful that she
stood transfixed and speechless. Even the empty milk cans,
stacked in a basket under the table, were wonderful because
there were so many of them. The big jar of peanut butter
was larger than any she had ever seen. There was something
new on the table, ten round, orange colored balls, smooth and
lovely. Speech returned to her in her curiosity.

"What's them?" Edith pointed to the table.

"Why Edith Thomas, aint you ever seen oranges?" Mrs.
Brand asked. Edith shook her head.

"No, I aint. What are they?"

"They're fruit, to eat. Miss Worthington's brung them
up as a treat for you kids today. What you out here for,
anyway?"

"Miss Bell wants to know is the meal ready."

"Yes." Edith ran back into the school room.

"She's ready, Miss Bell," she piped, her voice shriller
than ever. "We've got yellow balls today and we can eat
them!"

"All right, children, go out and get your cups." The boys
and girls marched out of the school room, scuffing their feet
against the board floor, and they returned to their seats,
each child holding a cup, spoon and plate. Mrs. Brand came
in with a large pitcher and one plate of sandwiches and the

children watched to see who would receive the first cup of cocoa.

"Maybe Miss Worthington would say grace for us," Miss Bell suggested. "Won't you, Miss Worthington?"

"I think it would be nice to have a Quaker grace, don't you?" Abby said. "In a Quaker home we bow our heads and are thankful without saying anything out loud. Shall we all bow our heads and be thankful together for this good food?" The children were very hungry and were disappointed to have a delay but they did as they were told and bowed their heads over the empty cups, all except Edith who was too excited to keep still.

"Thank you for bringing them pretty balls," she said.

Ploughshares, April 1932

"Why land sakes, if it aint Miss Evans coming up on a horse!" Will Beemis called to his wife. "Say, Ma, if I could use that horse a spell I could get the garden piece ploughed up." Nellie came to the door of the cabin to be sure he was telling the truth. Not that Will was in the habit of lying, but it sounded too good to be true. Claude began to whimper at the interruption to his meal. Sure enough, up the muddy road came a horse, carrying Miss Evans on his back.

"I guess she'll be glad though to set and rest long enough for you to use the horse, Pa." Nellie's heart quickened its beat. If Pa could plough the garden piece and have vegetables, she could can enough to last most of the winter. If they could have food to eat for next winter she believed they could get through without so much sickness. What with the extra meals Magnoly and John were getting in school, things had been a lot better. Maybelle looked kind of peaked, but every now and then John managed to bring something home to her, and how excited Maybelle was when he came in with the jar hidden under his sweater. Nellie never asked him how he got the cocoa, but she knew John was smart. Levoy might have got better if they could have given him food to make him strong.

"Hello!" Nancy called. "I thought I'd come and see how you are getting along today. Isn't this lovely weather?"

"You're a mighty welcome sight. Didn't know you could ride a horse," Will laughed. His fingers itched to get hold of the animal and hitch him to the rusty old plough. If he could just have that horse for about an hour! Nancy jumped down.

"You certainly have some mud around here. They told me when I started that I couldn't make it, but I guess a little mud wouldn't stop us, would it, Sandy?" She stroked the horse's nose and fed him a lump of sugar. "Claude is looking fine. Where's Maybelle?"

"She got so tuckered out playing this morning she lay down and fell asleep. She'll be waking up pretty soon. You better wait till she does."

"I'll wait till Mr. Beemis can plough his garden. That's what I've come for. And as long as I had a way to carry them I brought some other things, too. How do you like me in overalls? I couldn't ride up here in a skirt, so one of the boys loaned me this pair."

"You sure make a pretty looking boy." Nellie stood up holding the baby, "Come on in, Miss Evans, we aint very tidy, not expecting no company, but nothing will ever look as bad as the first time you come." Will helped Nancy remove the bundles from the saddle and carried them into the cabin.

"You've got some new steps, haven't you?" Nancy exclaimed. "They look awfully nice. Why, you've fixed the place up a lot." Nellie beamed, waiting until Miss Evans should notice the drapes. "Why! Mrs. Beemis, you've got curtains!" Nellie nodded, proud of her achievement.

"That cloth you give me I made up for Ruby. It made a real handsome dress. I couldn't decide whether to make up the other piece into curtains or a dress for myself, I aint had a new dress for so long, but then, I aint had curtains for longer, and there was just enough for them two windows. The other windows look kind of bare in comparison, but they're in the back and don't show so much. I just set here while I feed the baby and enjoy them curtains. Seems as though the view outside was prettier on account of them." They could hear Will whistling to the horse and the heavy clop-clop of Sandy's hooves.

"We aint had a decent garden for so long, Pa's determined he's going to have one this year. He's got a piece of ground cleared off and was waiting till Saturday for John to hold the plough while he hauled it, but Pa aint strong enough to do that and I kind of worried about it. This horse will make a lot of difference. Maybe we could buy some seeds off'n you. I want to do some canning later in the summer when the truck comes on. Aint no reason why I can't with Ruby to help me.

"You know, ever since you and Miss Worthington come to the cabin last winter and helped with the baby and Ruby, things has looked up for us. Course, we lost Levoy." Her voice trembled and the tears came into her eyes. "But I guess we can't blame anybody for that. Poor little kid, at least he aint coughing himself to death any more. Pa's fixed his grave so it looks real nice. Got a piece of board and carved his name on it. We're going to plant an azalea over him. But Ruby's pretty near well, and Claude here, while he aint fat like I wish he was, eats and sleeps good, and don't cry a lot. As for Pa, instead of his hanging around like a sick dog, he's been trying to fix up the cabin like you can see.

Listen to him out there whistling! Why, I aint heard him whistle since I can remember. He always was crazy about horses and ploughs and all them things. Never was happy in the mines but there wasn't anything else for him to do. His father was a miner and I guess he was just born in the wrong place. Pay was good at first. He aint never had no chance for farming, so he don't know so much about it, but I guess with half a chance he could turn his hand to it. He's kinda handy with any kind of tools."

Maybelle sat up on the bed and rubbed her eyes and, seeing a stranger in the room, she fell back on the pillow gradually turning her head so that she could stare at Nancy.

"Hello, Maybelle," Nancy called to her, "are you waking up? I've brought something for you." But the little girl was sleepy and she turned her face away again. Nancy opened one of the bundles and took out a rag doll. She held it up and called to the child.

"Look, Maybelle, it's for you." Maybelle looked at the dolly for a long time until she could resist it no longer. She climbed down from the bed and walked over to Nancy's chair. She had never seen anything so beautiful and she stood, perfectly still, without moving her hands, her eyes glued to the entrancing object. Nancy put the doll into Maybelle's hand and the child clutched it against her, rubbing her chin against its cotton head.

"Ooh, my dearie," she whispered, then she looked up again at Nancy. "Is it all mine?" she asked, fearful that it might not be hers, after all.

"All yours, Maybelle."

"Ooh, my dearie, dearie," whispered the child, hugging the cotton stuffing. Nellie looked at Nancy.

"Aint that a purty sight?" she asked. "Maybelle aint never had a thing to play with before." Nancy was bending down over the bundle again and she pulled out a piece of blue and white cotton cloth and a hank of green yarn.

"I guess you'll need this material right away," she said as she handed it to Nellie, "if you've made curtains instead of a dress. I thought maybe you'd like it, anyway, and here's some more yarn."

"Oh, say, Miss Evans, aint that cloth handsome! I just can't wait to cut that up." Nellie put Claude, who had fallen asleep in her arms, on the bed and held up the cloth against her faded, patched dress. "I don't mind if I do say it, I hated to give up a new dress for them curtains, though I've had a stack of pleasure out of them. Aint I lucky to get both, now! I've got the pattern you sent up before. You don't mind if I lay this out to cut up right away, do you? I'd ruther sew than eat, almost."

"No, I don't mind. Go right ahead. I forgot to tell your husband that I brought some seeds for the garden with me."

A New Upright, September 1932

Nellie Beemis stood at the door of the cabin, waiting for her husband to come home. It was getting late and although she knew it was silly to worry about him because there was nothing that could happen to Will, she couldn't help it.

She looked out over the garden and sighed with satisfaction at the thought of the jars of sweet, fresh peas and beans and tomatoes stored away for the winter. John was out there now, working till it got too dark to see. It was funny to see how the little boy took to the garden and with Will away most of the time John and Magnoly had done most of the work. John was a smart boy. It might be, she thought, if things kept on this way that there would be a chance for him yet. She saw Will coming up the road and he waved to her. He was tired, she could tell by the way he walked, but it was a different kind of weariness, he didn't come with the dragging step he used to from the mine. He looked younger and he had filled out some.

"Hello, Ma. Think I wasn't coming?"

"No, just happened to step out to see what John was doing. You come along so I waited." She wouldn't let on she had worried that a tree might have fallen on him or he'd cut his foot with the ax.

"Stayed a bit late to finish a chair I was making. Didn't have to finish it but seems as though I couldn't leave it till it was done. I get a piece of wood in my hands and I dunno what it does to my fingers. Gives them the itch so's I can't lay it down. Same's I've seen you with a dress you was making, I guess. Never could understand why you couldn't lay the thing down till morning and finish it when the light's decent, but guess we're two of a kind, Nellie!" They laughed. "Hope you've got something for supper. I'm pretty holler in here."

Ruby and Magnoly cleared away the supper while Nellie got Maybelle into bed. Then she came out and sat with Will on the steps.

"Getting dark early now, aint it? Guess summer's about gone."

"How many chairs you made now, Pa?"

"This one today makes six. It's the best I've done. I got the hang of the thing now. The others aint rickety as once them hickory rungs is set into the uprights you can't get them out, even if you wanted to. The other chairs is kinda uneven; this last one looks as good as anybody could make. Smooth and straight." Will rubbed his hands together as though he were feeling the chair. "Didn't think I'd turn into a chair-maker, did you, Nellie?"

"Can't say as I did, Pa. But seems like you can make

good in it and have a real knack. Going to make anything else besides chairs?"

"Sure, tables, stools now. Maybe sometime we'll be making all kinds of furnishings. Take a while, though. We aint got much space now. Talk about selling some of these things in Philadelphia. Dunno yet, just talk."

"It sounds good, anyhow. If you could have a job steady, doing something you liked I guess I could bear most anything. We need the money, but it aint so much that that was hard as seeing you slouch around all day with nothing to do, eating your heart out. Think the mine will open again?"

"Might and might not. You know how it is, but I'm rid of it. There's plenty to dig coal, too many, God knows, and I aint dying for the chance. Chopping down a tree is a sight better than hacking at a wall of coal. I aint afeared of hard work but around here there aint been no chance to try anything else but coal. What you making?"

"Oh, just knitting a suit like somebody showed me, for Claude. He's getting so big he's growed out of everything."

"Aint it too dark to see?"

"It don't matter. I don't have to see. Can tell by the feel."

"Well, Ma! Don't it beat everything? You and I can see with our fingers like they tell blind folks can. I suppose anybody can do things once somebody shows you how. That Bud Godlove teaching us to make chairs. Why it aint no trick to put rungs into uprights once you know about it from Bud. Who'd a thought this time last year you'd be knitting sweaters and I'd be making chairs? Well, listen. We're going to move."

"Move! What do you mean, Pa? Where can we move to? What about this garden?"

"We aint going yet, not till you get everything canned.

There's a house down near the shop we can have. I won't have to go so far to work and you can be around with the other folks and learn to weave on the loom like I was telling you. Soon as we get everything out of the garden we'll go. Be a lot better for all of us. This aint no place for people to live in the winter. It's all right in summer."

"How big's the house, Will?"

"It aint so big, be a room for the girls to have, though. What's the matter, Nellie? You crying?"

"No, I aint really. I was just thinking of leaving Levoy. Seems as though he was near and I hate to go off and leave him. It's kinda silly to cry about leaving him when he's dead if I can take the others into a better place. I'll go, any time you say."

Cod Liver Oil, October 1933

"All right, kids. Time to come in." Ruby stood at the door and called to the children who were playing outside. There was a chill in the air which meant that summer was over but winter wouldn't be so bad this year because there was this nursery school. She looked at the twelve children who came running to her; their hands and faces were dirty but they didn't have that permanently dirty look to which she had grown accustomed during the last years. There were black marks on Maybelle's stocky little legs, and smears on her face and dress, but her hair was soft and silky and her cheeks were pink. She was turning out to be quite a pretty child, Ruby thought.

The children took turns using the hand basin but they each had their own towel marked with different colored threads and hanging on separate hooks low enough for each child to reach his own. The toothbrushes were marked, too. Nursery school had been going only a week but already the

children were used to the routine of washing their hands
and brushing their teeth and took it as a matter of course.
All except Benny Miller who was new this morning and he
hung back not sure what to do. He had never washed his
own face in his life. Ruby kept her eye on him, and spoke
to the other children:

"You go on in the other room. My mother's getting your
lunch ready and you see how quiet you can sit." She took
Benny's hand. "You haven't any towel, have you? Well,
here's one and you can mark it with the thread yourself.
I haven't another toothbrush today but you can take this
washcloth and wrap it around your finger till we get you
one. You scrub your teeth that way, see?" Benny was
amazed. He found himself standing on a stool, bending his
head over the basin. He stuck one finger into the water and
it was warm. Warm water to wash in! "No, look, Benny,
like this. Take the cloth and wring it out. That's right.
Now, rub your face with it." The warm cloth felt good
against his sweaty skin and he rubbed vigorously. "Now,
Benny, take the soap and rub that on your hands." The
soap shot from his inexperienced fingers and slid along the
floor. "Never mind, take your hands out of the basin and
pick it up." He clung to the soap after that and liked to feel
the lather squeezing between his fingers. The water in the
basin turned dark.

"My! They was dirty," he exclaimed. He and Ruby went
into the other room of the old Hall which Ruby had fixed
up as a school room and joined the children who were waiting, wriggling and squirming in their chairs. She showed
Benny where he was to sit.

"Now, what do we do before we eat?"

"Sing!" Three of the children began before Ruby gave
the signal.

"Wait! Wait! All of you sing together!"

"Thank you, God, for food to eat," they chanted in several different keys. Perhaps they would do better after a while. They were so excited that they couldn't put their minds on the singing. After all, they were only babies of three and four. Ruby held up a big, amber bottle and unscrewed the top.

"You're going to like this better today," she announced. "Miss Worthington who came here on the first day of school told me how to make it taste good." She opened a smaller bottle and poured some drops into a spoon. "That's peppermint," she said as she emptied the spoon into the amber liquid and shook the bottle. "Now, who's ready for cod liver oil?"

"Me!" Even Benny, who hadn't the faintest idea what it was, shouted with the others. It might be honey, because somebody had told him that honey was yellow. Ruby started around the table and each child held up a spoon into which was poured the fishy, aromatic oil.

"Isn't it good!" Ruby said hopefully, "the peppermint makes it taste so nice." But the children were not convinced. They had been obedient but it didn't taste nice. It was just as fishy as ever. "You know," Ruby continued, "Miss Worthington says there aint,—says there isn't—anything so good for boys and girls as cod liver oil, because it makes your bones strong and your lungs strong and your cheeks pink. Miss Worthington knows everything and we're going to have it every day because she wants every nursery school in West Virginia and Kentucky to have cod liver oil. So! Now I guess we're ready for dinner, Ma."

Nellie Beemis brought in the hot plates and set them down on the table in front of the children. Hazel put her mouth down to the warm food and began to lick it with her tongue.

"Say, Miss Beemis," Donald called out, "look at Hazel

here 'side of me. She thinks she's a kitty." Arthur thrust his spoon under his spinach and lifted the whole serving into the air. It fell back on the plate with a flop, splashing the brown gravy over his bib.

"Children, you know how to eat better than that," Ruby spoke sharply. "Take your spoons and cut the spinach into little pieces, like I've showed you."

"I'm too hungry," Hazel apologized, sorry to have done wrong. "Cutting up takes too long." Ruby watched Benny to see how he got on with his dinner, but he was watching Billy next to him and doing as he did. Her eye fell on Florine. Florine was the one child in the school who was really difficult. The others were undisciplined and naughty but Ruby had no trouble with them. Florine never wanted to play nicely, nor co-operate with the others, nor do anything except knock the smaller children down. She had been born with a mean, unpleasant disposition. She was not eating but had pushed her chair back from the table and was kicking her leg up and down. Suddenly her hand shot out and grabbed Rosie's hair. Rosie began to howl.

"Florine's mean," shouted Arthur, glad to find someone sinning more grievously than he had. "Florine's mea—" Ruby cut him short.

"Go on with your dinner, Arthur, and you too, Rosie. She didn't really hurt you. Why aren't you eating, Florine?"

"It's nasty. I aint a going to."

"Have you tasted it?"

"I aint a going to. It's nasty."

"My mother doesn't cook nasty food. The rest are eating it and think it's good. You try it."

"You should be 'shamed, Florine." Maybelle solemnly put her spoon on her plate and spoke with her mouth full. "It makes Ruby cry when anybody says anything 'gainst her school. This food's awful good and it's my Ma who cooks it. You better just stick your spoon in and eat, like us is doing."

Fascinating as this interruption was the children were too hungry to be bothered with Florine's temper. They went on with their meal. Glancing furtively around to see whether anyone was looking, Florine picked up her spoon and took a mouthful. Her stubbornness vanished and she forgot her sulks as the delicious food slid down her throat. Ruby watched her and when the plate was empty asked her whether she would like some more.

"I guess mebbe so. I hadn't ever ate any of this before." When the second helping was gone, Florine called out:

"I aint filled yet. Kin I have another?"

Peaches and Corn Liquor, June 1934

"Gee, Ruby, you look awful pretty. Where'd you get that dress? Say! I guess I'm kinda proud to be taking such a swell girl to the dance tonight. You make me look kinda, I dunno . . . "

"You look awful nice yourself, Jimmie Brand. You got a new necktie, aint . . . You have a new necktie, haven't you?"

"Well, yes," he admitted, "it is new, but folks aint going to notice a necktie like a whole rig. My!" Jimmie's eyes glowed with admiration as he looked at Ruby, radiant in the peach chiffon dress which fell to her silver slippers. He had been so used to Ruby Beemis all his life, always the one black-haired member of the Beemis family, that he had never thought of her as pretty. She was just Ruby, in her poor, faded cotton dresses and her shabby, down at the heel shoes. He heard Ruby had been teaching all winter and done a good job. The folks around said their children looked better and acted better and that Ruby had a real knack with kids. He'd been off to Morgantown, working in the furniture shop and he didn't get home much. Ruby used to be plain, but she wasn't plain tonight. They walked into the Hall where Ruby had had her nursery school and where the dance was going to be. Other couples were standing around, waiting for the music to begin.

"Hello there, Jimmie! You come home? Nice evening."

"Hi, Ruby! Gee, aint that a pretty dress."

"Well, say, you two, you sure look nice together. Didn't know you was Ruby's beau. Where's Andy?" Ruby blushed and tried to be casual.

"Oh, Andy! He never was my beau, Silly. He couldn't come."

"I heard tell Andy's got religion up at the revival. Is it true?"

"Well, you can hear anything if you've got ears."

"You been going, too, aint you, Ruby? How come you wasn't converted along with Andy?" A group of boys and girls had gathered around, eager to learn more about the break between Ruby and Andy, eager to pump her for information.

"Oh, I went once or twice but I'm too busy to spend my time thinking about Hell-fire. Had enough when I burnt my leg. That preacher can get off a lot of high sounding words, but they aren't worth much."

"Is it true that he says dancing is a sin?"

"Yes, that's what *he* says," Ruby admitted, "but I guess he doesn't know much about music. Breathing's no sin, according to him, and dancing comes as natural as breathing to me. Singing hymns isn't dancing. There's more to music than just making sounds with your voice. Sure there is and these dances Miss Worthington's got going appeal to me more than any hymn singing at the church revival. I'm not going to have any religion that keeps me from dancing."

"What's Andy say about that?"

"Come on, Jimmie." Ruby touched his coat with the tip of her finger. "There's Miss Worthington now, talking to Mr. Clinton. Let's go over." They moved across the floor. "I'm not going to talk about Andy to that crowd."

"There aint no call for you to," replied Jimmie, glad to discourage all conversation concerning the absent boy-friend. Abby didn't see them at first. She was listening to Mr. Clinton who had found jugs of liquor in the back of the hall.

"It's just too bad," he was telling her, "I guess we're going to have some trouble tonight." She turned and saw the couple waiting to speak with her.

"Hello, both of you. Don't you look as handsome as can be!" Abby laughed. "That dress might have been made for you, Ruby. It fits very well, doesn't it?"

"Ma had to alter it a little. I can't imagine why anybody would want to get rid of it and send it down here. It looks like new. I never had anything so beautiful."

"How's the family?"

"They're just fine, Miss Worthington. Mother's so crazy about her loom and her weaving she's neglecting everything else. I don't know what she ever did without it before we moved down here. She goes to all the sewing and knitting clubs and the mothers' meetings and gets a heap of enjoyment out of everything. She don't stay at home at all. She's even fixed a pen over at the looms so she can take Claude along with her, when nobody is at home to look after him. Pa and John have got a good looking garden and they're just crazy about that mule. Pa loves it like it was one of his kids! Of course Pa's not at home so much. Spends most of his time in Morgantown in the furniture. Why, say, there he is now! What's he doing here? He told me he was going to some kind of meeting. Oh! the music's beginning."

"Well, run along and dance. I'll see you both again, per-

haps." The music swept through Ruby's body and its rhythm
lifted her so that she moved like a petal floating in water,
like a field of wheat bowing in the wind. She lost all sense
of time and space. There was nothing except music, except the rhythm to which her heart beat and her breath
came. She forgot the peach folds of her dress, which clung
to her hips and billowed around her legs, she forgot the silver shoes and sheer stockings. Her black hair brushed
against Jimmie's cheek, but she had forgotten that she was
close to him.

Will Beemis leaned against the wall and watched the
couples as they wound about among one another, his eye
following Ruby's black head as she floated along in Jimmie's
arms. It was not hard to see her, her light dress and dark
hair made her conspicuous to everyone and for Will Beemis
there was only one person in the room,—Ruby, his oldest
child. She had been born when there was some money to
spend and when things were going pretty well so that he
and Nellie could have a decent house with nice furniture.
He had thought it was nice then, but it was flimsy and cheap
compared to what he could make now.

It had nearly killed him to see his children wearing ragged clothes, going hungry, and to have Levoy die just because he couldn't have what he should. He remembered the
day Ruby burned herself and he thought she would die.
Then he had thought it would be better if she did, buried
up in that holler there wasn't any future for her.

He looked at the radiant young face, lying close to Jimmie's shoulder, as the couple floated past him. She was
eighteen and grown up and would be getting married herself
one of these days. She was getting what she wanted, now,
pretty clothes, books, music and she had turned out to like
teaching. There wasn't anything in the world too good for
his girl. Will Beemis sighed. It hadn't mattered that he had

had to go without things when the mine shut up, but he couldn't bear to watch Nellie and the children suffer. It wasn't right for a man not to be able to work and support his family. He had some pride about it.

The music stopped and Ruby came over to her father.

"Why, hello, Pa. What you doing here?"

"Oh, just thought I'd step in for a bit and see how things was going. Having a good time?"

"Just grand. The music's lovely." Ruby pushed back her hair and adjusted the shoulders of her dress.

"You're looking mighty nice," Will said casually. "Guess you've got a prize tonight, aint you, Jimmie?"

"I'll say so!"

"You going back to the shop pretty soon?"

"Yes, I'll be going back? Are you?"

"Oh, sure. I come and go. Just the kind of place for us, aint it? Anybody with a hankering for tools can't keep away from there long. I reckoned John needed some help on the garden, but I'll be going back tomorrow or the next day, likely. Well, go along, don't bother about the old man." He watched them as they went off together. "He'd make a good husband for Ruby. That Andy she's been going around with aint got no guts. Jimmie's got 'em and he's a smart one." He saw Jake Burroughs standing in the doorway and Will stuck his hands in his pockets. So Jake had come. Will strolled over to the front of the hall, noticing as he did so that Ruby was dancing with somebody else. That was all right. The boys would all want to dance with her, but he hoped she'd stick to Jimmie and forget Andy.

"Howdy, Jake," he drawled. "The young folks is having a good time, aint they?"

"Didn't expect to be seeing you here, Will. Didn't know you free-quented these shindigs. Thought you was in Morgantown?"

"Well, I can't say I come often, but just thought I'd drop in and have a look. I'm restless, you know; I come and go. What's brung you, Jake?"

"Oh, same's you, I guess. I like to see a pretty bit of flesh, myself. Your gal looks mighty fine tonight. Mebbe she'll give me a dance." Jake laughed loudly, blowing his breath, heavy with liquor, into Will's face.

"I guess she's got all her dances taken."

"Oh, that aint no matter. I guess I can cut in as good as anybody, even if I aint so young." Will nodded his head toward the door.

"Come on out, Jake. I'd like to have a word with you." The two men slipped out and walked around to the back in the warm dusk. Will could hear the music and the scraping of feet on the old floor. Ruby was in there. His hand closed around the jack knife in his pocket.

"Look here, Jake, what's your idea in bringing liquor to this dance?"

"What d'you mean, liquor?"

"You know damn well what I mean. Them jugs has been setting in the back here since last night. There aint going to be no drinking at this party."

"What's come over you, Will? Got the Jesus bug? Preacher got you all scared?"

"I aint been to the revival, if that's what you mean. But there aint going to be drinking at these dances, Jake Burroughs. Can't you leave these young folks alone when they're having a good time?"

"Can't have a good time without liquor."

"Looks like they was having a good time, don't it? There aint no call for you to be bringing your filthy stuff in. What's your idea? The Quakers is trying to put a stop to drinking at the dances."

"To hell with the Quakers. We could get along a sight

better without them sticking their damn noses into everything. They're worse than the preacher at the revival."

"I want to tell you something, Jake Burroughs. You got a grudge because the Quakers are agin your liquor. If those kids drank that powerful corn liquor of yourn, they'd be wallowing around over the floor like hogs. No, sir! I ain't going to stand for my gal dancing with a lot of stewed pups pawing all over her. You kin take your liquor home."

"You can't make me, Will Beemis."

"No? Mebbe not. But I want to tell you something. You're agin the Quakers because they're agin your liquor. Well, now, what's more important? For you to keep on selling it or for them to go on doing what they is doing? You can't see them for the dirt in your eye. You've been giving them a heap of trouble and I'm here to tell you to quit.

"What kind of a place was this afore they come? Everybody down and out, kids starving and dying of one thing and another. Nobody doing nothing cause there wasn't nothing to do. We'd be like it still if the Quakers hadn't come. Why did they? God knows, except they heard tell folks needed help. They fed our kids and give them clothes and they've got work for us that aint had any. They're trying to make us decent, self-respecting folks down here that don't need no more charity and then what happens? Somebody like you comes along, sore because liquor aint in their program. It gives me the belly-ache to see you sneaking your stuff into a dance hall full of young kids that aint got no judgment nor sense enough not to drink. After all the Quakers has done for me and my kids, I kin at least help them keep their parties decent."

"How come you know about the jugs, Will?"

"Never mind how I knew. I aint so dumb. Just because I was buried up there in that holler so long don't mean that my brain's dead. Come on, Jake, I'll help you clear out them jugs."

"I aint afeared of you."

"No, I aint much of an ogre, I reckon, but you let me help you clear them jugs out or else I'll tip every drop out of them. There's plenty of people right around who'll help me."

Later in the evening Mr. Clinton came over to Abby.

"Those jugs have disappeared, Miss Worthington. Do you know anything about them?"

"No, I do not. I saw Jake come in and then he disappeared. He couldn't have taken them away."

"Somebody has. They're gone."

Will stepped inside and looked until he saw the peach dress whirling over the floor. Ruby was dancing with Jimmie again. The music stopped and Will walked over to them.

"Well, guess I'll be stepping along home, now. You all right, Ruby?"

"Just fine, Pa. We're having an awfully good time. Do you want something?"

"Me? No, I aint wanting a thing. Just stepped in to see my gal all rigged up. A pretty good eyeful. Well, take care of her, Jimmie."

The Beemis Family, August 1937

Will sniffed the air as he came into the house. It was rich and spicy with the smell of tomatoes and it was pleasant to imagine winter coming on with plenty of tomatoes, crimson and juicy in their glass jars. Magnoly was standing over the stove, her face red with the heat, her hair curling in the steam. John came in from the garden lugging another basketful.

"You two young 'uns seem to be mighty busy," Will said. "Where the others?"

"Maybelle's got Claude over to the big house, out of the way. We're going to quit after canning this basketful John's just brought in." Magnoly wiped the sweat from her face with the back of her hand. "Never seen such good looking tomatoes before, have you, Pa?" Will picked one of them from the basket and held it in his hand, stroking the firm, smooth cheek with his rough fingers.

"That there fruit aint no smoother than tables I've made. Seems like this family goes in for smooth finishes. Your Ma's weaving beats us all, mebbe."

"Ma's written a letter to say she'll be home Tuesday. I stuck it on your bed. She says Ruby and the baby are just fine, and Jimmie's so proud! Wish I could see them. Imagine Ma being a grandmother and me being an aunt!"

"Say, aint I a grandfather? Men folks sure get neglected at a time like this. Your ma goes off and leaves me and you forget the kid's my own grandchild. Guess I don't count for much!"

"Aw, go along with you, Pa! You know that aint so. You wouldn't have had Ma stay home, now would you? Ruby needs her and aint we taking care of you all right?"

"Sure you are, Magnoly. I'm only teasing. I can't get over Ruby having a baby of her own."

Will left the hot kitchen and found the letter. He sat down on the bed and pulled the paper from the envelope. Nellie's large, uneven writing filled the pages:

"Dear Magnoly,

Just to say I hope to come home Tuesday. They're going to name the baby Abby, for Miss Worthington. Baby getting on good, so is Ruby. That Clinic she went to all the time has made a lot of difference, I guess. Jimmie so crazy about Abby he grins all the time. He's sure a good husband to your sister. He's one of the best men in the furniture business. Wish your Pa was still here but maybe this homestead is better. He and John can work together, but people here say they sure miss Will Beemis. Hope all's going well at home but then, I aint worrying with you there. You know what to do. Hope tomatoes will wait till I can get back to help. Miss my loom and will be glad to get back. Hug Claudie and tell Maybelle I've got something for her. Your loving mother, Nellie Beemis."

Will sat on the bed, holding the pages in his hand. He was disappointed Ruby hadn't named the baby for her mother. The first baby ought to be named for its grand-parents and it would have made Nellie happy to have the baby named for her. Well, it would have been nice, but he couldn't blame Ruby for calling her Abby. Nobody'd done so much for any of them as Miss Worthington had. If it hadn't been for her and the Quakers they'd still be back in the holler if they hadn't all died by now. There wasn't a thing to look forward to until the day she came into the cabin and helped with Claude and saved Ruby's life. Now there was everything to look forward to, even the new house which he was going to build himself. He had the plot of land on the homestead all picked out and the foundations staked. Any day now they'd be starting the digging. He knew just how it was going to look; he could see it as plainly as though it were an actual thing instead of a dream in his mind and a blue print in his pocket.

It was built of stone and clapboards, painted white. It had a lot of windows and a porch with vines growing up the posts, and shrubs by the steps. Inside the rooms were big and light, a room for him and Nellie, and a big room for her loom where she could teach her weaving. There was a room for Magnoly and one for John and one for May-belle and Claude. There was even an extra room for Maybelle when she got bigger or for Ruby and Jimmie when they came to visit. There was a bathroom with a big white tub.

He had given so much thought to the planning of this house that he knew it as well as the one he was in now. It was the culmination of all his desires, to build a home for Nellie and the children. It meant that he had what he wanted most. There was money enough so that Nellie could go and see Ruby when the baby came, just as any mother would want to. Magnoly was turning out to be smart enough when she had a chance. Here she was, running the house and looking after the little ones and canning the vegetables herself before Nellie got home. John was growing up to be a real farmer with an uncanny knack of making things grow. People were coming to him, young as he was, to ask him questions about soil and crops. Will was amazed to find how much the boy knew. Maybelle and Claude were just healthy animals, but they were clean and decently dressed and Will could take some pleasure in them. When the others were little he was hounded with fear because he never knew where the food was coming from. He couldn't have any fun with them. Nellie told him one day, just before she went to Ruby's, that she was so happy it almost hurt. "Seems like having this loom and this weaving has made me come alive," she said. "I like sewing and I like knitting, but you can't choose colors and patterns in them like you can on the loom."

Tears came into Will's eyes as he sat there, his head bowed over, resting on his hands. "I aint ever asked anything for myself," he thought. "All I've ever wanted was a chance to work so as to support the kids and give them the things they ought to have. If I coulda kept on at the mine and earned enough, I'da been satisfied. It was Hell when there wasn't any work. I guess I'm like Ma over her weaving. If I couldn't have made that furniture half of me would never have come alive. I'd have been half dead, and now they're making me boss on this here homestead I aint got another wish in the world. My kids are growing up to be respectable and people likes them. It's Miss Worthington and the others who knew what we was up against that I've got to thank. Ruby's done right to name her baby Abby, I guess."

Chapter XX

TREND OF AFFAIRS AT TWENTY SOUTH TWELFTH STREET

SIMPLE as it may seem to "dichotomize the cosmos" of the American Friends Service Committee into sections and group the activities under the headings of Peace, Home Service, Foreign or Social Industrial, this method will not include everything. As in every home there must be a piece bag and a hall closet into which to put everything which has no drawer nor closet of its own, so must this book contain a chapter to catch and hold things which could not be classified under specific sections.

There have been three Executive Secretaries since June 1st 1917, when Vincent Nicholson came into the small, downstairs room of the Friends' Institute. During the first year, surrounded by the hysteria and difficulties caused by the war, he interviewed the young men and women who applied for the work in France. He was the first to hold the position so that there were no precedents to follow. With nothing except the backing of his Committee he had to carve out his own methods and keep his head under the terrific pressure brought to bear by the military officials who had little sympathy with the conscientious objector. On August 1, 1918, Vincent Nicholson was called to the draft himself and he had to leave.

Wilbur K. Thomas, Pastor of the Friends Meeting at Roxbury, Massachusetts, was asked to take Vincent Nicholson's place until he should be released from the draft, but this release was a long time in coming. Vincent Nicholson resigned as Executive Secretary and on September 10, 1918, Wilbur K. Thomas was appointed to that position.

When he came into the office the Service Committee was sixteen months old. Work in France was at the mid-point, Russia was remote and mysterious, with information coming out at infrequent intervals. Service in Poland, Austria and Germany was still in the future. During Wilbur Thomas's period of service, he carried the burden and the responsibility of the great relief undertaking. It was largely through his endeavors that the American public became aware of the Service Committee. He made contacts in a remarkable way and he enlisted the sympathy and interest of the German-Americans who contributed large sums to the German-child-feeding, and at the beginning of that period of relief, he responded, without hesitation, to Mr. Hoover's request that the Service Committee should go into Germany. Millions of dollars passed through his hands and hundreds of persons came to the office, interviewed him, asked questions, offered their services and were accepted or refused. He travelled over the United States speaking on behalf of the Service Committee and he travelled through Europe visiting the Quaker centers, trying to understand how the organization which he represented might benefit the different countries in the most advantageous way. During the ten years of service, he was the tower of strength, tireless and dedicated to the difficult and diverse number of duties which he undertook, of the American Friends Service Committee.

He resigned as Executive Secretary on February 1, 1929. Anna B. Griscom spent six months in the office as temporary secretary until Clarence E. Pickett, Professor of Bible at Earlham College, took the position of Executive Secretary on June 15, 1929.

Clarence Pickett came to Twenty South Twelfth Street just before the stock market crash in the autumn. As soon as the depression brought panic and rapidly decreasing contributions he was faced with the problem of steering the Service Committee through the depression in spite of less money and more need. Almost immediately he was faced with the request to go to Marion, North Carolina, and help in that desperate situation. Two years later, in 1931, came the call from President Hoover to go into the coal fields. He has guided the Service Committee, not only through the depression, but through disillusion, through industrial break-downs and through European post-war chaos.

The Service Committee did not begin thinking about social and industrial problems in 1929. Under Wilbur Thomas it had carried on two programs in the coal fields, one in 1922 and one in 1928. He started the office in the direction toward which it has been going during the last eight years. Under Clarence Pickett this work has become as important and as outstanding as the great piece of German child-feeding. His vision and his wisdom have carried the Service Committee into the industrial areas of suffering and into broader education for peace. It was said in 1924 that the past was secure. One feels not only the truth of that statement but the safety of saying, "the future is secure."

Due to circumstances rather than to its point of location, Philadelphia has become the center of the Society of Friends in the United States. This has been unfortunate and efforts to remedy the situation have been made by establishing, at different times, branch offices of the Service Committee in Los Angeles, California, Richmond, Indiana, Chicago, Illinois, and Boston, Massachusetts. There are offices and secretaries in Chicago and Boston at the present time, and in April 1936 a house was bought in Washington, D.C., to be used as a student hostel, similar to the one in Geneva. Grace Lowry, formerly at the center in Paris, became the warden when it was opened in July.

Twenty of the twenty-nine Yearly Meetings in the United States nominate representatives who are members of the Service Committee. There is close co-operation between Twenty South Twelfth Street and Friends House in London where are located the offices of the Friends Service Council, of which Paul D. Sturge is General Secretary. Contacts with all parts of the world will be strengthened by the World Conference.

One of the great functions of the Service Committee has been to bring the Society of Friends closer together. It has, through its various pieces of work, especially the child-feeding in Germany, brought the Society of Friends to the attention of persons who were members of other denominations. When Rufus M. Jones returned in February 1930 from a visit in Europe he reported that he had found many people who were interested in the principles and beliefs of the Quakers and who had a great spiritual hunger for the deeper things of life but who did not wish to sever their church memberships. He conceived of a religious organization which might be termed "A Wider Quaker Fellowship." He was concerned with the fact that, while non-Friends were professing a great interest in the Society of Friends, Friends themselves were not sufficiently aware of the work of the Service Committee.

The Message Committee which had become the Foreign Service Section in 1925 was no longer in existence but a new one was appointed, consisting of six Friends, on March 27, 1930. One of the tasks of this new committee was to encourage inter-visitation among Friends and to find persons to visit scattered and isolated groups of Friends with the hope of bringing spiritual help and fellowship to those who had little contact with the Service Committee and the Society. Another task of the new Message Committee was to serve as a central organization for the non-Friends who were interested in the "Wider Quaker Fellowship."

In January 1932 an article was written by the chairman of the Message Committee, J. Passmore Elkinton, discussing the possibility of an International Society of Friends which would be an attempt to bring distant Yearly Meetings closer together and to decrease the confusion in people's minds when they inquired about the Society and found that there were branches and divisions. A letter was received in May 1932 from an individual who asked to join *the* Society of Friends, not a branch.

The name of the Message Committee was changed in March 1932 to the Fellowship Committee and a year later a proposal was received by this group that a World Conference of Friends should be held in 1935. Twenty-nine Friends were appointed to give this matter serious consideration and they became the nucleus of a large group which has organized the conference. Anna Griscom Elkinton was appointed chairman of this committee in July 1934 and the date of the conference was changed from 1935 to September 1–8, 1937. It has been due to her untiring efforts that the plans for the World Conference have gone through to completion. The number on the committee has increased to 385 and it has been necessary to limit the number of delegates to a thousand persons, each Yearly Meeting being allowed a certain quota.

The conference will be held at both Haverford and Swarthmore Colleges. The topics under consideration will be, the spiritual message of the Religious Society of Friends, the Christian and his relation to the state; the ways in which we can achieve economic, racial and international justice; the past and future contribution of Friends to education; and how Friends can co-operate internationally in a more effective way. Five Commissions were appointed to prepare outlines for study and these have been distributed all over the world, for the use of members of the Society whether they expect to attend the conference or not. This is not the first attempt to bring Friends together for spiritual and intellectual fellowship. Two years after the war, in August 1920, an All Friends Conference was held in London, and in September 1929 one was held at Penn College, Oskaloosa, Iowa.

In March 1935 a sub-committee of the Fellowship Committee was appointed to be responsible for the care and supervision of the Independent and United Meetings which had grown up in different parts of the country and in September 1935 it was decided to enlarge the Fellowship Committee and make it a Council "which shall be formed by the American Friends Service Committee in its capacity as a body representing all Friends in America . . . The controlling aim in the selection of its membership shall be to express in thought and action the essential spirit and the vital aims and ideals of Friends . . . Its primary scope and function shall be the promotion of the spiritual life and health of the Society of Friends, the closer co-operation of existing meetings, the integration where possible of its widely scattered membership, and the formation of closer relations of fellowship with religious seekers and friends of the Friends in all parts of the world . . . The Independent Friends meetings, now scattered over many parts of America, including Friends from different branches of the Society, have presented for some time a baffling problem in reference to the proper affiliation of these meetings, the status of their membership, the preservation of the full membership in the Society of Friends . . . and their right to incorporate new members. In this connection it is now proposed that the Council shall be a central meeting in America for the organization and assistance of these independent meetings."[1]

The official transition from the Fellowship Committee to the Fellowship Council was made at a meeting held in Washington, D.C., January 25th and 26th, 1936. Rufus M. Jones was appointed chairman and Leslie D. Shaffer was made secretary. His office has become the headquarters for the World Conference. In April 1936 a procedure for the organization of independent Monthly Meetings was prepared and the group at Cleveland, Ohio, was the first to establish itself in September. "In effect, the Fellowship Council is a central meeting, acting as representative of all Friends in America."[2]

Pendle Hill, a Center for religious and social study maintained by members of the Society of Friends, opened in the autumn of 1931 at Wallingford, Pennsylvania, under the directorship of Henry T. Hodgkin, former English secretary of the National Christian Council in China. After his death in 1933, it was carried on by John A. Hughes and later by Richard Gregg until the appointment of Howard and Anna Cox Brinton in 1936 as Directors. The relations between Pendle Hill and the Service Committee have been very close from the beginning and in May 1935 it was suggested that the Service Committee might provide field work in conflict areas for a small number of the Pendle Hill students. The Service Committee is now looked upon as a laboratory or work shop for Pendle Hill.

Through the generous gift of a Service Committee contributor, a house has been erected on a plot of ground

---

[1] From the Minutes of the Fellowship Committee, September 26, 1935.
[2] Annual Report, 1936.

adjoining Pendle Hill, to be known as the "Service Committee House" for the use of the Executive Secretary. It was completed in the early summer of 1937 and is now occupied by Clarence and Lilly Pickett and their two daughters.

On October 3, 1917, the American Friends Service Committee moved from the one room on the first floor of the Institute into two rooms on the second floor. After the crowded quarters downstairs the upstairs seemed spacious, for a short time. By 1927 the office occupied the entire second floor of the Institute and when work began in the coal fields in 1931 it was necessary to find more space in the Commercial Trust Building, next door to Twenty South Twelfth Street. Those offices are now being used by the Emergency Peace Campaign.

As the work increased it became obvious that the Friends Institute was not big enough and the Service Committee considered moving to a different location. By a strange coincidence, on the 2nd of October, 1935, eighteen years after the first removal into larger offices, an agreement was drawn up "between the Monthly Meeting of Friends of Philadelphia for the Western District and the American Friends Service Committee for the use of offices in the meeting house at Twenty South Twelfth Street."[3] This property was part of the same building as the Friends Institute but managed by a separate group of Friends.

The upper gallery which ran around the wall of the large meeting house was closed in, making accommodations for eight new offices, all against the windows of the building so that the rooms are light and airy. Room H, which had been used for the Interracial Secretary and for other purposes but was inadequate for the Executive Secretary, was transformed into a larger room and furnished with

[3] Minutes of the Board of Directors, October 2, 1935.

desk, chairs and couch made particularly for Clarence Pickett by the Mountaineer Craftsmen.

The new offices were opened officially at a house warming on February 28, 1936, and dedicated for the use of "one increasing purpose."

Chapter XXI

LOYALIST AND INSURGENT SPAIN

WHEN the first plans for writing an anniversary volume of the Service Committee were discussed in the early summer of 1936 one would have expected the book to close with the chapter on rehabilitation. All relief work in the coal fields stopped in June 1934 and the greatest project to be undertaken was the building of the homestead in Fayette County. One might have said, a year ago, that the Service Committee had graduated from feeding and emergency relief and could turn its attention in the future to rehabilitation schemes and attempts to improve industrial situations. No one could have dreamed that the experience in Germany would be repeated in 1937.

Friends were considering service in Spain before its Civil War. This interest "arose in the first place out of the rather belated response to the long-standing concern of our Friends, Russell and Maria Ecroyd, for a Quaker Center in Madrid. In the spring of 1936 Alfred B. Jacob, formerly an American Friend, now a naturalized British subject, encouraged by the Friends Service Council, visited Madrid, Seville, Albacete, Castellon and other parts to inquire as to the possibility of Friends' service. As an outcome of his report it was decided to liberate Alfred and Norma Jacob to go out with their two children to Madrid in the late summer for an experimental period of one year's service. The outbreak of civil war, in July, made this impossible, but Friends were appealed to from various quarters to take up reconciliatory service in Spain. In September Alfred B. Jacob, accompanied by John W. Harvey, brother of T. Edmund Harvey, visited the Spanish refugees in the South of France, and then went on to Barcelona where they made useful contacts . . .

"When the problem of refugees from the fighting areas became acute, Alfred Jacob returned home to put before the Spain Committee the possibilities of service. It was decided to approach the Save the Children Fund. A joint appeal for funds was made and the response being satisfactory a scheme for feeding children was set going in Barcelona, Tortosa, Valencia, Alcazar and Madrid. Clothing has also been sent to Burgos and canteens set up on that side of the Bilbao Front . . . Whilst the Spain Committee and the Save the Children International Union are cooperating also with other relief organizations in England as well as in Spain itself, they always emphasize their strict neutrality, and their desire to help the sufferers on whichever side they may find themselves . . . The American Friends Service Committee is much concerned over the situation." [1]

No one believed that the war would last very long but as winter came on and there were no signs that the war was going to stop it became evident that Alfred Jacob's program for child-feeding would not be sufficient for the increasing need and suffering. The appointment of a special committee on Spain was authorized by the Foreign Service Section on December 17, 1936, such a committee to make at once "the necessary arrangements in the office for care and forwarding of funds through the Friends Service Council, to make preparation for the receipt of gifts in kind and

[1] "Unity in Diversity," the Annual Report for 1936 of the Friends Service Council.

also to lay plans for the solicitation of funds from our own and various other groups interested." [2]

Sylvester Jones, a former missionary in Cuba, and a member of the Friends meeting at 57th Street, Chicago, was asked to go to Spain for the purpose of consulting with Alfred Jacob and investigating conditions. He sailed on the 20th of December and it was decided to make no decisions on the future work until his return, although tentative plans might be considered and committee organization might be made.

Other groups were interested in relief for Spanish children and nursing and expectant mothers, and representatives from the Association to Save the Children of Spain, the Ethical Culture Society and the Central Committee of the Mennonite Church were present at the meeting on December 17th. The Federal Council of Churches and the Church of the Brethren immediately expressed their desire to participate with the Service Committee, and a small Committee of ten which had been appointed as a Committee on Spain was enlarged. "The Spanish Committee united with the judgment of Dr. Barnes of the Federal Council of Churches, that whatever organization might be set up, the basic concern would be to administer relief as expression of the spiritual concern to demonstrate the power of non-violence to solve conflict." [3]

John F. Reich, who joined the staff of the Service Committee on November 15, 1936, to give part of his time to publicity, was asked in January to give the remaining third of his time as secretary for the Committee on Spain. By March 3rd it was arranged for John Reich to devote three-fourths of his time to Spain and one-fourth to publicity.

[2] Minutes of Foreign Service Section, December 17, 1936.
[3] Minutes of the Committee on Spain, February 3, 1937.

In January the following letter was received by Rufus M. Jones from Señor de Madariaga: "Recently I learned that the American Friends Service Committee is planning to undertake non-partisan relief work in Spain on behalf of the women and children. You have my most urgent encouragement. Please call on me for anything I can do to promote this work. The need is desperate. I hope you can be in the field soon, not only with food and supplies but also with the spirit of good will that characterizes Quaker relief. Unless food and supplies come quickly thousands of helpless people must suffer; unless the warring parties can be reconciled, my country will be torn apart. It was my privilege to know something of your child feeding work in Germany and other European countries following the war. It won my admiration and now that my own land needs the same ministration, I am happy that you have responded to the call."

Sylvester Jones entered Barcelona on the 3rd of January 1937, and visited children's colonies in the Loyalist territory; he entered Madrid on the 12th and was there during the siege. He left Spain on the 20th, came into France, and returned on the 22nd to the Nationalist headquarters at Burgos. He found 150,000 refugee children in Loyalist Spain in need of food and 30,000 war orphans, cared for by the Nationalists, in need of clothing and medical attention.

"It seems incredible. It is as though they had reached a ghastly impasse, with death as the only way out. It is a kind of insanity. All wars lead to mental unbalance and the worst of all is this civil war in which the passions are further inflamed by class hatred. Spain is stretched upon a cross. My rendezvous was also with life,—life that was left to struggle on after war had done its grim work. In the rebel territory are many thousands, how many I do not know, of war orphans. On the Loyalist side hundreds of thousands have fled the war-menaced towns and cities and trekked eastward toward the Mediterranean Sea into the already crowded populations of Barcelona, Castellon, Valencia and Alicante.

"Shall we send food to these undernourished orphans and refugee children and mothers who stretch out their hands in hunger to us? Shall we mediate a love that will reach those who suffer in the dark shadows of this modern crucifixion?" [4]

Sylvester Jones reached the United States on the 5th of February and was present at a Joint Meeting of the Board of Directors and the Committee on Spain held on February 8th. "The Joint Committee was united in proposing that the American Friends Service Committee undertake non-partisan relief work in Spain, especially for refugee mothers and children, with the co-operation offered by the Mennonites, Church of the Brethren and Federal Council of Churches of Christ in America.

"It further proposes that (1) as soon as $10,000 shall be raised, one or more workers should be sent to Spain. The tentative aim for the first year is to raise a minimum of $100,000 and to send from five to six workers. This goal is suggested with the knowledge that the need is far greater than can be met by the sum specified. (2) That materials and personnel be made available to established refugee agencies, both on the Loyalist and Rebel sides unless more satisfactory channels for service present themselves later." [5]

When a full report was made to the regular Service Committee Meeting on February 26 the Committee on Spain

[4] The Journal of Sylvester Jones, "Through Loyalist and Insurgent Spain," December 1936–January 1937.
[5] Minutes of the Joint Meeting of Board of Directors and the Committee on Spain, February 8, 1937.

was authorized, in consultation with the Board of Directors, to proceed as way opened. Directly after this meeting Henry Tatnall Brown offered his services as chairman of the Committee on Spain.

"Twenty-seven bales of clothing and one hundred cases of milk were shipped to Spain on May 1st. This was the largest shipment of clothing handled, at one time, by the Service Committee since post-war German child-feeding. The shipment consisted of about 12,000 new garments, 1,000 pounds of used clothing and 250 pairs of shoes. Eleven of the bales and the one hundred cases of milk were for distribution by Esther Farquhar in Loyalist Spain; sixteen bales by Wilfred Jones in Insurgent Spain." [6]

These two Friends, Esther Farquhar, at one time Professor of Spanish at Wilmington College, Ohio, and Wilfred Jones, son of Sylvester Jones, both well acquainted with the language and both social workers, sailed for Spain on May 5th. They were joined in Paris by Emma Cadbury who entered Spain with Wilfred Jones, going to Salamanca where they visited Count Vallellano, President of the Nationalist Red Cross. "We had a most satisfactory talk with him (on June 9th). He is really informed about the work for children and we feel that food and clothing sent from the United States can go through the Spanish Red Cross to those who most need it. But the headquarters for this distribution is at Burgos so we must take the invoice for the first consignment there and then we shall feel that the work is really starting. This afternoon we were taken to see two sets of refugee children who are at Catholic homes here and are being helped by the Red Cross. They were caught at summer colonies when the war broke out and could not get back to their parents in Madrid. But

[6] Minutes of the American Friends Service Committee, May 28, 1937.

the International Red Cross has made it possible for them to exchange cards with their parents.

"Now we think we can go to . . . Burgos to leave the invoice and to Vitoria to see the representative of the English Catholic Clergy's medical relief. Then I think I shall have done what I can about getting started and shall go back to St. Jean de Luz to meet Patrick Malin. We want first to get our 'safe conduct' for points out of the direct line between Salamanca and the International Bridge where we entered, and if they come tonight we hope to leave tomorrow morning . . .

"Later wounded men from the front were brought in autobuses,—stretcher cases in a big furniture van and other delivery cars and put on a train that had come in . . . I counted seven buses. The men in them had wounds on their heads, legs and arms, most of them limped or jumped on one foot with the help of a cane, some needed a man on each side to help them and a few were carried . . . They were a sorry sight . . . We wondered whether some of them were the laughing, cheering young men whom we saw going off to the front on our way to Salamanca . . . This has been the nearest that we have come to the war. In Irun we saw much destruction, although very many houses are intact and life goes on there as usual. In all towns there are 'Refugios' marked, sometimes by signs but in Salamanca by small white flags, and one sees directions telling how to act in case of alarm . . .

"One sees very well how the people feel that they are trying to save Spain from the terrors of Communism and the power of Moscow and to restore order where there had been chaos . . . We were allowed to look over the official photographs of the atrocities to human beings and the destruction of cities and churches perpetrated by the 'Reds' and could have had copies of them. But they were too terrible! We were shown a book published by a friend of the Reds, showing similar pictures of Nationalist atrocities but were told that these were really pictures of the World War. No! War does not convert one to war!" [7]

As a result of the interview with Count Vallellano, he asked Wilfred Jones to organize relief for the Basque children in and around Bilbao and he has offered free transportation of all goods across Spain. On receipt of this information $800 was cabled from Twenty South Twelfth Street to London to be forwarded from there to Wilfred Jones, and he has started feeding three hundred children a day at the cost of ten cents per child, the same amount which it cost for child-relief in the coal fields. The Nationalist Red Cross, which is a separate organization from the Loyalist Red Cross, is anxious for the Service Committee to increase the scope of its work in the Bilbao territory.

Esther Farquhar is located in Murcia, a town which is the seat of Murcia Province in Loyalist territory. There are 100,000 refugees in this one province, 25,000 in the town itself, who have fled from Malaga. They are housed wherever it is possible to put them, in homes and temporary shelters. Some of them have been put in large vacant buildings, the largest of which contains 4000. This building is called the Pablo Iglesias and is a nine-story factory which has been turned over for the purpose and these people are crowded on the nine floors without any furniture except mattresses. The people of the town are endeavoring to give these refugees one meal a day, although it is a heavy financial burden. Esther Farquhar and Francesca Wilson, who has been in Spain for some months under the Friends Service Council, are giving the children a lunch of milk and crackers.

With the help of a Spanish doctor Esther Farquhar has

[7] Letter written by Emma Cadbury, June 6–14, 1937.

organized a crèche, known as "The Drop of Milk," for one hundred babies. The one hundred cases of milk which were shipped in have been used for feeding these babies and two hundred more cases of milk, with fourteen cases of soap were sent as soon as a sufficient sum of money was available for their purchase. The size of this crèche will increase as supplies are secured.

Patrick Malin, Vice Chairman of the American Friends Service Committee, sailed for Spain on the ninth of June, with the expectation of visiting the relief centers on both Loyalist and Insurgent sides. He will bring back to the Committee in September a full account of the work that is being done by both English and American Friends and it is hoped that he will be available for lectures in the autumn and winter.[8]

"The American Red Cross has given us a letter of recognition as the agency doing their work in Spain on a nonpartisan basis and has encouraged their chapters to do everything they can to assist now."[9]

[8] The material for the latter part of this chapter has been supplied by John F. Reich.

[9] Letter from Clarence E. Pickett, July 21, 1937.

"I give you the end of a golden string;
 Only wind it into a ball,
It will lead you in at Heaven's gate,
 Built in Jerusalem's wall."

WILLIAM BLAKE

CHAPTER XXII

THE SWING OF THE PENDULUM[1]

"I THINK we've had about enough exercise, don't you?" Abby turned to the young man with whom she had been walking the deck. "I'm ready to sit down." The young man threw the blanket over her feet after she was in the chair and then stretched himself out in the chair beside her.

"Do you mind," he asked her, "if I ask you a few questions? Or are you too tired to talk?"

"Mercy, no! I'm never too tired to talk, David. It's the most extraordinary sensation to be going abroad again to do relief work. You know it's just twenty years ago this spring that the Service Committee emerged out of a concern for reconstruction work in France. It will be twenty years ago in September since I sailed. After spending the last six years in an attempt to do away with the need for relief by rehabilitating the coal areas it seems particularly extraordinary to have the pendulum swing back again. I suppose Spain won't be just like France during the World War although I don't know why it shouldn't be. War isn't very original in its forms of devastation,—air raids, houses and villages destroyed, children hungry and separated from their families,—the kind of desolation which never seems to matter to those who instigate fighting. But here! I have

[1] Many of the topics of the discussion in this chapter are taken from answers to the questionnaire which was sent out last winter. These have been woven into the narrative in an attempt to evaluate the American Friends Service Committee.

started to talk without giving you a chance to ask me a question! I am sorry, David."

"But, Miss Worthington," David Wilson spoke eagerly, "don't you see that that's just what I want? Think how much you know and I don't. You've been with the Service Committee for so long and have so much background for this work we're going to, whereas I've known the Service Committee at long range all my life and never had a close contact with it. I used to hear about the Mission in France from my uncle, Tyler Wilson. Did you know him?"

"Know him! I should think I did. He was in a hospital near where I was that first year, '17 and '18, and he used to come up often on Sunday afternoons. You're his nephew?"

"Yes, he's father's second brother. He used to tell me a lot about his experiences. You must have had an awfully good time in France."

"Well, I suppose we did, David, looking back on it. But at the time we were under a terrific strain and tension. It was cold and we didn't have much variety in the food and we did have to work to the bone. It's never exactly restful to be living in a war zone. It's all like a dream now and yet here I am, going right back to it in Spain."

"How did you happen to go to France, Miss Worthington, if it's not too impertinent of me to ask?"

"No, it's not impertinent, David, but it's a very difficult question to answer. I don't believe any of us realized exactly why we were going although it was different, of course, for the men, because they had to face the decision of whether or not to join the army. They had strong convictions, many of them, against war before they went but it was interesting to talk with them after they had been in France for a while and had seen what war was like. Building new houses in that scene of confusion and of destruction made them realize to the full the futility of war and the reason for the Quaker testimony against war. I tried to think at the time that I was dedicated to a great cause but I am sure that the reason I went in the beginning was that France was the most exciting place on the earth in those days. Everybody wanted to go and it offered something which would get me out of the rut I was in. I wasn't very happy and this was a chance to break away. There was nothing very noble about my reason."

"Do you think that my uncle, for instance, and the others who went had more of a religious motive impelling them than the young men of today who go to a work camp or are peace volunteers?"

"It was a more obvious religious motive, David, because there was a religious issue at stake in 1917. But who knows a person's religious life? I talked with hosts of boys in the Mish but I don't suppose I knew more than two or three well enough to discuss religious principles and ideals. As far as I was concerned, religion played a small part in my life when I first went to France, although I was drawn to work with the Quakers because of their spiritual motives. After months of experience I became awake to the real implications of a religious motive and I understood how it was that the Service Committee had been created. It was not only an organization which provided activities for men who had been released from military service but it was doing a much bigger thing; it was releasing creative and spiritual energies in the men and women, wearing the red and black star, to further the building of the Kingdom of God.

"You have to remember all the time that we in 1917 were keyed up by the emotional, hysterical atmosphere in which we were living. We could hardly stop to think what we were doing, nor why. Everyone had gone mad and we were mad, too. Religious emotionalism was all tied up with it. It wasn't until after the war when I was trying to feed German children that I was able to think clearly about my feelings toward the Service Committee.

"Perhaps the world is just as mad now, but the boys and girls in the work camps and other fields of the Service Committee, are not driven by hysteria or emotionalism. I should say that they come because they are interested in helping to unravel the complex social and industrial tangle. They may be studying economics in college and want some practical experience to augment their theoretical knowledge. The Service Committee has become a laboratory for a limited number of young people. It is safe to say that their first motive is an intellectual one. Behind that there is undoubtedly a deeper reason. Those whom I have seen during the last few years seem to me just as religious as we ever were. One girl whom I knew particularly well in the coal fields told me frankly that she came down because she wanted to see the situation for herself and understand more clearly than she could by reading reports. A purely intellectual curiosity. When that was satisfied she saw the deeper meaning that her service in the coal fields might have. Almost as interesting as rehabilitating a group of down and out miners was watching that girl grasp the religious significance of her task. When I see the young people who are dedicated to this attempt to build the Kingdom of God and then listen to some long-faced theologian who says that boys and girls of today have no religion, I know he is wrong."

"During the short time that I've been on this boat, Miss Worthington, I've been trying to analyze my reasons for going to Spain. There were a few reasons, of course, that were more or less obvious. Having been brought up in Mexico I can speak Spanish. I have specialized in sociology and economics and I have had a little experience as a social worker, and I know that the children are in need.

"I ought to have a sufficiently religious background. I lived in Mexico where my parents were missionaries. They sent me to a Quaker College. I have heard a lot about the Service Committee from my uncle and from my sister who was a Home Service worker for three summers while she was in college. My older brother was one of the first boys to go on a Peace Caravan. I was delicate and wasn't allowed to do these things. After I left college I got sidetracked and out of touch with Friends but last summer I went to one of the Institutes of International Relations and I was perfectly thrilled; it brought me back into touch with the Quaker out-reach and when I heard about the trip Sylvester Jones made into Spain last winter, I was determined to offer my services, which I did, to the Committee. I looked on it as a well-equipped social service bureau for the Quakers.

"But I'd never been to Philadelphia and I'd never met Clarence Pickett. When I came on, a month ago, we'd been corresponding, of course, but he was just a well-known name to me. I was pretty sure of myself, when I went into his office, because I had given a lot of thought to Spain. The children needed help and I could speak Spanish. It was all pretty simple, but I hadn't been in his office for ten minutes before I knew that there was more to it than I had thought. He and I talked casually at first, to get acquainted. He showed me a pair of shoes on his desk and said a miner had made them. All that was needed was sufficient money to set up a good shoe factory. He showed me the desk that the Mountaineer Craftsmen Association had made for him when the office was fixed over, and he showed me the red and black star hanging against his window. He didn't show me, but I saw, the pictures of Hitler and Gandhi that he has pinned, side by side, on his wall, showing in a startling way the two methods of action,—violence and non-violence.

"While we were talking the phone rang several times. He had to go out and speak to someone who was in some kind of trouble. There was a pile of correspondence on his desk that he said he had to read before he could go home. And yet, in spite of all these interruptions and the thousand things he must have had on his mind, he seemed to be giving me every bit of his attention and made me feel as though I were the one person who mattered. Busy and tired as he must have been by the end of the day he took me home with him to spend the night. He and his wife entertained me as though they had nothing else to do.

"I can tell you that if I never see him again in my life the few contacts which I have had with him during this last month will influence me as long as I live. It isn't just because of his interest in my particular problems, either. His finger is on the pulse of the whole Service Committee every minute and he cares so much about every one connected with it, the secretarial staff, the office force, the miner who has learned to make shoes, the man who made his desk, the children we are going to feed and those of us who are going. And behind all this intense interest in the different activities one feels the deep, spiritual quality of the man himself. He made me realize a person ought to have more than just proper qualifications of language and training for this job. I've been changing my point of view during these few weeks."

"It's too bad that you didn't know Wilbur Thomas as well. He's quite a different type of man from Clarence Pickett but he also has had a profound effect on the Service Committee. All during those awfully difficult years when the

CLARENCE E. PICKETT

committee was getting underway and undertaking the stupendous mission in Germany and Poland and Austria it was he who put it through. Of course, actually, we on the field did a good deal of the work, but he managed all the many threads of it in the office at Twenty South Twelfth Street and he brought it before the public. Although work in the coal fields began before Wilbur Thomas left, the major job on his hands was the organization of relief and reconstruction; he helped to shape the Service Committee as we know it today, and Clarence Pickett fell heir to it just at the beginning of the depression. Splendid as his contribution has been, it must not overshadow the ten years of really outstanding leadership which Wilbur Thomas gave."

"It's wonderful, Miss Worthington, to be able to talk to someone who has known the Service Committee from the beginning, as you have. Would you mind telling me which piece of work has meant the most to you? Clarence Pickett told me you had been in France, Germany and the coal fields. Is that correct?"

"Yes, that's correct. I'm almost exhibit A. 'I tried it once and have used no other since!' To tell you the truth, I don't believe I can tell you. The fields were all so different that it's like saying which of three friends is one's favorite. They all have their own personalities and rich experiences. France, of course, came first and for that reason, perhaps, has remained in my mind as a vivid and dramatic adventure for which I was the least prepared and therefore was forced to put the most effort into the job. The war was going on during the first year; it was the end of an era and the beginning of a new one. Probably the experience in France had more influence on my own personal life than the other experiences have had because that was the turning point in my whole career.

"Child-feeding in Germany has always been considered by the public as the most important piece of work the Service Committee has done. People judge things by quantity and the fact that we were feeding a million children a day is an impressive one. Not least impressive is the fact that there was a small personnel of foreign workers in Germany and that most of the job was done by the German volunteer workers themselves. Then it was done at a time when feeling against Germany was still high and it was an unusual gesture of friendship to feed children of our recent enemies.

"I sometimes wonder just how effective this gesture has been through the years, on a large scale, I mean. Yet one of the finest by-products of Service Committee work is the German Yearly Meeting which I visited during the summer of 1935. They are a valiant group of Friends, as much so, indeed, as the early Friends in England. I wish the Service Committee could have more influence in behalf of these Friends. We encourage them to stick to their ideals and to remember that others have faced what they are facing, but that is cold comfort. But I suppose I expect too much of the Service Committee.

"Relief in the coal fields has been, to my mind, the greatest thing which the Service Committee has done because the relief itself has been the smallest part of the undertaking. This time the Service Committee has put the emphasis on the re-creation of individuals and has tried to evolve projects which would give the man of the fámily a chance to become a wage-earner once more."

"I gathered from Mr. Pickett, Miss Worthington, that you were responsible for some of these new projects and that the rehabilitation scheme was your idea."

"Oh, goodness, no! Anybody who spent any time down there could see right away that the coal industry was a dying concern and that thousands of men were never going to have work again. It took no brains to see that, just common observation. Relief wouldn't do anything of permanent value because what was needed was to do away with the demand for relief. There were a great many of us working on the problem of the miner's future. We tried one thing and another, in very small groups, and whatever has been done of value has been done as a result of group planning. We've gone along on the trial and error method to a large extent. I've been more interested in this experiment than anything else I've done because it has shown that an individual can be taught a new trade, that he can make the adjustment to something else in order to be a self-supporting and self-respecting man.

"This mission to Spain on which you and I are going is only a temporary one, I imagine. When the war is over the country will slowly pick itself up again, just as France and Germany did. It's natural, of course, that the Service Committee should be giving relief at a time like this, but I want to see it specialize now in creative rehabilitation, not only for unemployed families but for out-worn ideas. It's too early in the game to tell how long child-feeding will be necessary. I am going for a short time, only, just to help organize the work and start the ball rolling. This is a job for you younger people to tackle.

"I believe the Service Committee ought to be even more awake than it is to situations of conflict. It waited to go down to West Virginia until after Grace Abbott had started investigations and until she came and told about the conditions down there in 1931. Then the Service Committee sent Clarence Pickett down. Why wasn't the Committee aware long before that and why wasn't someone sent down ahead of Grace Abbott's Bureau so that we could go to her and ask for her co-operation? I've been worrying about Spain for months and English Friends have been on the job there from the beginning, almost, but here it is May 1937 and the fighting began in July 1936. We're only just going in ten months after the war started. We have a reputation for being first on hand in a crisis but we don't deserve any such honors.

"What did we do about Italy and Ethiopia? Not a thing. We have had no effect whatever in changing Japan's policy toward China. Of course we're a minority group, only a hundred and twenty-five thousand Quakers in the world and the Service Committee is a small part of that number, but we have a reputation that is far greater than we are, and I believe we could do more than we think we could. The League of Nations went to pieces and we all agreed it was a tragedy of the first water, but that was all we did about it. Splendid as our work has been in the coal fields we have hardly touched the surface of conflict problems. Take the share-croppers, for instance, or sweat shops. I can think of only three or four outstanding cases where unique attempts have been made to come closer to such conditions and there ought to be more such attempts. Bill and Ruth Simkin went down to Crown Mine near Morgantown in 1932 and lived in a miner's house, became members of that kind of a community, put up with every inconvenience and disadvantage in order to try to raise the level of the whole group and to understand it. Wilmer and Mildred Young with their children have gone down to the Delta Co-operative Farm in Mississippi to live among the share-croppers, and this takes a tremendous amount of courage because they are bringing up their children away from good schools, good doctors, and playmates of their own cultural background.

"It takes far more nerve to give this kind of service than it does to go into Spain for a few months. Harry and Rebecca Timbres gave this same kind of service in Russia where he obtained a post as medical doctor under the Soviet Government. They lived in a Russian town and their children went to a Russian school. You probably heard, just as we left, that Harry died of typhus and gave his life for this brave adventure.[2]

"The Home Service Volunteers, the Peace Caravans and the Work Camps are all steps in the right direction, but they are not enough. The Service Committee is a capitalistic concern and it is forced to be so because it depends on the wealthy people for contributions. Hugh Moore has an uncanny gift for getting money and he tells individuals that giving money to the Service Committee is the best method of investing their cash. Not that I want to put Hugh out of a job, but after twenty years the Service Committee ought to be so vital a part of the Society of Friends that it would be endowed to carry on experiments in industrial sections and labor areas and try to organize factories and mills on an absolutely Christian basis. I think I may be unfair to criticize the Service Committee unduly. It is, after all, an organ of the Society of Friends and its function ought to be to act as a clearing house for all requests from the Society. It's far ahead of most of the Society which clings to old orders and is willing to sit back on its reputation and considers the Service Committee much too radical. The Society of Friends began as the most radical movement in England and I don't want it to lose that growing, vital, fearless quality."

"One of the things I have noticed particularly, Miss Worthington, since I came to Philadelphia has been the difference between Friends in the West and in the East. Having grown up in Mexico I didn't have much contact with any Friends except my family until I went to a western Quaker college. Perhaps their principles and ideals aren't so dif-

[2] The death of Harry Timbres actually occurred after the two workers had left for Spain.

ferent, but their methods of worship certainly are. A meeting that is organized on the pastoral system is just a different thing from Arch Street where there is no pastor at all."

"It would be a good thing, David, if more Friends could travel back and forth and become better acquainted with these groups. The World Conference may do a lot in that direction, in helping Friends to feel more closely unified, and the Fellowship Council with its emphasis on inter-visitation and its creation of a central meeting which any group can join, will do a beneficial service. Some people think that the most important thing the Service Committee has done, is, not the relief work in France, or Germany, or the coal fields, but the closer amalgamation of the Society. The Committee has done that. Theological and petty differences have been forgotten to a large extent in a common interest but I hate to think that the Service Committee was created for the primary purpose of bringing Friends together. That has been the by-product of a much larger piece of work. The Service Committee is a means to an end, not an end in itself. If it were it would become a stagnant pool with no fresh current of life pouring through it.

"For all the differences among pastoral and non-pastoral Friends, or conservatives and radicals, there are two basic principles in the Society which are greater than any disputes among factions of thought. The first is the principle of peace, i.e., that we should so live as to do away with the occasion for all war. That is not a negative ideal which implies that we don't fight when war comes, although that is included in our doctrine, but it is a positive way of life which means that we do our utmost to prevent a war from coming. The second ideal is the knowledge that the light of Christ dwells in every man, i.e., no man is better than another, therefore no person has any right to exploit or use another individual and we're all potential sons of God. They're such simple ideals that we don't take them seriously enough. If we did we'd transform the universe."

"But you're just re-stating the golden rule, Miss Worthington."

"That's all. And there is no difference between Christianity and Quakerism. Don't let a fence of denominationalism hide you from the love of God which is universal and timeless."

"Is it going to take me twenty years to gain the wisdom which you have acquired? Since seeing Clarence Pickett and now after talking with you all my ideas are shot to pieces. This child-feeding in Spain keeps adding on a new significance all the time and I begin to see that I am not really equipped for the job. Perhaps I'm like your friend in the coal fields who came out of curiosity and nothing deeper."

"The Service Committee has the effect of shooting every preconceived idea to pieces. After you've been in Spain a few months you'll find that the process of growth is still going on. Every theory you started with will have to be changed or scrapped. But it won't take you twenty years, David. I believe that young people are better equipped today than we were when we started off in 1917. You'll get your bearings far more quickly than I ever did, and you'll find much sooner the deeper significance underlying your apparently mundane service.

"I have a feeling that your generation is going to have even more difficult problems to face than we did twenty years ago, or have had during these years which have been the aftermath of the war. We have made a start only, beginning with relief and coming along gradually to rehabilitation. The pendulum has taken another swing and it is men and women of your age who will have to put your brains together and see how you can stop this pendulum. We have done great things but they haven't been enough.

"There will always be suffering and there will always be young people in search of adventure, impelled by curiosity and intellect to reach the bottom of social conditions. I believe a religious concern is a mature form of intellectual interest and cannot be separated from the other reasons which send a person into service. Do you remember what George Fox said? 'I saw that there was an ocean of darkness and death, but I saw also that there was an ocean of light and love which flowed over it.' That is what the Service Committee has done and will continue to do. It is an ocean of light and love which flows over the ocean of darkness and death."

APPENDIX

April 6. The United States entered the World War.

April 30. A committee meeting is called in the Young Friends building at 15th and Race Streets, Philadelphia. Present: Alfred G. Scattergood, temporary chairman, Charles J. Rhoads, Henry W. Comfort, Anne G. Walton, Jesse H. Holmes, Lucy Biddle Lewis, Arabella Carter, William H. Cocks, L. Hollingsworth Wood, Homer L. Morris, Vincent D. Nicholson, Henry J. Cadbury, J. Barnard Walton. An organization was formed to be called "Friends National Service Committee."

May 11. The name is changed to "The American Friends Service Committee."

May 28. Grayson M.-P. Murphy, Chief of the American Red Cross in France, asks for a Commission of two Friends to sail with him to France.

June 1. Vincent D. Nicholson becomes Executive Secretary of the AFSC in one room of the Friends Institute at 20 South 12th Street, Philadelphia.

June 2. J. Henry Scattergood and Morris E. Leeds sail for France on the S.S. *Touraine* for the purpose of investigating opportunities for relief work.

June 11. Rufus M. Jones becomes chairman of the AFSC. Charles F. Jenkins becomes Treasurer of the AFSC.

June 23. First group of workers sail for France: George V. Downing, Edith Coale, Douglas Waples, Eleanor Cary, Ernest L. Brown, Howard and Katherine Elkinton, William and Mary Duguid.

July 1. Tom E. Jones travelling as field worker in the United States.

July. Lydia Lewis, Anna J. Haines, Emilie C. Bradbury, Esther White, Nancy Babb and Amelia Farbiszewski sail for Russia.

July 17. Reconstruction Unit #1 begins its training at Haverford College under the directorship of L. Ralston Thomas, Richard Mott Gummere and Robert Brown.

August 28. 14 members of the Unit sail for France.
Six members of the Russian Unit reached Buzuluk, Russia.

August. Dr. James A. Babbitt is the Director of the Unit.

September 4. 49 members of the Unit sail for France.

September 6. Charles Evans appointed to serve as representative in France.
Samuel Bunting to be assistant to Vincent D. Nicholson.

September 13. 12 members of the Unit sail for France.

September 16. 11 members of the Unit, 5 of whom were women, sail for France.

October 3. Sub-committee on re-organization of AFSC recommends appointment of an Executive Committee; this adopted.
F. Algernon Evans becomes Assistant-Secretary.
Request made to the Friends Institute that the AFSC have the use of two upstairs rooms.
Arthur C. Jackson made purchasing agent.
Rebecca Carter appointed to be in charge of the women's work department, and assistant to the Executive Secretary.
Mary H. Whitson appointed to have charge of the store room at 1515 Cherry Street.

November 8. Paul J. Furnas appointed as Field Secretary, successor to Tom Jones.

November 13. All of the members of Unit #1 with the exception of 3, had arrived in France.

The red and black star adopted as the official emblem.

Name of the Executive Committee changed to the Executive Board. Appointment of a Publicity Committee.

November 22. Florence P. Yarnall made chairman of women's work.

1918

January 15. Request from Homer Folks, Director of the Division of Civil Affairs of Red Cross, for another Unit of 300 men.

February 20. Letter sent to Mennonites and Church of the Brethren asking them to co-operate in Friends relief work.

March 12. $25,000 sent for famine relief in Russia.

May 15. English Friends in Russian Unit reach Vancouver, B.C.

May. Charles J. Rhoads and William C. Biddle sail for France.

May 23. Report received that the attitude of military camps is growing more hostile to conscientious objectors. Unit #2 to be under William C. Biddle.

July 10. Charles J. Rhoads appointed as successor in Paris to Charles Evans.

August 1. Vincent D. Nicholson having been drafted and called to Camp, Wilbur K. Thomas is appointed to act as Executive Secretary.

August 22. F. Algernon Evans resigns.

September 10. Resignation of Vincent D. Nicholson and appointment of Wilbur K. Thomas to take his place as Executive Secretary.

September 17. Report made that 56 boys who have been released from camps are at Merion Hall, Haverford College. As the number is increasing all the time, it is necessary to find larger accommodations which are secured by leasing Rosedale Farm, Kennett Square, Pa.

October 4. 5 members of the Russian Unit leave Buzuluk, for Omsk, Siberia.

October 13. Letter received from Carolena M. Wood expressing her concern for service in Germany.

November 21. Two members of the Mennonites and two of the Church of the Brethren appointed as associate members of the AFSC.

Number of persons in France: men, 258; women, 40; total, 298. 5 in transit.

December 14. Rufus M. Jones and J. Henry Scattergood sail for France to visit the work of the Reconstruction Units.

December 16. Cable received from the Russian workers, sent from Irkutsk, Siberia, on November 22nd.

1919

January. Work begun in the Verdun area.

April 18. Carolena Wood sails for Europe, to enter Germany.

May 22. Rufus M. Jones asked to write *Service of Love in War Time.*

July 7. Carolena Wood, Jane Addams and Alice Hamilton reach Berlin.

August 6. Frederick Kuh sent from France to Vienna.

August 22. Wilmer J. Young appointed to succeed Charles J. Rhoads as chief American Friends Service Committee representative at Grange-le-Comte and Chief of the Friends' Bureau of the American Red Cross.

September 25. Report that 6 workers are in Serbia with 7 more on the way.

Russian workers return from Siberia.

November 1. Herbert Hoover writes asking AFSC to go to Germany for child-feeding.

November 6. Decision made to accept Mr. Hoover's request.

December. Two English and two American members of French Unit go to Germany to distribute photographs and money to the families of German prisoners in France.

Elizabeth Marot comes into the store room.

1920

January 2. American workers for Germany reach Berlin: Alfred G. Scattergood, head of mission, Moses M. Bailey, Robert W. Balderston, Julia E. Branson, Albert J. Brown, Richard L. Cary, Arthur M. Charles, Catherine M. Cox, Harold Evans, William Eves, 3rd, Jesse H. Holmes, Arthur C. Jackson, Herman Newman, Caroline L. Nicholson, Caroline G. Norment, Henry S. Pratt, J. Edgar Rhoads, James G. Vail, Emma T. R. Williams.

February 26. First meal served to German children.

March 10. Blanche Cloeren comes to the office as stenographer.

April 1. Work in France closed.

April 29. Appointment of a Home Service Committee.

Decision to undertake work in Mexico.

June 6. Friends Meeting started in Geneva.

June 26. Conference of returned members of French Unit at Richmond, Indiana.

July 22. Decision to send two nurses' aides to Châlons Maternity Hospital, Châlons-sur-Marne.

August 12–20. All Friends Conference, London.

October. William Fogg in Poland.

October 30. Anna J. Haines sails for Russia.

November 11. Report that a hospital at Petch, Serbia, has been opened.

1921

January 21. William Fogg made head of the Polish Unit.

February 4. S. Edgar Nicholson appointed representative of the AFSC in Richmond, Indiana.

April 5. Meeting with German-Americans to organize $3,000,000 campaign for child-feeding in Germany.

May 5. Francis Bacon appointed head of German Unit in place of Alfred G. Scattergood.

May 14. Rufus M. Jones and Wilbur K. Thomas sail for Europe to visit Quaker relief centers.

July. William Fogg leaves Poland. Florence M. Barrow head of Unit.

October 28. Arrival in Russia of Unit, headed by Murray S. Kenworthy, for famine relief.

1922

January 26. Home Service Committee introduces the subject of need for relief among miners in West Virginia.

January 26. Transfer made from Poland to Russia of Rebecca Janney and Harry G. Timbres.
Clarence E. Pickett appointed Field Secretary for Home Service.

April 1. The hospital at Petch, Serbia, turned over to Serbian authorities.

April 20. The decision made to undertake some form of relief among miners' children in West Virginia after hearing report from Walter Abell and Andrew Pearson.

Report that requests have been received from college students and teachers asking for summer work.

June 17. The new Châlons-sur-Marne Maternity Hospital dedicated.

June 19. The decision made to include a few children of miners in Pennsylvania in the relief program.

July 31. Child-feeding in Germany handed over to the D.Z.A. (Deutsche Zentral Ausschuss für die Auslands Hilfe).

August 24. Agreement made to start feeding program for miners' children.

September 1. AFSC working in Russia independent of the American Relief Administration.

Center is opened at 5 Place de la Taconnerie, Geneva.

September 21. Child-feeding in West Virginia and Pennsylvania discontinued.

Report made that Douglas L. Parker is in Mexico City, acting as representative of the AFSC, while he is Professor in Union Theological Seminary in that city.

Report made that the office at Dorotheenstrasse, Berlin, is open with Gilbert MacMaster as American representative of the AFSC.

November 23. Report made that Luella Jones is continuing work in the coal fields of West Virginia and that Emily C. Seaman and Mary Liddle are supervising work in Pennsylvania.

1923

January 25. The Central Committee of New York City agrees to make the AFSC the distributing agency for its funds in Austria.

Report made that all work among miners in Pennsylvania is closed.

April 1. Work in West Virginia closed.

April, May, June. Murray S. Kenworthy, acting Secretary during absence of Wilbur K. Thomas in Europe.

August 14. Dr. Otto Wiedfeldt, German Ambassador to the United States, asks the AFSC to do child-feeding in Germany, and the Committee agrees to undertake it.

September 24. Margaret E. Jones comes as Assistant Secretary.

September 27. Report given of plans for the formation of a National Committee of which General Henry T. Allen has agreed to become chairman. The purpose of this committee is to appeal for funds for child-feeding in Germany.

October 31. Robert Pretlow agrees to do field publicity work for AFSC.

December 15, Henry Tatnall Brown, with his wife and Dr. Haven Emerson, sail for Germany where Henry T. Brown will act as head of child-feeding mission.

1924

January 28. First carload of Allen food reaches Berlin.

February 15. Cable from 20 South 12th Street authorizes Henry T. Brown to increase child-feeding to 1,000,000 per day.

March 27. Request made that the Friends Centers in Europe should be continued.

Concern expressed by L. Hollingsworth Wood that work should be done for Negroes.

The Central Relief Committee has turned over $100,500 to AFSC for work in Austria.

April 19. Conference held in Frankfurt a/M. of Friends and friends of the Friends.

May 22. All work in Poland finished except model orphanage at Kolpin.

Douglas Parker has left Mexico and Annie P. Carlyle has taken his place as representative of AFSC.

June 14. D. Robert and Elizabeth Yarnall sail for Germany where he will be head of German child-feeding in place of Henry T. Brown.

July 17. O. Edward Janney expresses concern that the AFSC should undertake educational peace work.

Report made that a Friends Center has been established in Paris at 20 Avenue Victoria where Alfred and Grace Lowry are in charge.

All work in Poland has been turned over to new Polish-Friends Eastern Borders Committee. The Center at Warsaw, Widok 26, is in charge of Wilmer and Mildred Young.

The Center at Vienna, Singerstrasse 16, has Emma Cadbury as American representative and Headley Horsnaill as representative of English Friends.

July 17. In Russia the location at Borisoglevski 15, Moscow, is retained as a Center. Mabelle Phillips is chief in Buzuluk, Nancy Babb in Totskoe, and Alice Davis and Nadia Danilevsky in Sorochenskoe.

September 19. The records of General Henry T. Allen's Committee are given to the AFSC.

September 25. A special meeting held to discuss the future of the AFSC.

October 1. Discussion how those persons who want to join Friends can be brought into the Society without joining any particular branch.

October. Ethel Mather from England at the Geneva Center.

October 7. German child-feeding turned over to the D.Z.A. who expect to continue feeding until April, 1925.

October 22. Proposed that the AFSC should be arranged in defined sections: European, Interracial Service, Peace and Home Service.

November 20. Report made that several of the former German workers have remained in Germany as representatives of the AFSC.

Desire to have an AFSC representative at Geneva is mentioned.

1925

January 22. Anna J. Haines reports that she is going to Russia to work in the Health Department of the Government.

May 28. The AFSC is organized into four sections, Foreign, William Eves, 3rd, chairman; Interracial, Raymond Bye, chairman; Peace, Vincent D. Nicholson, chairman; Home Service, J. Barnard Walton, chairman.

July 23. Report made that Henry Harris, from England, is in charge of Warsaw Center as representative from both England and America.

September 24. Report made that Anna J. Haines is teaching in the Nurses' Training School, Moscow.

Gilbert MacMaster is now the only American representative in Berlin.

October 1. Thomas Q. Harrison begins travelling and speaking for the AFSC, in co-operation with the Fellowship of Youth for Peace.

November 10. Lloyd Balderston sails for China and Japan as representative of the AFSC.

November. Emma Cadbury, Bilbert MacMaster and Fred Hankinson visit Bulgaria.

Ethel Mather leaves Geneva. Margaret Lester, from America, takes her place.

December 1. Regional office of the AFSC is opened in Richmond, Indiana.

December 2. The Society of Friends is organized in Germany with Heinrich Becker as Clerk.

4 AFSC workers to go and assist Dr. C. Telford Erickson in establishing an agricultural school in Kavaja, Albania.

1926

January 28. Report made that Wilfred and Mary Conard and their daughter are helping at the Geneva Center.

$1000 appropriated toward the building of the model Friendship village in Pootung, across the river from Shanghai.

Report made that a branch office of the AFSC has been opened in Boston and it is hoped to secure O. Ben Gerig as secretary.

February 1. Support for an AFSC representative in Mexico is discontinued.

March 25. Decision made to incorporate the AFSC.

Rufus M. Jones announces that he has been asked to go to China under the auspices of the Y.M.C.A. to attend a conference celebrating the 40th anniversary of the beginning of their work in China.

March 31. The agricultural school in Poland is turned over to the Polish Ministry of Agriculture.

April 29. The report from Lloyd Balderston after his return, recommends helping to support Rufus Jones so that he can be an AFSC representative in China and elsewhere; financing a trip of Mr. Kagawa from Japan to China; help support plan of Friendship village; encourage Henry T. Hodgkin to give all his time for international service.

Thomas Q. Harrison is made field worker for the Peace Section, no longer co-operating with Fellowship of Youth for Peace.

May 27. Funds are in hand to bring three Japanese students to the United States for study.
The Interracial Section asks for a secretary.

June 18. Rufus M. Jones and family sail for China.

June. Bertram and Irene Pickard come to Geneva to take charge of the Center.
AFSC exhibit at the Sesqui-centennial, Philadelphia.

September 23. AFSC sending friendship dolls to Japan in co-operation with the Federal Council of Churches.
Two Japanese students are under the care of the Interracial section, one in Earlham College and one in Smith.

October 5. Helen R. Bryan is assistant secretary of AFSC for Interracial section.

November 26. The Home Service Section tells of the Student-in-Industry project for the next summer.

1927

January 5. Report made that the Near East Relief has allocated $5000 for Bulgaria, to be administered by Friends.

January 27. Report made that plans are underway to establish a Quaker student Hostel in Geneva.
Mr. Hasegawa, Japanese friend, is travelling and speaking for the Interracial Section.

February 2. The Foreign Service Section agrees to help English Friends in financing a Center in Salonica, Greece.
Proposal of Peace Section's plan to send out college students on Peace Caravans during the summer.

March 24. Rufus M. Jones receives the medal of the German Red Cross for child-feeding in Germany.
Rufus M. Jones makes his proposal for a Wider Quaker Fellowship.

April 28. A letter is sent from the AFSC to Governor Fuller of Massachusetts asking him to reconsider the case of Sacco and Vanzetti.

The sum of $1000 is appropriated to Harry and Rebecca Timbres for a trip to Russia.

May 26. The Board of Executives and Membership of German Society for Study of Children's Diseases present an Honorary Testimonial to Wilbur K. Thomas because of German child-feeding.

Report given that there are over 100 Friends in Germany.

The announcement is made that members of the American Legion are trying to put Rachel Davis Du Bois out of her teaching position in the Woodbury, N.J. High School because of her peace and interracial activities.

June 1. Ray Newton becomes secretary of the Peace Section.

June 4. Mr. Hasegawa sails for Japan.

June 18–21. Conference held at Haverford College for 24 boys and girls who are going out on Peace Caravans for 10 weeks.

June 21. The sum of $1000 received from sale of Russian Industries is allocated to Nancy Babb's hospital in Totskoe.

Ernest L. Brown, Chairman of Home Service Section.

July. Student Hostel in Geneva is opened with the prospect of 5 American Friends to live there as students. Alexander and Edith Wilson are wardens.

6 Students volunteer for Student-in-Industry project.

September 7. The Young Friends Committees in Richmond, Indiana, 20 South 12th Street and 15th and Race Streets, ask to be represented on the AFSC.

Branch office of the AFSC opened in Los Angeles, Calif.

September 15. Crystal Bird becomes field representative for the Interracial Section.

October 5. The Fellowship of Reconciliation invites the Foreign Service Section to join in sending a small delegation to Nicaragua.

Decision made to give $60 to the support of a Japanese student in the National Y.W.C.A. training school.

October 14, 15. Peace Conference held in Richmond, Indiana, preceding the Five Years Meeting.

October 27. Elbert Russell and Carolena M. Wood are to be the representatives of the AFSC on the trip to Nicaragua.

Anna L. Curtis is working for the AFSC in New York Yearly Meeting.

November 10. Clement and Grace Biddle establish the Geneva Study Scholarship for teachers of history in Friends schools and colleges.

The Peace Section arranges to co-operate with the Peace Association of Friends in Richmond, Indiana, in the editing of *The Messenger of Peace*, with John O'H. Harte as editor.

December 1. The Peace Section plans to hold Oratorical Peace Contests for children.

1928

January 1. Paris Center is moved from 20 Avenue Victoria to 12 Rue Guy de la Brosse.

January 4. Agreement made to appeal through Friends' papers for funds and clothing to send to miners in Western Pennsylvania.

January 26. The office is authorized to secure one or more representatives to supervise the distribution of food and clothing for miners.

The peace section is considering the case of Rosika Schwimmer who has been denied citizenship in the United States because of her objection to war, and refusal to defend the country in case of war.

February 2. The headquarters for miners' relief is opened in Barnsboro, Pa., by Edith Hall, Sophia Dulles, Edith Coale, Eliza Cope and Mary Kelsey.

March 22. 750 miners' children are being fed daily.
Rufus M. Jones resigns as chairman of the AFSC.

April 26. A book of recitations entitled *Peace Crusaders* for use in the oratorical contests sponsored by the Peace Section is being prepared by Anna B. Griscom.
Report is made that 1000 miners' children are being fed and 475 families are receiving second-hand clothing.
Funds have been guaranteed for sending out two Prohibition Caravans.
Report is made that Dorothy Verplank is the secretary of the AFSC Branch office in Los Angeles.
O. Ben Gerig, secretary of the Boston Branch of the AFSC, resigns.

May 2. Report is made that the AFSC has become an incorporated body under the laws of the State of Pennsylvania.

May 15. Report is made that a Branch office for the Eastern Central States,—Ohio, Indiana, Illinois, Michigan, Tennessee—has been organized with headquarters at Richmond, Indiana, and Murray S. Kenworthy as secretary.

May 24. The Student-in-Industry project is given up.
Henry J. Cadbury is nominated as chairman of the AFSC, and accepts the appointment.

June 1. Lucy M. Thruston, from Baltimore, is to work with the Peace Section and the two Peace Committees of Baltimore Yearly Meetings in supplying peace material to newspapers.

June 6. Rufus M. Jones is appointed as Honorary Chairman of the AFSC.

July 3. Proposal brought to the AFSC that there should be a Friends Center in Washington, D.C.

July 26. The Interracial Peace Committee, organized by the AFSC is started, with Alice Dunbar-Nelson as secretary.

There are thirteen caravan teams on the field.

20 Home Service workers.

Margaret E. Jones resigns from the AFSC.

Helen R. Bryan resigns from the AFSC.

Irene Pickard is warden of Geneva Hostel.

Gladys M. Scott is made book-keeper in place of Helene Wittmann who has gone to Geneva.

September. John Harte resigns as Editor of *Messenger of Peace.*

September 20. Hugh and Elizabeth Borton arrive in Japan to serve as representatives of the Foreign Mission Board of Arch Street Yearly Meeting and the AFSC.

September 25. Discussion of the increasing number of independent meetings and the need for finding some way by which they can have some kind of central affiliation.

September 27. The AFSC agrees to finance Amy E. Sharpless until June, in co-operation with the three Young Friends' Committees (Arch Street, Race Street and Five Years Meeting) as a travelling field secretary for the Peace Section.

October 1. *Quaker Adventures,* a series of radio talks which the Service and Publicity Committees of the two New York Yearly Meetings had been asked to broadcast, and edited by Edward Thomas, is in book form and on sale.

October 3. Dorothy Verplank resigns as secretary of the Los Angeles Branch office.

October 5. *Peace Crusaders* edited by Anna B. Griscom is on sale.

October 8. Henry Harris has resigned from the Friends Center in Warsaw.

October 25. The decision is made to hold an All-Friends Conference at Penn College, Oskaloosa, Iowa, in 1929.

November 7. John W. Dorland has been secretary of the Los Angeles Branch office.
Report is made that Helen R. Bryan is the secretary of the Committee on the Interests of the Colored Race of the Race Street Yearly Meeting.

November 22. Report is made that Blanche R. Howland is the secretary of the New England Branch Office.

December 27. The work among the miners in Barnsboro, Pa. is completed.
Milton C. Davis is appointed secretary of the Interracial Section in place of Helen R. Bryan.

1929

February 1. Wilbur K. Thomas resigns as Executive Secretary.

February 15. Anna B. Griscom becomes Acting Secretary.
Decision is made to discontinue the Interracial Section.

March 6. The AFSC authorizes the transfer of all AFSC files and records to Haverford College.
Anna L. Curtis becomes Publicity Secretary.

March 21. Margaret E. Jones gives two days a week to the work of the Home Service Section.
Clarence E. Pickett is nominated for Executive Secretary; the statement is made that he is willing to serve and he is appointed.
Report is made that Center at Salonica is closed.

April 25. Harry and Rebecca Timbres accept the invitation given by Rabindranath Tagore, through Charles F. Andrews, asking them to come to India and serve in Tagore's ashram, Santiniketan.

June 15. Anna B. Griscom resigns as Acting Secretary and Clarence E. Pickett comes into the office to give one day a week.

July 25. Report is made that there are 12 Peace Caravans in the field.

September 1. Clarence E. Pickett begins full time work for the AFSC.

September 3–9. All Friends Conference, Oskaloosa, Iowa.

September 6. Announcement is made that Margaret Dorland Webb has been refused citizenship in the United States, while her husband, John R. Webb, who holds the same views on war that she does, has been accepted.

October 1. Alfred Lowry resigns from Paris Center.

October 17. Request is received from the Federal Council of Churches that the AFSC should take charge of relief among the families suffering from the textile mill strikes in Marion, North Carolina.

October 24. The AFSC approves of the Home Service Section undertaking this program.

October 24. Report is received that the orphanage at Kolpin, Poland, has been liquidated.

November 9. Frank D. Watson and J. Lawrence Lippincott leave for Marion, N.C., the former to make a survey of the situation and the latter to take charge of relief.

November 15. Work started in Marion, N.C.

December 5. Lawrence Lippincott reports that Hugh Moore is acting head of Unit, Winifred Wildman and Ruth Biddle are social workers, and Betty Fowler is the nurse. Feeding about 900 people.

Report is made of a plan for a Quaker Peace Institute which will train the Peace Caravaners.

December 12. Carolena M. Wood sails for the Philippine Islands and she expects to join a deputation of English Friends in April to visit among Friends in China.

1930

January 23. Report is given that 175 families (1000) people are being fed at Marion.

February 5. Charles F. Jenkins resigns as Treasurer of AFSC.
Murray S. Kenworthy resigns as secretary of AFSC Branch office in Richmond, Indiana.

March 27. The Message Committee is organized.

March 29. Clarence E. Pickett sails to visit European Centers.

June 5. William R. Fogg is appointed as Treasurer of the AFSC.

June 9–21. Peace Institute at Haverford College. This is the first Institute of International Relations.

June 21. 12 Peace Caravan teams start out.
32 Home workers are placed.

July. Gilbert MacMaster resigns from the Berlin Center.
Richard and Mary Cary come to Berlin to take charge of the Center.
Mabel Ridpath is warden of Geneva Hostel.

August 1. Work in Marion, N.C., is closed.

September 1. Elizabeth Marsh comes to be secretary of the Home Service Section.

September 10. Report is made that Mary R. G. Williams has given funds to the AFSC to provide a scholarship for travel, study and teaching in the Friends Schools at Ram Allah, Palestine.

September Ruth Outland is the first person to hold this new scholarship, and sails for Palestine.

September 25. Special Committee is appointed to study the Industrial Situation. This is later called the Economics Commission.

October 8. Rabindranath Tagore arrives in the United States to visit among Friends, accompanied by Harry Timbres.

October 26–November 2. Rabindranath Tagore stays in the home of William C. Biddle and Lucy Biddle Lewis, Lansdowne, Pa.

November 1. Effie McAfee sails for Paris as representative of the AFSC.

December 7. William C. Biddle, Bernard G. Waring, J. Hoge Ricks and Dr. S. C. Mitchell appointed to visit the President of the mills at Danville, Virginia, in regard to doing relief work after the strike.

December 22. Request received that AFSC should undertake child-feeding in Philadelphia among school children of unemployed parents.

Decision is made that the AFSC will not undertake relief in Danville, Virginia.

1931

January 1. Hugh Moore becomes financial secretary of AFSC.

January 7. Report is made that a gift of $10,000 has been received from Mary and Margaret Campbell, the income of which is to be used for a foreign scholarship.

February 4. Wray Hoffman is working under the care of the Home Service Section in an attempt to find employment in repair of churches for unemployed men. This resulted in 920 men being given "made work" in 100 churches in Philadelphia.

February 26. The AFSC will sponsor the work of Charles P. Howland in the preparation of a brief concerning the citizenship cases of Dr. MacIntosh and Miss Bland.

Report is received that French Friends have started a Peace Caravan.

The AFSC is helping to serve breakfasts to school children in Philadelphia and is co-operating with the "Made Work Committee" and with the Board of Education.

March 4. The Home Service Section has a sub-committee on Unemployment.

March 26. A Committee is appointed to co-operate with other groups in making a study of German reparations and war debts.

April 1. The Interracial Peace Committee is discontinued.

April. Corder and Gwen Catchpool from England go to the Berlin Center.

May 6. A Committee is appointed to visit President Hoover and Secretary Stimson in regard to disarmament.

May 13. Grace Abbott, head of the Federal Children's Bureau, and Mr. Fred Croxton, chairman of President Hoover's Unemployment Committee ask the AFSC to undertake relief and rehabilitation in the bituminous coal regions of West Virginia and contiguous areas.

May 28. Peace Section co-operates with 60 other peace organizations in preparation for the Disarmament Conference in 1932.

June 4. The Coal Committee is appointed.

June 8–July 3. Two Institutes of International Relations held at Haverford College.

June 12. Harry and Rebecca Timbres sail for India.

Douglas V. Steere, Chairman of Home Service Section.

July 14. Report made that 14 Caravan teams are on the field.

77 home service workers have been placed.

August 4. Rufus M. Jones, Henry T. Brown, Lucy Biddle Lewis, Clarence Pickett and Fred Croxton meet with President Hoover to discuss financing the coal relief project.

August 5. AFSC makes the decision to undertake this piece of relief work and rehabilitation.

August 25. Bernard G. Waring is appointed as "Coal Chief" and Henry T. Brown is appointed chairman of the Coal Committee.

August 27. Bernard Waring, Clarence Pickett, William C. Biddle and Fred Croxton meet with the Governor of West Virginia.

August 28. The same group meets with the Governor of Kentucky.

August. Establishing of the Dutch Yearly Meeting.

September 1. $225,000 has been received from the American Relief Administration to be used for relief in the coal fields.

September 24. Hugh and Elizabeth Borton return from Japan to spend a year of study in the United States.

Report is made that the permission to renew the lease of the Moscow Center has not been granted.

Mahlon Harvey will take Emma Cadbury's place during her temporary absence from Vienna.

Opening of Pendle Hill, at Wallingford, Pa.

September 24. E. Raymond Wilson has been made a member of the staff and is travelling for the Peace Section.

September 28. 6 school districts in Kanawha County, West Virginia, start receiving food.

Harry and Rebecca Timbres have reached Santiniketan.

September 30. 1000 children begin to receive food daily in Monongalia County, West Virginia. Anna J. Haines and Mary Skinner from the Children's Bureau are making investigations.

Eleanor Stabler Clark will take charge, one day a week, of the distribution of clothing.

November 4. Three Yearly Meetings in Canada organize the Canadian Friends Service Committee.

Malcolm Ross will spend three months in the office doing publicity work for the Coal Relief Section.

Homer L. Morris is in Harlan County, Kentucky.

The Federal Council of Churches has endorsed the relief carried on by the AFSC and is soliciting funds for it.

November 19. 17 Counties have been surveyed with regard to underweight children. It is estimated that between 12 and 16 thousand must be fed before the end of the winter. Between 10 and 25 thousand adults need food.

Charles and Maud Woodruff and Donald Graham are working in the store-room.

1932

January 7. Elizabeth Marot resigns from the store-room after 13 years of service.

Paris Center has charge of arrangements for Gandhi's Meeting.

Child-feeding started in Illinois and Tennessee. Homer L. Morris is making a survey for rehabilitation projects.

February 26. Report is made that the unemployment situation is serious in Germany. Requests have been received asking the AFSC to carry on relief, similar to that in 1920, in Germany, but the AFSC cannot raise funds for such an undertaking while it is doing relief at home in the coal fields.

February 27. A second French Peace Caravan has been sent out.

Bill and Ruth Simkin are on their way to Crown Mine, West Virginia, to establish their home in that community.

28,000 people being fed, school and pre-school children and expectant mothers.

Carolena M. Wood speaks of the concern of German Friends for a group of Jews in Berlin who have been persecuted.

March 24. The Message Committee is changed to the Fellowship Committee.

The statement is made that 100,000 men will not return to the coal industry.

The Friends Center in Frankfurt a/M. has sent two groups of children from unemployed German families to Alsace.

April 1. Report is made that a total of 1,300,000 meals have been served in 38 counties and 6 states. The greatest number of meals per day has been 40,000.

April 29. A special meeting is held to celebrate the 15th Anniversary of the AFSC.

May 26. Hugh and Elizabeth Borton are no longer representatives of the AFSC.

Gilbert MacMaster will devote his time to visiting Minority Sections.

Hannah Clothier Hull has been given the one ticket for the Disarmament Conference which was designated for the Society of Friends.

20,000 children are being fed.

Suggestion is made that the products of the rehabilitation work might be taken in a truck to various Quaker hotels for display and sale.

June. 15 Home Service Workers have a short conference at Pendle Hill. 64 workers placed for the summer.

June. Institutes of International Relations are held at Haverford College, Wellesley College and Northwestern University.

Eight Peace Caravans on the field, two of which were Mennonite teams.

22 Austrians, members of the Forum, visit England.

September 7. All relief is closed in the coal communities and the staff have left, except 3 who are working on rehabilitation projects.

September 22. The meeting house at Bad Pyrmont, Germany, is being rebuilt as headquarters for the German Yearly Meeting of which there are 200 members.

Report is given that feeding has been done in 6 states, 41 counties, 690 schools. 33,000 children have been on the feeding list and a total of 2,000,000 meals have been served.

Bernard G. Waring resigns as "Coal Chief."

The Governor of Kentucky has asked the AFSC to do a similar piece of work in several counties during the coming winter. Counties in West Virginia have sent in a request for the same thing.

October 5. Invitations are received from West Virginia and Kentucky asking the AFSC to return to carry on relief.

October 27. Child feeding is opened in Logan County, West Virginia.

November 30. The Home Service Section has a concern that the Summer Volunteers need a definite training period before they start out on their work.

December 21. The Paris Center is feeding 50 children in Germany one meal a day, using French money and personnel.

December 22. Report is made that French Friends are establishing their own Yearly Meeting.

The AFSC has been invited into 16 counties of West Virginia and Kentucky. In 2 counties of West Virginia the AFSC has taken over the entire relief program. In the others it is doing only feeding for children.

The report is made that one family has been settled on a 10 acre farm.

1933

January 27. Raymond Wilson and Guy Solt are travelling in the middle west to raise money for the Mid-west Institute of International Relations.

January 28. S. Howard Pennell is in charge of coal relief. 15,000 children are being fed.

February 23. Work has begun on the garden projects in the coal fields.

Arrangements are being made for Edith T. Maul to exhibit furniture in New England and the two Philadelphia Yearly Meetings.

19,000 children are receiving one hot meal a day.

March 20. Committee appointed to consider plans for a World Conference of Friends.

March 31. Total feeding enrollment, 25,783.

April 27. Mahlon and Vivian Harvey will take up the work of the Paris Center in place of Effie McAfee.

April 29. A Quaker letter is sent out by the Fellowship Committee to isolated Friends.

May 25. The report is made that French Friends have established a center at Le Havre under their own care. Since the relief work in Berlin has been closed, Germaine Melon is directing relief in Paris for German refugees, under the name of Entr'aide.

A garden project for the unemployed in Yardley, Pa., is under the leadership of Hans Burkhard.

An award of $3000 from the Woodrow Wilson Foundation is given to the Peace Section in recognition of the Institutes of International Relations.

June–July. Institutes of International Relations are held at Duke University, North Carolina, Wellesley College, Massachusetts and Northwestern University, Illinois.

June 14. Institute is held at Pendle Hill for the purpose of training the Home Service Workers. 78 workers are placed during the summer.

July. There are 6 Peace Caravans out on the field.

9 members of the Forum come to America from Vienna with Riki Teller.

The first institute of Race Relations is held at Swarthmore College.

July 21. The Peace Section agrees to co-operate with Devere Allen, editor of *The World Tomorrow*, in the development of an international news release service, called the Nofrontier News Service.

August 21. The Board of Directors of the AFSC authorizes Clarence E. Pickett to accept the position which has been offered by the Department of the Interior. This will be the development of Subsistence Homesteads under the TVA.

September 3–9. Institute of International Relations for Labor Leaders is held at Haverford College.

September 28. Report is made that the Hostel at Geneva has moved from Chemin Krieg to 18 Avenue Bertrand.

AFSC makes an agreement to retain Clarence Pickett for part time in the office.

October 9. Announcement is made that the Elmhirst Foundation has given $1000 for health work in Logan County, West Virginia.

October 16. Death of Richard Cary in Berlin.

October. Olga Jones is director of the Coal Section.

October 26. Clarence Pickett announces the 5 point program for the winter of 1933–1934 in the coal fields: (1) child-feeding, (2) Health program, (3) training miners for new skills, (4) Friendly Advisers for conflict areas, (5) providing leaders for subsistence homestead colonies. The Federal Council will co-operate with the AFSC in projects #4 and #5.

November 15. Gilbert MacMaster is at the Berlin Center in place of Richard Cary.

November 22. Elizabeth Marsh will take Clarence Pickett's work while he is in Washington, with the assistance of Grace E. Rhoads, Jr.

November 23. Report is made that a Quaker school for German children will be established at Ommen, Holland.

December 2. The AFSC has been asked to go into 9 counties in Kentucky to do child-feeding.

E. Raymond Wilson, Field Secretary of the Peace Section, has headquarters at 203 South Dearborn Street, Chicago.

December. Winifred Way Wencke in charge of Friends Health Service, Logan, West Virginia.

1934

January 24. It is recommended that the Peace and Home Service Sections establish a work camp during the summer in Westmoreland County, Pa., which will provide young people with first-hand knowledge of social and industrial problems.

Report is made that David Telfair has been suspended from Ohio State University because of his refusal to take military training.

January 25. Friendly Advisers, Harold Marley and family, move to Blue Diamond, Kentucky.

February 4. Stanley and Marie Hamilton move to Shadyside, Ohio, as Friendly Advisers.

February 20. Letter from Emma Cadbury tells of Civil War in Vienna and the need for relief.

February 22. A Social Order Section of the AFSC is created at the suggestion of the Social Order Committees of the two Philadelphia Yearly Meetings.

13,000 children are being fed one meal a day.

The AFSC is working on the Trade Training Program in co-operation with the Federal Relief Administration and Subsistence Homestead Division.

Homer L. Morris, former Field Director for the Coal Section, is working with the Subsistence Homesteads.

A Committee is appointed to follow the situation among German Friends and to keep American Yearly Meetings in touch with developments in Germany.

Clarence E. Pickett, with Henry J. Cadbury as alternate, is appointed to represent the AFSC on the American Christian Committee for German Refugees. This was organized by the Federal Council of Churches.

February 24. Harry and Rebecca Timbres sail from India for U.S.A.

April. The Quaker School at Ommen, Holland, opens.

April 21. Report is made that $5000 has been given to the Peace Section for the purpose of establishing Institutes of International Relations on the Pacific Coast during the summer of 1935.

Wilmer J. and Mildred Young have been appointed as directors of the Friends Service Camp.

Report is made that money for Austrian relief has been supplied by the International Federation of Trade Unions.

April 26. Clarence and Lilly Pickett sail for Europe to visit Friends Centers. He is also under commission by the Government to visit homestead experiments in Germany, Austria and England.

May 24. Trade Training shops are organized in Morgantown, West Virginia, Clearfield and Westmoreland Counties and in Tygart Valley.

Report is made that Mrs. Roosevelt is giving to the AFSC, money which she receives for her radio talks.

June 1. Child-feeding in the coal area is ended.

June 7. Henry J. Cadbury resigns as chairman of the AFSC. Henry Tatnall Brown succeeds as chairman.

June 13–17. Home Service Workers' Conference at Pendle Hill.

June–July. Institute on American Labor and World Recovery at Haverford College. Institutes of International Relations held at Duke University, North Carolina; Atlanta, Georgia; Northwestern University, Illinois; Wellesley College, Massachusetts. Institute of Race Relations held at Swarthmore College, Pa.

14 Peace Caravans on the field.

June 16. Report is made that 1,600,000 meals have been furnished to Kentucky school children.

Friends Service Camp opens at Greensburg, Pa. 41 men and 14 women making a water system for the Westmoreland Homestead.

July. Elizabeth T. Shipley is in Paris making a study of the German refugee situation.

July 7. Anna Griscom Elkinton is made chairman of the World Conference Committee.

August 1. Mary Cary withdraws from her work at the Berlin Center.

September 1. Clarence Pickett will give only one day a week in Washington.

September 27. A request has been received that the AFSC should establish a Center in Spain but the AFSC does not accept the proposal.

The AFSC approves receipt of money with the Friends Service Council, from the German Organization, Brüder in Not, for relief in Austria.

Report is made that the Coal Section has had charge during the summer of 2 educational projects for 150 girls, using money which was given by the Federal Government.

Howard Pennell has been made Manager of the Clearfield County Subsistence Homestead.

October 15. Guy Solt is travelling for the Institutes and has been made a member of the staff for the Peace Section.

October 24. The possibility of having work camps for junior boys is suggested.

November 8. The Carnegie Corporation has appropriated $5000 to the Peace Section towards the support of the Institutes of International Relations for 1935.

December 1. There are between 3 and 4 thousand refugees in Paris who need help. The administration of relief has been turned over to French Friends and Henri Van Etten is acting as chairman.

Vienna is still caring for 1000 families.

Report is made that since the starting of the Home Service Section there have been 670 men and women workers.

There are five Government Subsistence Homesteads started, and one in formation, in the coal fields. Each will accommodate 200 families at a cost of $2500 per family.

Harold Chance has been made secretary of the AFSC branch office in Boston.

December 27. The suggestion of using young Friends as internes in the European centers is made by Douglas V. Sture.

1935

January 15. Homer L. Morris becomes secretary of Coal Committee.

January 21. Edwards and Marjory Dickinson arrive in Shadyside, Ohio, to work with the Hamiltons.

February 11. Classes begin at the "People's University" at Shadyside, Ohio.

February 28. Announcement is made that Paul D. Sturge will succeed Carl Heath as General Secretary for the Friends Service Council, London.

Property at 2410 Wyoming Avenue, Washington, D.C., is turned over to the AFSC by Mrs. Anne Hubbard Davis, to be used as an International Hospitality House.

March 16. Lucy Meacham Thruston reports that in the "Trend of World Affairs," news releases are being sent to 700 subscribers through 135 newspapers.

May 1. The American Legion attacks the personnel of the Institutes calling them un-American and communistic.
Henry Tatnall Brown retires as chairman and Rufus M. Jones is appointed in his place.
A close co-operation is arranged between the AFSC and Pendle Hill. The AFSC will provide field work for a limited number of Pendle Hill students.

May 7. Death of Alfred Lowry.

May 21. Mrs. Roosevelt speaks at the closing exercises of the People's University.

June 5. The Social Order Section is established and will include the work of the Home Service Section, the Coal Committee, and Economics Commission. Homer Morris is secretary.
Emily Cooper Johnson, Chairman of Peace Section.

June 12–16. Conference at Pendle Hill for 54 Home Service Workers.

June. 4 Service Camps: For junior boys at Westmoreland County; Neffs, Ohio; Kensington, Philadelphia and Bedford Street Mission, Philadelphia.

June–July. Institutes of International Relations are held at: Duke University; Wellesley College; Atlanta, Georgia; Northwestern University; Reed College, Oregon; Mills and Whittier Colleges, California; Haverford College; Grinnell College, Iowa.
Four Peace Caravans are on the field.

June. A Maternal Health Clinic is added to the Health Service in Logan County, Virginia.

July. Institute of Race Relations at Swarthmore College.

August 1. Elizabeth Marsh Jensen resigns and is succeeded by Ruth Outland.

September 25. A committee is appointed by the Peace Section to consider the question of neutrality in the Italian-Ethiopian situation, from the Quaker point of view.

September 26. Louisa Jacob, who has been at Nürnberg, will take charge of the Vienna Center during Emma Cadbury's absence in the United States.

The American-Christian Committee is trying to raise $400,000 for relief for non-Jewish German refugees and the committee has asked the AFSC and its representatives in Vienna, Paris, Prague and Berlin to help with the distribution of funds. The AFSC agrees to this.

September 28. Pauline Trueblood has 6 travelling Quaker Libraries and Richard C. Brown has made a Quaker Bibliography. A handbook of the Society of Friends is being prepared.

October 1. E. Raymond Wilson is made Dean of the Institutes of International Relations.

October 2. The name of the Social Order Section is changed to the Social-Industrial Section.

Western District Monthly Meeting at 20 South 12th Street, gives permission to the AFSC to use the gallery of the Meeting House for additional office space. Room H in the Institute will be altered for an office for the Executive Secretary.

October 10. The Peace Section reports that it is interested in the project of a nation-wide religious pacifist program.

November 8. Report is made that the Nofrontier News Service has built up a circulation of 7,445,000.

1936

January 8. The project of the Peace Section is named the Emergency Peace Campaign.

Arthur E. Morgan, on behalf of the TVA, asks the AFSC to establish work camps in that area during the summer. The Board agrees to do this.

The AFSC agrees to study the possibility of retirement funds for the staff.

January 22. Ray Newton is appointed Executive Director of Emergency Peace Campaign.

January 23. Report is made that Prince Pierre Kamsarakan has asked the Vienna Center to help with relief for Russian emigrants in Vienna. Since the Russian Revolution in 1917 there have been 800 Russian Jews and 300 Russian Christians living in that city.

January 25. The Fellowship Committee and World Conference Committee meet together in Washington, D.C., and the Fellowship Committee officially becomes the Fellowship Council, with Rufus M. Jones, chairman; Leslie D. Shaffer, Secretary; and Mary E. Gaunt, Office Secretary.

February. Albert and Anne Martin sail for Germany to be the American representatives of the AFSC in the Berlin Center.

February 5. Chicago Friends ask to open a Center in that city, to be recognized as a branch office of the AFSC. Alfred Cope will be secretary.

February 27. Richard Gregg is asked to spend some time among the southern share-croppers and report the situation.

Request is made that Edith T. Maul, field representative and salesman of Mountaineer Craftsmen Co-operative Association furniture, should have a centrally located show and sales room.

February 28. House-warming of new offices in the Meeting House.

March 12. Death of Carolena M. Wood.

March 20. A letter is read from Szechwan Yearly Meeting (West China) asking that the AFSC send Rufus Jones out for a period of six months to lecture in West China Union University.

March 21. Report is made that Albert and Anne Martin have arrived in Berlin.

Wilmer and Mildred Young and David and Mary Richie expect to visit among share-croppers.

April 8. A 15 room house at 1708 New Hampshire Avenue, Washington, D.C., has been purchased for $23,000 to be used as a Quaker student Hostel.

April 16. Report is made that industrial leaders have pledged $25,000 for 3 years to be used for rehabilitation program development in Fayette County, Pennsylvania. This is in the center of the unemployment region where 96 out of 152 mines have been shut down.

Report is made that the Arkansas share-croppers receive, per tenant family, $212 per year, $37 of which is cash. Wilmer Young suggests possibilities of homesteads for share-croppers and poor landlords. The Youngs plan to live at Delta Co-operative Farm, Mississippi.

Campbell Award is given to Barbara Cary as a student-interne in Berlin.

April 21. Emergency Peace Campaign is launched publicly at a meeting in Philadelphia.

April 24. Funds of the Brüder in Not are to be transmitted through the Berlin Center to Germans living in Czechoslovakia.

The MCCA has acquired a salesroom in the Co-operative Center, 1504 Race Street, Philadelphia.

May 6. Pendle Hill and the AFSC jointly purchase land adjoining Pendle Hill for a house for the Executive Secretary.

May 21. $10,000 more has been received for Fayette County.

May 22. Garden Clubs are being started in one of the worst unemployment areas of Fayette County.

The Resettlement Administration has agreed to make a study of the economic and human resources in Fayette County.

278 meetings have been held for the Emergency Peace Campaign.

June 3. Plans are discussed for the 20th Anniversary of the AFSC in April 1937.

June 18. A special fund has been donated for ambassadors at large. President Comfort will go to France in 1937 to give a series of lectures. Question is discussed of sending Rufus M. Jones to China, Japan and South Africa, and one or two persons to Scandinavian countries.

June 18–21. Conference at Pendle Hill for 65 Home Service workers.

June. 190 Service Work Campers are in 7 camps. There are 2 junior camps, one for boys in the Cumberland Homestead, in the TVA, and one for girls, at Tunesassa, Quaker Bridge, N.Y. The other 5 are at Clinch River, in the TVA; Kensington, Philadelphia; Bedford Street Mission, Philadelphia; the Big Jim Mission, Norman, Oklahoma, and Dillonvale, Ohio.

June–July. Institutes of International Relations are held at: Swarthmore College, Pa.; Wellesley College; Duke University; Northwestern University; Grinnell College; Bethel College, Kansas; Whittier College; Mills College; Reed College; Nashville, Tennessee.

July 5–25.   Institute of Race Relations at Swarthmore College.

223 Peace Volunteers are spending 8 weeks in 23 states under the Emergency Peace Campaign.

July 15.   The International Student House in Washington, D.C., opens with Grace S. Lowry as director.

August 1.   The first Richard Cary Memorial Lecture is given at German Yearly Meeting by Hans Albrecht, the Clerk.

August.   Harry Timbres takes a medical position in Russia.

September 1.   Robert and Dora Willson, at the Tygart Valley Homestead, are no longer representatives of the AFSC.

September 13.   Cleveland, Ohio, Independent Meeting is affiliated with the Fellowship Council.

September 23.   Desire is expressed that there should be a co-ordinating committee of the work carried on in the Orient by all American Friends.

September 24.   Alfred and Norma Jacob had been appointed by the Friends Service Council, London, to take up center work at Madrid, Spain. Emma Cadbury had planned to go with them to investigate the situation. Due to the Civil War this plan has been given up.

September 24.   The National Birth Control League has given a grant to finance a Birth Control Clinic at Logan, West Va.

Wilmer and Mildred Young and their family have reached the Delta Co-operative Farms, Mississippi.

September 25.   The Speakers Bureau of the Peace Committee is helping to arrange for a second series of meetings for the Emergency Peace Campaign to be held in 500 cities during October and November.

October 22. The change in policy of the Resettlement Administration makes it impossible to use their funds for purchase of land and construction of buildings in Fayette County. The money was to be used for the purpose of developing educational and community projects for securing cash income in the community. Additional funds are therefore needed.

John Harvey and Alfred Jacob, sent to Spain by the FSC, report that there is no step which can be taken in Spain, at present.

November 15. John F. Reich is appointed to give two-thirds of his time to the AFSC for publicity work.

World Events edited by Devere Allen has been enlarged to 4 pages and the circulation has increased to more than 20,000.

December 2. The FSC has asked Alfred Jacob to undertake relief work in Spain to administer funds raised by English Friends and the Save the Children Fund.

In the United States the Ethical Culture Society offers to bear half of the expenses involved in sending an investigator to Spain and the Mennonites offer to co-operate with Friends in work for Spain.

The Board agrees to send Sylvester Jones to Spain for a survey of what is to be done.

Donald Stephens has been secured for 3 months to raise funds to buy the property at Fayette County.

Decision is made to move the Geneva Hostel from 18 Avenue Bertrand to the old Palais des Nations.

December 10. Decision is made to raise additional funds for a salary for Wilmer and Mildred Young.

The MCCA has merged with the Arthurdale Industries.

Two students have spent a term at Pendle Hill and expect to spend the next term, one at the Logan Health Center and the other at Delta Farm.

December 17. Decision is made to appoint a special committee on Spain.

The sum of $2500 is received to finance moving the Geneva Hostel.

December 18. Emphasis is laid on the necessity for maintaining a neutral attitude in regard to any activities which the AFSC may undertake in Spain.

December 20. Sylvester Jones sails for Spain.

December. George Selleck is secretary to the AFSC Boston branch office.

1937

January. Gilbert MacMaster resumes relations with Foreign Service Section, to visit Berlin Center whenever possible and to attend Minorities' Congresses.

January 3. Sylvester Jones arrives in Barcelona.

January 6. Ray and Babette Newton are released for another year of service for the Emergency Peace Campaign.
John F. Reich is asked to give remaining one-third of his time to secretarial work of Committee on Spain.

January 20. Sylvester Jones enters Burgos, Nationalist Territory.

January 21. Report is made by Clarence E. Pickett that a meeting of the Rehabilitation Committee has been held with a group of industrialists in Pittsburgh, to discuss the matter of Fayette County.

February 3. AFSC will take out compensation insurance which covers all paid employees of the AFSC in Pennsylvania.

February 5. Sylvester Jones reaches the United States.

February 8. Committee on Spain and Board of Directors unite in proposing that non-partisan relief in Spain should be undertaken as soon as funds are available in cooperation with the Mennonites, Church of the Brethren and the Federal Council of Churches.

February 12. Rufus M. Jones, Alvin T. Coate and Patrick Malin for the Society of Friends; Paul H. and Rufus D. Bowmen for the Church of the Brethren; A. J. Neuenschwander and C. L. Graber for the Mennonites, present statements in behalf of these 3 historic peace churches to President Roosevelt. The purpose of the visit is to put on record the fact that these 3 churches oppose war.

February 15. David W. Day arrives in Fayette County as manager of the homestead project.

February 18. The rehabilitation Committee authorizes the incorporation of Friends Service, Inc., which is organized for the purpose of buying and holding property.
The purchase of the Craft Farm, 200 acres in Fayette County, Pa., for $7500 is approved.

February 25. The option is closed on the 200 acres.

February 26. AFSC recommends that relief should be taken into Spain as soon as funds are available.

March 3. John F. Reich is asked to devote three-fourths of his time to the Committee on Spain, the remaining one-fourth to publicity for the AFSC.

March 18. The Foreign Service Section authorizes the AFSC to co-operate with Hertha Kraus in her placement work for German refugees in the United States.

March 20. Report is made that there are 100 persons who have expressed their desire to become members of the Wider Quaker Fellowship.

April 1. President and Mrs. Comfort sail for France.

April 7. The Committee on Spain reports that it is getting out its first general appeal for funds. Funds are also being solicited through the channels of the Church of the Brethren and the Mennonites.

April 14. A letter is read from the State Department which recognizes the AFSC as an official relief agency, authorized to send workers to Spain. Assistant Secretary of State says that his department will facilitate the issuing of passports.

April 23. Celebration of the 20th Anniversary of the starting of the AFSC.

May 4. Henry Tatnall Brown, William Eves 3rd, Mary B. Moon and Clarence E. Pickett are received by Ambassador Luther before his return to Germany.

Esther L. Farquhar and Wilfred V. Jones sail to Spain to undertake relief work, she in Loyalist territory and he in insurgent.

May 12. Harry G. Timbres dies of typhus fever in Russia.

May 15. Emma Cadbury leaves Vienna to join Wilfred Jones in Paris so that they may enter Spain together where she will bring the purpose of the AFSC relief program before officials.

May. Esther L. Farquhar goes to Barcelona and joins Francesca Wilson from the FSC.

May 27. Report is made that 12 homesteaders have been accepted for the Fayette County project.

May 28. Report is made that the Advisory Board, consisting of citizens in Logan, West Virginia, is trying to raise $4500 toward the support of the Friends Health Service.

June 4. Emma Cadbury and Wilfred Jones enter Salamanca, Spain.

June 5. Douglas Steere sails for Scandinavia.

June 9. Emma Cadbury and Wilfred Jones interview Count Vallellano, President of Nationalist Red Cross, who offers cordial co-operation to AFSC.

Patrick Malin sails to spend the summer investigating conditions in Spain.

June 12. Clarence and Lilly Pickett move into their new house.

June 14. Emma Cadbury leaves Spain.

June 16–20. Workers Conference at Pendle Hill for 29 Home Service Volunteers. Thirty-nine workers have been placed for the summer.

June–July. Institutes of International Relations are held at: Bethel College, Kansas; Duke University; Grinnell College; Cheyney State Teachers' College, Pa.; North Central College, Naperville, Illinois; Mills College; Wellesley College; Whittier College; Reed College, Oregon; Nashville, Tennessee.

June–August. Volunteer Work Camps are held at: Fayette County Homestead; Delta Co-operative Farm, Hillhouse, Mississippi; Friends Neighborhood Guild, Philadelphia; Hull House, Chicago; the TVA; Tunesassa, Quaker Bridge, N.Y. This camp is composed of Friends, Members of the Mennonites and Church of the Brethren.

July 5–24. Institute of Race Relations at Cheyney State Teachers' College.

August. Mabel Ridpath resigns as warden of the Geneva Hostel. During September Roger and Irene Soltau will take charge; from October until August 1938 James and Anne Forsythe will take charge.

September 1–8. Friends World Conference at Swarthmore and Haverford Colleges.

Contributions to the American Friends Service Committee

1917–1926

Friends	. . .	$ 1,858,734.26
Non-Friends	. .	10,386,298.14
In kind	. . .	12,939,414.99

1927–1936

All Sources	. .	2,192,127.25
Total		27,376,574.64

Disbursements, 1918–1925

Austria	$	378,086
France		917,529
Germany		7,673,764
Poland		187,266
Russia		1,572,707
Total		10,728,707

Disbursements, 1927–1936

Administration . . .	$	321,203.86
Home Service		56,860.07
Foreign Service . . .		307,731.47
Interracial		12,888.73
Peace		293,885.61
Fellowship Committee and Council . . .		3,790.79
Relief and Rehabilitation		990,529.19
Total		1,986,889.72

Disbursements, 1917–1936

$12,715,596.72.

Figures taken from Jones, Lester M., *Quakers in Action*, p. 156, and from material prepared by M. Elizabeth Kerns. This does not include final total of disbursements.

INDEX

Abbott, Grace, 224, 313, 339.
Abel, Walter H., 212, 325.
Addams, Jane, 75, 76, 78, 322.
Albania, 329.
Albrecht, Hans, 355.
Alien Immigration Act, 169.
All Friends Conferences, 289, 324, 335, 336.
Allen, Devere, 181, 345, 356.
Allen, Henry T., 83, 326, 327.
Allen, William, viii.
Ambassadors at Large, Quaker, 145, 354.
American Christian Committee for German Refugees, 347, 351.
American Farm School, 151.
American Friends Service Committee, 52, 124, 125, 290, 342.
anniversaries, 342, 354, 359.
branches in U.S.A., 286, 329, 331, 333, 334, 335, 349, 352, 357.
corporate activity, viii, 10, 129.
house, 291, 354, 359.
incorporated, 333.
organized, xvii, 14, 20, 305, 319.
reorganized, 128–132, 284, 327, 328, 329, 333.
represents Friends in America, 289.
Secretaries: Vincent D. Nicholson, 5, 284, 319; Wilbur K. Thomas, 20, 284–285, 335; Clarence E. Pickett, 285–286, 335.

Treasurers: Charles F. Jenkins, 11, 319; William R. Fogg, 337.
American Interracial Peace Committee, 170, 334, 339.
American Legion, 196, 197, 350.
American Red Cross
coal fields, 213.
France, 5, 16, 17, 319, 322.
Poland, 112.
Russia, 46, 63.
Spain, 301.
American Relief Administration, 46, 66, 68, 78, 81, 82, 112, 228, 325, 340.
Andrievka, 42, 43.
Appel, Baronin Friederika (Riki Teller), 150, 344.
Armistice, 20, 98, 128, 202.
Arthurdale, 232, 240, 356.
Atherton-Smith, Mrs., 148.
Austria, vii, 19, 20, 119, 146–153, 347, 348, 349.
Austrian Unit, 78, 128, 146–147, 152, 325, 326.

Babb, Nancy, 6, 43, 44, 45, 62, 69, 139, 320, 327, 331.
Babbitt, Dr. James A., 76, 320.
Bacon Francis, 324.
Bad Pyrmont, Meeting House at, 143, 343.
Bailey, Moses M., 323.
Balderston, Lloyd, 134, 328, 329.
Balderston, Robert W., 323.
Barnsboro, Pa., 217–218, 333, 335.

363

RENEWALS 458-4574

DATE DUE

FEB 1 7			
MAY 0 2			
GAYLORD			PRINTED IN U.S.A